Using English Grammar: meaning and form

EDITION WITH ANSWER KEY

Other titles of interest include:
Using Idioms, *J. B. Heaton and T. W. Noble*
Using Phrasal Verbs, *D. Britten and G. Dellar*
English Syntactic Structures (+ workbook), *F. Aarts and J. Aarts*
International Expressways, *S. Molinsky and B. Bliss*

Using English Grammar: meaning and form

EDITION WITH ANSWER KEY

Edward G. Woods

The Institute for English Language Education
Lancaster University

and

Nicole J. McLeod

The Institute for English Language Education
Lancaster University

English Language Teaching

Prentice Hall
New York   London   Toronto   Sydney   Tokyo   Singapore

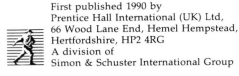

First published 1990 by
Prentice Hall International (UK) Ltd,
66 Wood Lane End, Hemel Hempstead,
Hertfordshire, HP2 4RG
A division of
Simon & Schuster International Group

Typeset by Cambridge Photosetting Services
Printed and bound in Great Britain at the University Press, Cambridge

---

Library of Congress Cataloging-in-Publication Data

Woods, Edward G., 1937–
    Using English grammar: meaning and form/Edward G. Woods,
Nicole J. McLeod.
        p.   cm. — (English language teaching)
    "Edition with answer key."
    ISBN 0-13-941395-2: $9.00
        1. English language—Grammar—1950–   2. English language–
–Textbooks for foreign speakers.   I. McLeod, Nicole J., 1936–
II. Title.   III. Series
    PE1112.W66   1989   89–25478
    428.2'4—dc20   CIP

British Library Cataloguing in Publication Data

Woods, Edward G., 1937–
    Using English grammar: meaning and form.
    1. English language. Usage
    I. Title   II. McLeod, Nicole J. *1936–*
    428

    ISBN 0-13-941395-2

To Dal.
To Chris, who said it was possible;
To John, who sent me all over the place;
EGW

For Cathy, Lisette and Geoff.
njm

Contents

Acknowledgements

Our thanks to Chris Candlin for his interest and support in this project; also our thanks to colleagues and friends who have been prepared to try out some parts of the book in their classes and who, with their students, often inadvertently, have been sounding boards for the ideas and tasks in the book.

Nobody who has been teaching English for any length of time can claim to be completely original and we therefore happily acknowledge our debt to the many writers of grammar books before us. At times, we have been very conscious of their influence on our work; at other times the influence has been more indirect.

Finally, we would like to thank David Haines for encouraging us and keeping us at work on the book and Isobel Fletcher de Téllez for combing the manuscript so thoroughly and commenting so perceptively. We would also like to thank Pat Drennan for her illustrations.

All these people have contributed to this volume – credits are theirs and debits are ours.

Edward Woods
Nicole McLeod
1989

Introduction

1. Aims of the course

The aim of this course is to help intermediate and more advanced learners towards an understanding of the importance of grammar in expressing what they want to say and interpreting correctly not only the basic meaning of what has been said to them but also the force of the utterance or piece of writing.

Meaning and form are both important in language. We see form as important because it helps people to express attitudes both to what they are saying and to the people to whom and about whom they are talking or writing.

When using language people make choices. For example:
  whether to use the active or the passive;
  whether to use the full relative or the reduced relative;
  whether to use the *will* future or the *going to* future; etc.

The aim of this grammar is to help learners to understand how to make these choices for themselves.

2. To the teacher

The grammar aims to be practical; but we feel that in order to be able to use grammar efficiently learners must understand the underlying system of grammar. This is also important if learners are to become able to help themselves and to monitor their own progress. Therefore, you will find that some explanations introduce more technical terms than is usual in a grammar of this kind; and that some tasks check the rules rather than just give practice.

You will find several kinds of tasks. For example:
  understanding of rules;
  gap-filling practice;
  relating task to text;
  free practice tasks.

3. To the student

You may find that some of the explanatory notes in this grammar give rather more technical terms than you are used to and that some of the tasks concentrate on the system rather than the use. This is because we feel that now you are at an intermediate level you should be able to start helping yourself to learn. To do this, you need to have some knowledge of the system that lies behind the form and the use of the grammar.

You may also find that some of the explanations will be quite new or different from those you learned in the past. This is because, as we learn more about the system of English, it becomes possible to find explanations that are better or clearer than the rules we used to learn.

The aim of this grammar is not just to give you lots of easy practice with sentences but to help you to think carefully about the grammar and why you should use one form rather than another.

SECTION 1: Sentence organisation

Correct use of grammar is important in helping to convey messages properly. At a very formal level, this means putting the words in the right order in a sentence. Central to this organisation is the verb. A sentence must contain a verb that is both finite (i.e. a verb that has a full form showing tense, number etc.) and lexical (i.e. a verb that conveys meaning).

The other elements in the sentence are formed around this verb. Many of these elements have fixed positions; but some, such as adverbials or adverbial phrases, are moveable.

In Section 1 we look at the following:

the different types of verbs, and how each type affects the order of other words in the sentence;

the various positions possible for adverbs in a sentence.

UNIT 1.1
VERB CATEGORIES:
transitive, intransitive, intensive

The agent collected the rent.
The older people left.
Thatcher became Prime Minister in 1979.

Verbs can be **transitive, intransitive** or **intensive**.

Look at these examples:

Transitive	Intransitive
The agent collected the rent.	James went to Rome.
They've given the keys to the owner.	He cried bitterly.
The older people left the street.	The older people left.

In the left-hand column of the chart above, the verbs are being used **transitively**. This means that they are all followed by a **direct** object, which answers the question WHO? or WHAT? after the verb; in these cases, the **rent**, the **keys** and the **street**.

In the right-hand column of the chart, the verbs have **no object**. There is nothing which answers WHO? or WHAT? after the verbs as in the left-hand column. If anything follows these verbs, it is an adverbial phrase which answers the questions WHERE? or HOW? and in other cases WHEN? These verbs are being used **intransitively**.

Some verbs are always used **transitively**. You **cannot** say, for example:
   *The agent collected.
   *They've given.
These sentences are incomplete. Verbs such as **collect** and **give** always need an **object**.

Some verbs are always used **intransitively**, for example:
   James went . . .
   The book fell . . .
Verbs such as **go** and **fall** are **never** followed by an object.

Some verbs can be used either **transitively** or **intransitively**, for example:
   The older people left. *(Intransitive)*
   The older people left the street. *(Transitive)*

There is a group of verbs which are known as **intensive** or **linking** verbs (see Unit 1.2). They are not followed by a direct object, but by a **complement**. The **complement** tells you more about the subject and is sometimes a description of the subject.

Look at these examples:
   Thatcher became Prime Minister in 1979.
   Romy is a teacher.

Some intensive verbs are: **appear, be, become, feel, look, seem, smell, sound, taste**.

Learner dictionaries indicate whether verbs can be used transitively, intransitively or intensively.

2

Unit 1.1 Verb categories – TASKS

Task one

Read the following sentences and identify the category of verb by writing the verb in the appropriate column in the following table. An example has been written for you.

Example:
David Livingstone **lived** and **died** in Tanganyika (now Tanzania).

(a) We **receive** numerous queries from policy holders.
(b) A deed of covenant **saves** you money.
(c) Patricia and her friend **went** to St Ives for their holiday.
(d) D'Arcy **invited** the artist to Oxford.
(e) Cardinal Heenan **was** a close friend.
(f) On the banks of the river, the women **clean** the pots and pans.
(g) All kinds of criminals **wait** for the tourists.
(h) The children **swam** naked in the pool.
(j) The six brothers **own** twenty-two houseboats.
(k) Andy Kennedy **takes** a slow boat to China.

Transitive	Intransitive	Intensive
	Lived *Died*	

Task two

Read the following text and fill in the missing words by selecting one of the verbs below which fits the category stated in brackets.

have turned, is wearing, see, are tramping, are walking, traverses, is shivering, covered, is, seems

Dawn. Everyone of us (a) . . . . . . (*intransitive*). White legs (b) . . . . . . (*intensive*) pink from the cold wind off the North Sea. We (c) . . . . . . (*intransitive*) along the edge of the ocean.

Each of us (d) . . . . . . (*transitive*) high-top trainers, socks, shirts, sweater, rain-jacket and day-pack. This (e) . . . . . . (*intensive*) inadequate for the weather. The wind (f) . . . . . . (*intensive*) wet and we can (g) . . . . . . (*transitive*) our own breath. We are about to walk across the North Sea.

We are in Holland, and this is a walk as Dutch as the Nation itself. It (h) . . . . . . (*transitive*) a kind of countryside that once (j) . . . . . . (*transitive*) half of Holland.

Three dozen of us (k) . . . . . . (*intransitive*) along the outermost dike.

UNIT 1.2
VERB CLASSES: lexical and primary verbs; modal auxiliaries

Nurse Lane continued with her knitting.
Romy and Alan became neighbours.
I don't do that any more.
John has sent the application off.
He was arrested last night.
Payment must be received on or before
19 April 1988.

What do verbs DO? Some verbs tell us what is happening or they describe something; other verbs act as supporters to main verbs and help to show the tense or whether the form is a question; while others qualify what the main verb does.

1. Verbs and meaning

Look at these examples:
   (a) She **applied** for the senior post.
   (b) Nurse Lane **continued** with her knitting.
   (c) Romy and Alan **became** neighbours.
   (d) Churchill **was** Prime Minister in 1953.

The words in bold type are **verbs**. In examples (a) and (b), they are telling us what the subject **did**. In (c) and (d), they form a **link** between the subject and information about the **subject**. The words that follow the verbs are descriptions of the **subject**. **Neighbours** and **Prime Minister** here are not the **object** of the verb, but the **complement**. They don't tell us what the subject is doing as in (a) and (b). They tell us **more about the subject**.

Look at these examples:
   She applied for the senior post.
In this example, **applied for the senior post** answers the question, WHAT did she do? Verbs like this are **extensive**. They go out from the subject.
   SHE ————→ applied for the job.

Now look at this example:
   Churchill was Prime Minister in 1953.
In this example, **was Prime Minister in 1953** answers the question WHAT happened to Churchill? or WHO was Churchill? Verbs like this are **intensive**. They go back to the subject.

   Churchill ————→ was Prime Minister in 1953.

Both of these types of verb (**extensive** and **intensive**) are called **lexical verbs** (see also Unit 1.1). They carry the **meaning** of the action or description.

There must be a lexical verb in every sentence.

2. Verbs as supporters

Look at these examples:

> I **don't** do that any more.
> John **has** sent the application off.
> He **was** arrested last night.

The verbs in bold type here do not have any meaning themselves but support the **lexical verbs**. They are **primary verbs** and are used as follows:

do is used to express negation or questions (see Unit 2.1).

have is used for the perfect forms (see Unit 2.17).

be is used (a) for the continuous forms (see Units 2.3, 2.4, 2.7, etc.)
        (b) to form the passive (see Units 2.23, 2.24)

The **primary verbs** help us to show the following:

whether we are asking a question or saying something in the negative;

what aspect of time we are talking about;

when we are using the passive.

3. Verbs as qualifiers

Look at these examples:

> Payment **must** be received on or before 19 April 1988.
> The north-east **can** expect rain later this evening.

The verbs in bold type in this group show degrees of obligation, ability, etc., and qualify the **lexical verbs**. They are known as **modal auxiliaries** (see Units 2.25–2.34).

Sometimes sentences carry all three classes of verbs. Then you put them in the following order: **modal auxiliary, primary, lexical**, as shown in the table below.

	Modal	Primary	Lexical	
The soldier			stood	to attention.
The house		has	been	empty for years.
Tom	will		be	very rich.
That car	must	have	cost	a lot.

WARNING BOX

> As well as supporting other lexical verbs, the **primary verbs – to do, to have** and **to be** – also function as **lexical verbs** themselves:
> > I'll **do** the washing-up.
> > Mary **has** three children.
> > Picasso **was** Spanish.
> Sometimes the verb **to be** has two parts as a **primary** verb:
> > She **is being** given a better job.
> > She **has been** seen in Calais.

Unit 1.2 Verb classes – TASKS

Task one

Read the following sentences and identify the classes of the verbs in bold type by placing them in the appropriate column in the table. An example has been written for you.

Example:
Irving Berlin **has written** over 800 songs.

He **was born** in Russia on 12 May 1888. His parents **brought** him and his six brothers and sisters to America in 1894. They **lived** with other immigrants in the Bronx in New York. When he **was** fifteen he **left** home and **worked** as a waiter and singer. He **became** famous when he **wrote** 'Alexander's Rag-Time Band'. Many people **know** the words of his songs, even when they **don't know** the name of the writer: 'I**'ve** never **seen** the sun looking so bright' and 'I **don't want** to get up in the morning' are just two. He **has been married** twice. His first wife **died** shortly after they **were married**. Although he **became** very rich, the father of his second wife **wasn't** happy that Berlin **had grown up** in a poor immigrant family with little education. He **said** his daughter **mustn't marry** Berlin. But the couple **ignored** him.

Modal auxiliary	Primary verb	Lexical verb
	Has	Written

Task two

Using words from the following list, complete the advertisement below. Each word may be used more than once. State the class of each verb as you use it.

should, take, rush, seems, consider, is, have, would, suggest, engineered

No one (a) . . . . that buying a Mercedes-Benz (b) . . . . . . a decision you (c) . . . . or (d) . . . . . . lightly. Far from it. It (e) . . . . . . only when you (f) . . . . . . the time to consider the facts that a Mercedes-Benz (g) . . . . . . such an obvious choice. (h) . . . . . . the 300E for example.

Like all Mercedes-Benz cars it (j) . . . . . . not (k) . . . . . . to perform a few specifics superbly well but to perform every function superbly well. Avoiding extremes in any single area in pursuit of the very highest competence overall.

Few cars (l) . . . . . . the ability to strike the same balance between comfort, handling performance, safety, reliability and re-sale value.

6

UNIT 1.3
VERB FORMS:
participles

Wanting something rather cheap, she went to the market.
Asked about an agreement, Sir Geoffrey refused to comment.

1. Verb forms which indicate time

All **lexical verbs** have forms which show **present** or **past time**.

Look at these examples:
> The problem **seems** insoluble. (**Present**)
> We **wrote** to you for advice. (**Past**)

Forms which indicate **time** in this way, without the support of primary verbs, are known as **finite** forms.

All **lexical verbs** also have **non-finite** forms which end in **-ing** or **-ed**. These are generally known as **participles** and are made up as follows:

the stem of the verb + **-ing**
(**present participle**) want + **-ing**;
the stem of the verb + **-ed**
(**past participle**) ask + **-ed**.

WARNING BOX

> To simplify things, we have said that the **past participle** is formed from the stem of the verb + **-ed**. This is the **regular** form. But there are many **irregular** forms, such as the following:
> > Go (**gone**)
> > Say (**said**)
> > Put (**put**)
> For a full list see Appendix 4.

Although non-finite forms are called **present** or **past participle**, they **do not** indicate **time**. We can see this in sentences where they are used in forms with the support of primary verbs.

Look at these examples:
> The French are electing a new President. (*Present Continuous*)
> The French were electing a new President. (*Past Continuous*)
> Thatcher has attacked the press. (*Present Perfect*)
> Thatcher had attacked the press. (*Past Perfect*)

In all these cases, it is the **primary verb** which reflects the **time**.

2. Participal phrases at the beginning of the sentence

Look at these examples:
> **Wanting something rather cheap**, she went to the market.
> **Asked about an agreement**, Sir Geoffrey refused to comment.

The first part of each sentence does not indicate whether we are talking about a **present** or **past** event; it is in the second part, where there is the **finite verb**, that we can find this information.

Look at the examples in the following chart:

Participle phrase	Finite clause
Wanting something rather cheap,	she went to the market. Robert is going to the charity shop.
Asked about an agreement,	Sir Geoffrey refused to comment. Sir Geoffrey will refer you to his report.

In both cases we can see that the same **participle phrase** can appear with **finite clauses** that reflect a different **time**. This will become clearer if we expand the participle phrases.

Look at these examples:
    Because she **wanted** something rather cheap, she went to the market.
    As he **wants** something rather cheap, Robert is going to the charity shop.
    When he **was asked** about an agreement, Sir Geoffrey refused to comment.
    If he **is asked** about an agreement, Sir Geoffrey will refer you to his report.

The expansion of these examples shows the following three things:
(a) the time element is reflected in the **finite verb** in the main clause;
(b) the present participle phrase is an abbreviation of an **active** clause;
(c) the past participle phrase is an abbreviation of a **passive** clause.

3. Present participle versus infinitive after verbs of senses

After verbs, such as **see, watch, hear, notice, feel**, etc., we can use either the infinitive or the present participle.

Look at these examples:
    Frankenstein watched his man-made person **coming** to life.
    Frankenstein watched his man-made person **come** to life.
The difference is the sense of duration of the activity. In the first example, the writer is focusing on the **process** itself as the creature became alive. In the second example, the focus is on the **result** of the process. (Other uses of the non-finite form are discussed in Unit 4.12.)

WARNING BOX

> This use of the participles is formal and usually used only in writing. It is **unusual**, therefore, for the participle phrase to be used with **I** or **you**.
>
> A sentence must contain a **finite** form. When the form of the **lexical verb** is **non-finite**, the **primary verb** or **modal verb** is in the **finite** form:
>   Day-Lewis **has** appeared in many films.
>   This house **was** built in 1900.
>   We **must** receive an answer by Monday.

Unit 1.3 Verb forms – TASKS

Task one
Read the following text and identify the verb forms in bold type by putting them into the correct column in the table below.

There are a lot of kitchen companies out there, **offering** you all sorts of deals. But we at Wilson & Glick **are** not among them. **Compared** with our rivals, our kitchens **are built** from better materials. They **have** adjustable legs and wall brackets to ensure a perfect fit. Yet, as **displayed** in our showroom, our kitchens **cost** far less than those of our rivals. What we **have** to offer comes in at about half the price of more commonplace kitchens. So if you're **interested** in higher quality, but you're **looking** for a lower price, call us.

Finite	Non-finite

Task two
Rewrite the sentences below so that the part in bold type becomes non-finite. Some examples have been written for you.

Examples:
As Tarzan swung from the tree, he fell.

Swinging from the tree, Tarzan fell.

When he was last seen, he was driving a blue Audi 100.

When last seen he was driving a blue Audi 100.

(a) **While the jockey holds the reins,** he controls the horse.
(b) **Because she was hurt by the fall,** she couldn't phone for help.
(c) **Because Mehdi wants a holiday in France,** he has written to his friend there.
(d) **As Balan lives in Madras,** he often visits the Parthasarthy temple.
(e) **When Philby was found out,** he escaped to Moscow.
(f) **After she was given a computer as a present,** she quickly became an expert.
(g) **When he was awarded the top prize,** Malcolm decided to give up his job.
(h) **When she saw the house,** Anne immediately wanted to buy it.
(j) **Because she was seen by a top Hollywood producer,** she thought she would become a big star.
(k) **As she was leaving the university,** Esme had an accident with her car.

Task three

(a) *Think of ten things you like to do or wish would happen to you. Express them through the use of one of the non-finite forms. Some examples have been written for you.*

Examples:

Walking through the park in the rain.

Playing football with his friends.

Given a lot of money.

(b) *Now think of something somebody else might do or might have done, while doing the above or as a result of what had happened to them. Some examples have been written for you.*

Examples:

Walking through the park in the rain, Jane saw a wild bear.

Playing football with his friends, Ken hurt his knee.

Given a lot of money, kathy would travel round the world.

UNIT 1.4
ADVERBS, ADVERBIAL PHRASES: position in the sentence

The wedding is in May.
Put the fish stock and the red chilli in the liquidizer.
He struggled on bravely.
The doctor sees only private patients on Thursday.

The position for **adverbs** or **adverbial phrases** is usually at the **end** of the sentence. You may have been told that when there is more than one **adverb** or **adverbial phrase**, the correct order is **manner** (answering the question HOW?), **place** (answering the question WHERE?), then **time** (answering the question WHEN?).

For example, we can say:
He works **at home on Thursdays and Fridays**.
He works **hard at home**.
He works **hard on Thursdays and Fridays**.
but it is **unlikely** that we would say the following:
He works *on Thursdays and Fridays at home*.
He works *at home hard*.
He works *on Thursdays and Fridays hard*.
However, there are occasions when we can change the order (see Unit 5.9).

It is often said that **adverbs** and **adverbial phrases**, especially those of time, can be put at the beginning of the sentence. This is true. It is not true, however, that it is not important whether they come at the beginning or the end of a sentence because the message will not be the same (see Unit 5.9). Furthermore, it is not always possible to move the **adverbial phrase**.

Look at the examples in the following chart:

Column 1	Column 2
The wedding is **in May**. The wedding is **in Keswick**. John has behaved **badly**. Put the fish stock and the red chilli **in the liquidizer**.	Lord St John retired from the House of Commons **in 1987**. He struggled on **bravely**. The doctor sees only private patients **on Thursday**.

In the chart above, we can move the **adverbial phrases** in the sentences in column 2, but we cannot move those in column 1. *Look at the sentences in column 1 again.*

We can say
The wedding is in May.
John has behaved badly.
Put the fish stock and the
red chilli in the liquidizer.

We can't say
*In May the wedding is.
*Badly John has behaved.
*In the liquidizer put the fish
stock and the red chilli.

Why can't we change the **adverb** position in these sentences? Look what happens when we take away the **adverb**. We **can't** say the following:

11

Unit 1.4 Adverbs, adverbial phrases

The wedding is.
John has behaved.
Put the fish stock and the red chilli.

None of these sentences is complete. They have no meaning at all. The **adverbial phrase** is necessary to make the **form** of the sentences grammatically acceptable and to give them some meaning. Thus, it can't be moved from its position at the end of the sentence because it is essential to the sentence in both **form** and **meaning**.

Now look at the sentences in column 2 again.

In these sentences we can put the **adverb** or **adverbial phrase** at the beginning of the sentence.

What happens when we take away the **adverb** or **adverbial phrase** at the end of the sentence?

Look at these examples:

Lord St John retired from the House of Commons.
He struggled on.
The doctor sees only private patients.

All these sentences are grammatically acceptable in **form** and in **meaning**. The **adverbial phrases** that have been taken away are not necessary to make the sentences grammatically complete (but, of course, they do affect the meaning). It is for this reason that in these sentences we can move the **adverbial phrase** to the beginning of the sentence, as follows:

In 1987 Lord St John retired from the House of Commons.
Bravely he struggled on.
On Thursday the doctor sees only private patients.

Unit 1.4 Adverbs, adverbial phrases – TASKS

Task one

Read the following statements and put the words in the correct order.

(a) the house last week they sold
(b) was in June the wedding
(c) from all over the country seamen at Dover gathered have
(d) in many parts of the world Elizabeth Taylor houses has
(e) any more Alice here live doesn't
(f) for a few days Spencer in Cookham remained
(g) on didn't being he like own his
(h) in love two years later with Patricia fell he
(j) the bugle beautifully in the army played Scottie
(k) the casserole into a warm oven put

Task two

Read the following sentences and underline the adverbial phrases which are essential for the formal completion of the sentence and, therefore, cannot be moved.

(a) The king died in 1979.
(b) She carefully placed the chair by the door.
(c) I shall be in London on 25 May.
(d) Roy has gone to Karachi for three years.
(e) They travelled slowly down the Ganges.
(f) *Spycatcher* has been published in America.
(g) The two old ladies stood at the gate for hours.
(h) The party was in the Great Hall.
(j) We're moving our shop to Gage Street.
(k) He dropped the typewriter on to the floor.

Task three

(a) *Make a list of dates*, e.g. in May, on 26 June, on Monday, next year, last month, this week, etc.
(b) *Make a list of things to do*, e.g. visit Aunt Mabel, write the essay, paint the house, mend the bicycle, go to the cinema, etc.
(c) *Write a short story about some friends, the things they do and when they do them.*

UNIT 1.5
ADVERBS OF FREQUENCY: position in the sentence

John has seldom known the misery of poverty.
Has Eddie Eagle ever skied before?
Peter took his driving test three times.

There are two groups of adverbs which answer the question HOW OFTEN?

Look at these examples:
   John has **seldom** known the misery of poverty. (HOW OFTEN? general)
   Peter took his driving test **three times**. (HOW OFTEN? specific)
These **adverbs** never affect the formal **completion** of a sentence. They will, of course, affect the **meaning**. In the chart below, you can see the position they usually have in a sentence.

General	Specific
John has **often** known the misery of poverty. The dog **always** woke them up with its barking. He must **never** go there again.	Peter took his driving test **three times**.

When a **specific number** of occasions is stated, the adverbial phrase goes at the **end**. In the case of the more **general frequency**, the adverbs go immediately **before** the **lexical verb** (see Unit 1.2). When there are **primary** verbs and **modal auxiliaries**, then the adverb goes **between** them and the **lexical verb**.

Look at the examples in the following chart:

	Modal	Primary	Adverb	Lexical	
The dog John He	 must	 has	**always** **often** **never**	woke known go	them up with its barking. the misery of poverty. there again.

In the question form, when the frequency is unknown, we use the word **ever**.

Look at these examples:

    Q: Does Pauline ever go to the theatre?

    A: Yes, she goes once a week.

        No, she never goes.

        Yes, she sometimes goes to the theatre, but she usually goes to the cinema.

    Q: Have you ever eaten gado-gado?

    A: No, I haven't ever eaten it.

        No, I've never eaten it.

As with the other adverbs of frequency, the position of the word **ever** is **before** the **lexical verb.**

WARNING BOX

Ever is **not** used in a positive answer. The following answer is **wrong**:

    Q: Have you ever eaten gado-gado?

    A: ***Yes, I have ever eaten it. (Wrong)**

When the verb **to be** is used as a lexical verb and without an auxiliary, the general frequency adverb goes **after** the verb:

    Antonio is **always** late.

    Jane was **never** happy.

    I have **never** been here before..

    You must **always** be on time.

The relationship of meaning among the adverbs of frequency can be seen in the diagram below:

    always 100%

    usually ....

    often ....

    sometimes 50%

    seldom ....

    rarely ....

    never 0%

Unit 1.5 Adverbs of frequency – TASKS

Task one

Read the following sentences and state whether the adverbs are in the right or wrong position. An example has been written for you.

Example:

Spencer worked usually at night. Wrong.

(a) As a child, I went never into the city alone.
(b) Wherever he went, she was always by his side.
(c) Jonathan has six times run the London Marathon.
(d) Four times I have visited Rabat.
(e) In Rome, Barry often ate at the 'Vincula'.
(f) The newspaper is delivered always late in the holidays.
(g) He couldn't get there during the snow always.
(h) Joan attempted to swim the Channel four times.
(j) Once home, Wordsworth rarely went out in the evenings.
(k) Have you been ever to China?

Task two

Work round the circle in the diagram below as often as you like and see how many correctly formed sentences you can find. You must keep the phrases in the order you find them. You can start anywhere.

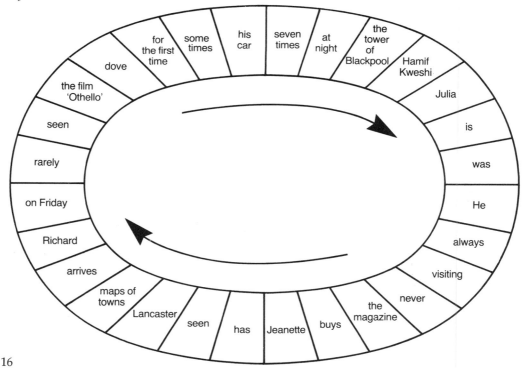

16

Section 2: Verbs

UNIT 2.1
VERB FORMS: positive, negative, interrogative

We can divide verb forms into two types: those with only one main verb and those with an auxiliary such as a form of the verb **to be** or **to have** or one of the modals such as **can, will**, etc. The **Simple** forms, **Present** and **Past**, are of the first type; all the other forms are of the second type.

When the verb form has only one part, then we use a form of **to do** to make the negative and question or interrogative forms. When the verb form includes an auxiliary or a modal, then there is no need to use **to do**; the auxiliary is used to form the negative and question forms.

Look at the following chart:

Forms that use do/does/did

Positive	Negative	Question

Present Simple

I You We They	**study** English at school	I You We They	**do not (don't)** **study** hard	**Do**	I you we they	**study** hard?
He She	**studies** English at school	He She	**does not (doesn't)** **study** hard	**Does**	he she	
It	**works** well	It	**does not (doesn't)** **work** well	**Does**	it	**work** well?

Past Simple

I You He She We They	**studied** English at school	I You He She We They	**did not (didn't)** **study** English	**Did**	I you he she we they	**study** hard?
It	**worked** well	It	**did not (didn't)** **work** well	**Did**	it	**work** well?

Forms that do not use do/does/did

Positive	Negative	Question

Present Continuous

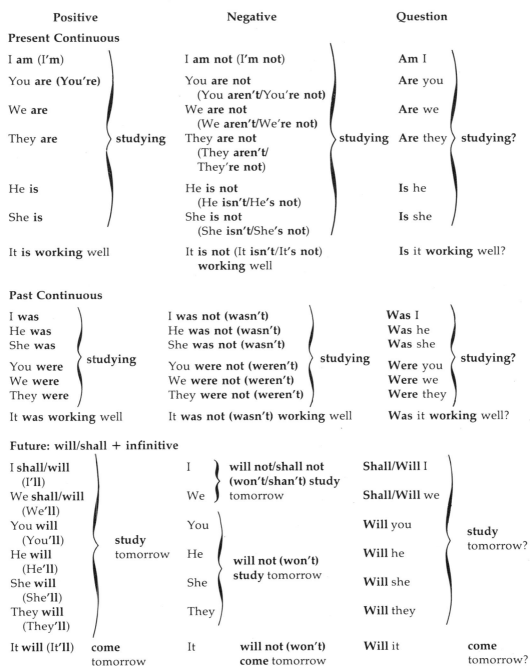

I am (I'm)

You are (You're)

We are

They are ⟩ studying

He is

She is

It is working well

I am not (I'm not)

You are not
   (You aren't/You're not)

We are not
   (We aren't/We're not)

They are not
   (They aren't/
   They're not) ⟩ studying

He is not
   (He isn't/He's not)

She is not
   (She isn't/She's not)

It is not (It isn't/It's not)
   working well

Am I

Are you

Are we

Are they ⟩ studying?

Is he

Is she

Is it working well?

Past Continuous

I was

He was

She was

You were ⟩ studying

We were

They were

It was working well

I was not (wasn't)

He was not (wasn't)

She was not (wasn't)

You were not (weren't) ⟩ studying

We were not (weren't)

They were not (weren't)

It was not (wasn't) working well

Was I

Was he

Was she

Were you ⟩ studying?

Were we

Were they

Was it working well?

Future: will/shall + infinitive

I shall/will
   (I'll)

We shall/will
   (We'll)

You will
   (You'll)

He will   ⟩ study
   (He'll)   tomorrow

She will
   (She'll)

They will
   (They'll)

It will (It'll) come
   tomorrow

I

We ⟩ will not/shall not
      (won't/shan't) study
      tomorrow

You

He

She ⟩ will not (won't)
      study tomorrow

They

It   will not (won't)
      come tomorrow

Shall/Will I

Shall/Will we

Will you

Will he   ⟩ study
           tomorrow?

Will she

Will they

Will it   come
           tomorrow?

Continued

Unit 2.1 Verb forms

Positive	Negative	Question

Present perfect

I You We They } **have studied** English	I You We They } **have not (haven't) studied** English	**Have** I **Have** you **Have** we **Have** they } **studied** English?
He She } **has studied** English	He She } **has not (hasn't) studied** English	**Has** he **Has** she }
It **has worked** well	It **has not (hasn't) worked** well	**Has** it **worked** well?

Past Perfect

I You He She We They } **had studied** it before	I You He She We They } **had not (hadn't) studied** it before	**Had** { I you he she we they } **studied** it before?
It **had worked** before	It **had not (hadn't) worked** before	**Had** it **worked**?

Future Perfect

I **will** (I'll) You **will** (You'll) He **will** (He'll) She **will** (She'll) We **will** (We'll) They **will** (They'll) } **have studied**	I You He She We They } **will not (won't) have studied**	**Will** { I you he she we they } **have studied?**
It **will** (It'll) **have worked** well	It **will not (won't) have worked** well	**Will** it **have worked** well?

UNIT 2.2
PRESENT SIMPLE

Mary goes on holiday next week.
Water freezes at 0°C.
But love is a risky business.
Don't you insist on Walker's Crisps?
He doesn't take sugar in his tea.
The plane leaves at 6.00 a.m.
Liverpool plays Everton next Saturday.

The **Present Simple** form is used to express **statements of fact**. It does not include any notion of specific time and is not necessarily concerned with the present time. The **Present Simple** is used:

to express general truths or facts. For example:
    Water **freezes** at 0°C.
    But love **is** a risky business.

to describe habits or habitual actions. For example:
    He **doesn't take** sugar in his tea.
    Don't you **insist** on Walker's Crisps?

to express feelings and opinions. For example:
    I **think** English grammar is boring.
    She **likes** coffee with sugar but **prefers** tea without.
    Geoff **doesn't like** cats very much.

Speakers and writers use the **Present Simple** to express **ideas** and **facts** that they perceive to be **objectively true**. If the speaker or writer wants to include information about **time**, then s/he adds an expression of **time**. For example:
    Mary goes on holiday **next week**.
    This programme returns **next week at the same time**.
    The plane leaves at **6.00 a.m.**
    Liverpool plays Everton **next Saturday**.
The speaker here is certain that what s/he said is a **fact** even though the events will occur in the future.

There is one other use of the **Present Simple** form which you may hear or read but which you will probably not need to use. The **Present Simple** form is used for sports commentaries, demonstrations such as experiments or cookery demonstrations, declarations, etc., which refer to events which begin and end at the moment of speaking. For example:
    And Keegan scores!
    I add some sugar and mix it in with the butter.
    I pronounce you man and wife.

WARNING BOX

Remember to add **-s** to the verb when it is in the 3rd person singular:
    He wants;
    She likes;
    The plane leaves.

Unit 2.2 Present Simple – TASKS

Task one

(a) *Underline the verb in each of the following advertising slogans.*

The old technology is dead.

HUNTERS STAND OUT IN ANY CROWD

 Our Label Spells Style

(b) *You will notice that all the verbs you have underlined are in the Present Simple tense. Can you give a reason why the advertisers have chosen to use this tense?*

Task two

Read the following text and fill in the missing words with any verb you think is appropriate.

It is a fact that:
(a) The United States (i) ...... the most extensive road system in the world. The proportion of cars to people (ii) ...... almost ridiculously high. With 500 cars to every thousand of population, there (iii) ...... one to every two people. This (iv) ...... babies, children and old people. There (v) ...... approximately thirty-six cars per mile of road.
(b) (i) Australians ...... more meat per year than any other nationality.
  (ii) Over 50% of Italians ...... their own homes.
  (iii) 21% of Germans ...... reading to any other leisure pastime.
  (iv) 17% of 3-year-old children in Japan ...... to school.
  (v) On average, every French person ...... 4.9 books per year while every Austrian ...... 2.6.

Task three

The statistics that appear in Task two were compiled by questioning people about their habits and possessions. What questions do you think the people were asked? Fill in the missing words in the following questions to make them questions that might have been asked:

(a) How much meat ...... you ...... every week?
(b) ...... you ...... your house or ...... you ...... the house you ...... in?
(c) What ...... you ...... in your leisure time?
(d) How many 3-year-old children ...... there in the school?
(e) How many books ...... you ...... in a year?

Task four

(Extension task)
Listen to a news broadcast in English (for example, BBC World Service, Voice of America or a local radio service in English) or to people speaking English, or watch an English television programme. Find as many examples as you can of the Present Simple form in the texts you have listened to and try to decide why the speakers have chosen to use the Present Simple form each time.

UNIT 2.3
PRESENT CONTINUOUS 1

The windscreen wipers aren't working
properly.
It's raining again.
We are looking for someone who wants to
make money.
The Chancellor is planning to make tax cuts.

The **Present Continuous** form of the verb is used when the speaker or writer views the event as occurring within a **limited period of time**. The use of this form includes some idea of **duration** and clearly indicates that **time** is an important consideration.

Look at this example:

The windscreen wipers **aren't working** properly.

The speaker sees this as a **temporary condition**. The problem started recently and the speaker expects the mechanic to find the fault and repair it.

Many grammar books state that the **Present Continuous** form is used to describe events that are happening **at the moment of speech**. But this is only a partial explanation of the meaning of this form. It would, for example, explain the difference in meaning between the following two statements:

It's **raining** again.
It **rains** a lot in England in the winter.

The first describes an action that is happening **at the moment of speech**; the second makes a **general statement of fact** that the speaker believes to be true. (See Unit 2.2 on the Present Simple tense.) It would not, however, explain why it is correct to say both of the following:

She **lives** in London.
She **is living** in London.

The speaker here has a choice of making a **general statement of fact** or making a statement of fact which includes the idea that 'living in London' is seen to be a **temporary state** or at least seen as a condition that has a **definite duration**.

We can see, then, that the **Present Continuous** form is used when the speaker or writer sees the event as happening **between two points of time**: either the **time of speaking** or writing or the time when the event **started** or **was planned in the past** and some point of time in the **future**. This explains why it is possible to use the **Present Continuous** form to talk about **events in the future**.

Look at the following examples:
They **are leaving** at 5.00 a.m. next Monday morning.
The **plan has already been made** and the event will take place at a **definite time** in the **future**.
The Chancellor **is planning** to make tax cuts.
This statement suggests that the Chancellor **has made the plan** and will implement it at a **definite time** in the **future**.

Continued

COMMISSION SALES

We are looking for someone who wants to make money. They will have to find some of their own projects and make their own sales. Our product is a necessity in every home. Its quality is superior and its prices competitive.

We are looking for someone who wants to make money suggests that the company has **started** to look for a new employee and that there is a definite **time limit** for looking; after that, they will offer one of the applicants a job with the company. So the period of looking for new employees will be of a **limited duration**.

Unit 2.3 Present Continuous 1 – TASKS

Task one

(a) *Read the job advertisement below and underline the verbs.*

(b) *State how many are in the Present Continuous form.*

Relational Databases	We are currently operating a number of specialised systems enabling a better understanding of customer requirements and are planning a sophisticated database which will determine the travel needs and preferences of the 20 million passengers who fly with British Airways each year. We are looking for people with skills in ORACLE or DB2 – or any other modern relational database. **Ref. RJ/408/31**

(c) *Why did British Airways choose to use so many Present Continuous forms in this advertisement?*

(d) *If they had used the Present Simple and Present Perfect forms instead, what impression would have been given?*

Task two

(a) *Below is a report from a weatherman on a television programme. Some of his words were not transmitted clearly and are missing in the transcript. Complete the text by filling in the missing words with the correct form of the verbs from the following list:*

stand, look, be, bring, shine, see, come, expect

As you can see, I (i) . . . . . . on the pier at Brighton. The sun (ii) . . . . . . at the moment but if we (iii) . . . . . . at the satellite picture we can (iv) . . . . . . that there (v) . . . . . . a depression which (vi) . . . . . . in from the Atlantic and should reach Ireland and Southwest England by the middle of the afternoon. This depression (vii) . . . . . . a lot of rain and by this evening we can (viii) . . . . . . rain in most parts of Wales and England.

(b) *How many '-ing' forms did you put into the passage?*

(c) *Which four blanks should not be filled with a Present Continuous form?*

Task three

Tom and Anne are planning a timetable for the week for a class in Intermediate English Language Skills. They want to include one more guest speaker and a one-hour visit to a local school during the week. They do not want the learners to miss any of the scheduled activities and the learners will not want to have a class on Friday afternoon because that is traditionally a free period and many of them have already made plans to go away for the weekend.

The following is a copy of their timetable and below is a conversation between Anne and Tom. Work with a partner and fill in the missing parts of the conversation. Be prepared to explain why you use the Present Continuous form when you need to use it.

Unit 2.3 Present Continuous 1 – Tasks

English for Communication class: Week three

	Monday	**Tuesday**	**Wednesday**	**Thursday**	**Friday**
9.00	Reading	Writing	Conversation	Grammar	Listening
11.00	Listening	Grammar	Reading	Writing	Discussion
1.00			Lunch		
2.00	Guest Speaker: Mr James	Project Work	Individual Tutorials	Project Work	Free Period

Anne: Ms Kelly has agreed to come and speak to the class next week. When can we fit her talk in?

Tom: What is she (a) . . . . . . about?

Anne: Modern approaches to grammar. What about Friday afternoon?

Tom: No, that is a free period for the learners. Some of them are (b) . . . . . . to go on a trip. But what about Wednesday afternoon?

Anne: No, that's not possible either. They're (c) . . . . . .

Continue this conversation with your partner until you find a time when Ms Kelly could give her talk and a time for the school visit.

UNIT 2.4
PRESENT CONTINUOUS 2

Life is being a bit difficult.
He's having lunch so he may be late for the meeting.
I'm always forgetting things.
We're seeing him tomorrow about the new courses.

In Unit 2.3 we looked at some of the common uses of the **Present Continuous** form and we saw that the most striking characteristic of this form is that it is used to express the idea that an event is of **limited duration**.

Look at this example:
> *Cagney and Lacey*, the series with the two believable policewomen, will return to your television screen on BBC1 this week. This time they deal with the problems of a mental patient with no place to go. Off-duty, life **is being** a bit difficult for both partners with each of them facing personal problems.

We are expected to understand by this use of **is being** that they will find ways of solving their problems, that the difficulties they have will be resolved.

Certain verbs, often called **state** verbs in contrast to **event** verbs, do not normally occur in the **Present Continuous** form. This is because their normal meaning does not include the idea of temporary or **limited duration**.

The verbs which **do not** usually have a **Present Continuous** form are verbs of the **senses** which we **cannot control** (such as **hear, see, smell**), verbs of **mental activity** (such as **think, know, realise**), verbs that express **feelings** or **emotions** (such as **like, want, hate**), verbs of **possession** (such as **belong, own, possess**) and **concern, consist, contain, seem**, and **matter**.

Below is a list of some common verbs that are **not** usually used in the **Present Continuous** form:

be	hate	mean	see
believe	hear	need	seem
belong	know	prefer	suppose
forget	like	realise	think (when the
have (when the	love	remember	meaning is **believe**)
meaning is **possess**			understand
or **suffer from**)			want

These verbs are not normally used in the **Present Continuous** form because they are not seen as temporary states or as having limited duration. If, for example, we believe or think or know something, we expect to continue to believe, think or know those things for an indefinite period. We make these statements as **facts**, not as temporary states or events.

However, when these verbs express an **event** or an **action**, or have a meaning that **denotes an action**, then they can be used in the **Present Continuous** form just as any other **event** verb.

Look at these examples:
> I **think** that's brilliant.
> I **am thinking** of going to Spain for a holiday.

In the first case the speaker is expressing an opinion which s/he believes to be a **fact** which has no time limit. In the second case the speaker is using **think** to mean **consider** or **plan** and knows that this planning time will end when s/he makes a decision and either goes or does not go to Spain for a holiday.

WARNING BOX

> **Have** is never used in the **Continuous form** when it means **to suffer from**:
> > I **have** a headache.
> > He can't come to class because he **has** a fever.
>
> **Have** can be used in the **Continuous form** when it means to **have someone do something**:
> > I'**m having** my hair cut on Wednesday.
> > They'**re having** the house painted.

Unit 2.4 Present Continuous 2 – TASKS

Task one

Look at the following pairs of sentences and decide why the speaker or writer has used the Present Simple form or the Present Continuous form in each case:

(a) He's having lunch now so he may be late for the meeting.
(b) I have a headache so I don't want to go to the meeting anyway.

(c) This perfume smells horrible.
(d) Well, stop smelling it then.

(e) I'm seeing him today about the agenda for the meeting.
(f) Cats see in very dim light.

(g) Some babies cry a lot at night.
(h) The baby's crying; it's your turn to go and see what's wrong.

Task two

Read the following text and fill in the missing words with either the Present Simple form or the Present Continuous form of the verb in brackets.

(a) What . . . . . . *(do)* an old English sheepdog . . . . . . *(look)* like without its coat? In the case of the wonderful Heinecken ad which . . . . . . *(be)* on television currently – where the dog . . . . . . *(get)* on with the business of painting the room while the master . . . . . . *(sit)* back and . . . . . . *(have)* a drink – it . . . . . . *(look)* just like actress Penny Stead.
(b) 'A few years ago I joined the Monsters etc. agency who . . . . . . *(deal)* with people of extreme heights' . . . . . . *(say)* Penny, who is only four foot seven inches tall.
(c) 'They . . . . . . *(need)* someone who . . . . . . *(look)* convincing as a dog and I . . . . . . *(have)* the job.'
(d) The actress . . . . . . *(live)* in London with her husband and three Yorkshire terriers.
(e) 'I . . . . . . *(come)* from a circus family and used to help with the horses and sideshows,' she . . . . . . *(say)*. 'I . . . . . . *(do)* lots of ads, including the Panda for a new airline, but you never . . . . . . *(see)* me as I really . . . . . . *(be)*.'

UNIT 2.5
PAST SIMPLE 1

Lucy Souter retained her title . . . she defeated Liz Irving. . .
Edinburgh and Cardiff made an immediate impact when the event was held at London's Alexandra Palace.

Regular verbs in English form the **Past** tense by adding **-ed** to the **stem** or **infinitive** form. For example:

Lucy Soutter <u>retained</u> her British Under-23 Open title last night when she <u>defeated</u> Liz Irving of Australia 7-9, 9-6, 9-2, 9-6 in 62 minutes at Lamb's Squash Club in London.

However, there are a number of very common verbs which are **irregular** and form the **Past** tense in different ways. For example:

Edinburgh and Cardiff, making their first appearance in the competition, <u>made</u> an immediate impact when the event was <u>held</u> for the second time, at its new venue of London's Alexandra Palace.

You will know most of these **irregular** verbs already but on the following page there is a task in which you will put the **irregular** verbs into a systematic scheme which will help you to remember them. (See also Appendix 4.)

To check how to make questions and negatives in the **Past Simple** form, see Unit 2.1.

Unit 2.5 Past Simple 1 – TASKS

Task one

In the chart below are some of the most common irregular verbs. Fill in the missing words to complete the chart.

Stem/infinitive	Past Simple	Past Participle
be	was/were	. . . . . .
become	. . . . . .	become
. . . . . .	began	. . . . . .
bet	. . . . . .	. . . . . .
. . . . . .	. . . . . .	bitten
break	. . . . . .	. . . . . .
. . . . . .	brought	. . . . . .
. . . . . .	. . . . . .	bought
. . . . . .	chose	. . . . . .
come	. . . . . .	. . . . . .
cost	. . . . . .	. . . . . .
. . . . . .	cut	. . . . . .
do	. . . . . .	. . . . . .
draw	. . . . . .	. . . . . .
. . . . . .	drove	. . . . . .
. . . . . .	. . . . . .	eaten
fall	. . . . . .	. . . . . .
. . . . . .	fed	. . . . . .
. . . . . .	. . . . . .	felt
find	. . . . . .	. . . . . .
. . . . . .	forgot	. . . . . .
get	. . . . . .	. . . . . .
. . . . . .	. . . . . .	given
. . . . . .	went	. . . . . .
have	. . . . . .	. . . . . .
. . . . . .	. . . . . .	heard
. . . . . .	hid	. . . . . .
hit	. . . . . .	. . . . . .
. . . . . .	. . . . . .	held
keep	. . . . . .	. . . . . .
. . . . . .	knew	. . . . . .
. . . . . .	led	. . . . . .
leave	. . . . . .	. . . . . .
. . . . . .	. . . . . .	lent
. . . . . .	let	. . . . . .
light	. . . . . .	. . . . . .
. . . . . .	. . . . . .	lost
. . . . . .	made	. . . . . .

Continued

Stem/infinitive	Past Simple	Past Participle	
mean	. . . . . .	. . . . . .	
. . . . . .	met	. . . . . .	
. . . . . .	. . . . . .	paid	
put	. . . . . .	. . . . . .	
read	. . . . . .	. . . . . .	
. . . . . .	rang	. . . . . .	
run	. . . . . .	. . . . . .	
. . . . . .	. . . . . .	said	
see	. . . . . .	. . . . . .	
. . . . . .	sold	. . . . . .	
send	. . . . . .	. . . . . .	
. . . . . .	. . . . . .	shown	
. . . . . .	shut	. . . . . .	
sit	. . . . . .	. . . . . .	
. . . . . .	spoke	. . . . . .	
spend	. . . . . .	. . . . . .	
. . . . . .	. . . . . .	stood	
. . . . . .	took	. . . . . .	
teach	. . . . . .	. . . . . .	
. . . . . .	told	. . . . . .	
think	. . . . . .	. . . . . .	
. . . . . .	. . . . . .	understood	
. . . . . .	wrote	. . . . . .	

Task two

(a) *Now sort the verbs in the above chart into three groups. In Group 1 put the stem of all the verbs that have a different form in each column; for example,* **fly, flew, flown**. *In Group 2 put the stem of all the verbs that have only two forms, one for the infinitive and the same one for both the Past Simple and the past participle; for example,* **buy, bought, bought**. *In Group 3 put the stem of all the verbs that have the same form in all three columns; for example,* **bet, bet, bet**. *Some examples have been written for you.*

Group 1	Group 2	Group 3
fly	buy	bet

(b) *Can you think of two common verbs that do not fit into any of the three groups you have made?*

(c) *In which group would you put regular verbs?*

UNIT 2.6
PAST SIMPLE 2

In 1849 Edward Frankland, the British
chemist, made a momentous discovery.
If we found a solution . . . it would
probably not be a simple one.
Could you please give her a message for me.

The **Past Simple** form of the verb is used to indicate events or to describe actions or states which are in some way **remote** from the time of speaking or writing. In other words, there is a **distance** between the time of speaking or writing and the time of the event or state being referred to. This **distance** can be in terms of **time**.

Look at these examples:

He **wrote** to me two weeks ago but I only **answered** the letter yesterday.

In 1849 Edward Frankland, the British chemist, **made** a momentous discovery. He **found** that when he **heated** zinc with an organic compound, ethyl iodide, he **produced** an evil-smelling liquid that readily **formed** a vapour and **caught** fire. It **was** the first time that anyone had identified a compound that **was** organic but also **contained** a metal.

Capra **graduated** from the University of Vienna in 1966 and **spent** the next two years in post-doctoral research at the University of Paris.

In the three examples above, the distance or remoteness is one of **time**. In the first case, the action took place two weeks ago and yesterday. In the second example, it all took place over a hundred years ago. And in the third, the action was over twenty years ago.

If you have been taught that in **reported** or **indirect speech** you must always change the verb tenses from, for example, Present to Past Simple or from Past Simple to Past Perfect, this is not completely true because the decision to change the verb tenses depends on what **meaning** the speaker or writer intends to convey and on what **time** is being focused on. For example:

Owen said he **has** to go home at one o'clock.
Owen said he **had** to go home at one o'clock.

In the first case, it is probably before one o'clock and the speaker is focusing on the time Owen is going home, which is still in the **future**. The speaker, therefore, uses the Present Simple form of **have** to indicate this fact. In the second example, the time is probably past one o'clock and the speaker is therefore **reporting** both what Owen **said** and the fact that he **has gone** home already. (See Units 2.43, 2.44 for more details of reported speech.)

The **distance** can also be in terms of **possibility** or **probability**. For example:

If I **won** a lottery I would buy a new car.
If we **found** a solution to the problem of how to measure the performance of a system adequately, it would probably not be a simple one.

In the first example, the speaker thinks there is very little chance of winning the lottery. In the second, the writer is indicating by the use of **found** that the chance of a solution is unlikely.

Unit 2.6 Past Simple 2

In this unit we concentrate on the first type of **distance** or **remoteness: time**. (See Units 2.35–2.39 on **conditionals** for a discussion of the second type of distance: **probability**.)

When we speak or write about events, actions or states that occurred in **past time** and when there is a **focus** on the **time** or a **definite time** is given, we use the **Past Simple** form. There are three basic meanings of the Past Simple form:

State
> Pete **was** a very competent lecturer at Stirling University.
> Carole **was** very busy.

Single event
> Lisette **planted** a holly bush in the garden.
> They **found** some new evidence in the case against the three defendants.

Habit or repeated events
> Esme **went** to Spain for her holidays every year.
> Joan **worked** extremely hard on the course.

We can add **adverbials** of **time, frequency** or **duration** to all of these to specify the time of the action or the state. For example:
> They **found** some new evidence in the case against the three defendants **yesterday**.
> Pete **was** a very competent lecturer at Stirling University **for three years**.
> Lisette **planted** a holly bush in the garden **last month**.
> Carole **was** very busy **last week**.
> Joan **worked** extremely hard on the course **last term**.
> Philip **practised** the piano **every day for three hours when he was a young man**.

Unit 2.6 Past simple 2 – TASKS

Task one
Read the following text and fill in the missing words with the correct form of the verb in brackets. Use only the Present Simple (see Unit 2.2) or the Past Simple forms to fill in the blanks.

(a) All the world ...... *(love)* a lover – but I have always thought that the English really ...... *(prefer)* their animals. It ...... *(be)* surely not without significance that, as long ago as 1822, Parliament ...... *(make)* cruelty to animals a crime, but it ...... *(take)* another 67 years before MPs ...... *(get)* around to making cruelty to children also an offence. The Royal Society for the Prevention of Cruelty to Animals – ...... *(notice)* that 'Royal' – ...... *(date)* from 1824. The National Society for the Prevention of Cruelty to Children ...... *(date)* from 1884. Both ...... *(be)* admirable organisations – but why the disparity?

(b) This national obsession with animals ...... *(show)* itself in the law. If an ordinary domestic pet is following its natural bent, 'doing its own thing', the owner ...... *(is)* not usually liable for any damage or injury caused, unless it ...... *(can)* be proved that he has been negligent. And this ...... *(be)* not easy.

(c) For instance, one day a girl was crossing an unfenced, unhedged public footpath – where she ...... *(have)* every right to be – that crossed a farmer's field. Two young, unbroken fillies ...... *(be)* in it. They ...... *(be)* not vicious but undoubtedly playful with a habit of galloping up to people and gathering around them. They ...... *(do)* so this time. Unfortunately, one filly ...... *(bump)* against the girl and ...... *(knock)* her to the ground. She ...... *(sue)* for damages, claiming that the farmer must have known his beasts ...... *(be)* likely to do this.

(d) But she ...... *(lose)* the case. The Appeal Court ...... *(rule)* that the farmer 'had not been lacking in reasonable care' – i.e., had not been negligent.

Task two
(a) *All of the following sentences are correct. Look at the pairs of sentences and decide what the speaker meant to say about the time of the reported event, action or state.*
   (i) He said that he was very depressed.
     He said that he is very depressed.
  (ii) She said it was raining.
     She said it is raining.
 (iii) They said their office is on Main Street.
     They said their office was on Main Street.

(b) *If you know any native speakers of English or if you have an English teacher, try this experiment. Start a conversation with the person and occasionally ask them to repeat something you pretend you did not hear. Check whether they change the verb tense when they complete the sentence, 'I said. . .' If you do this a few times you will find that sometimes they do change to the Past Simple form but often they simply repeat the words in the same form as the original.*

Task three
Yesterday I was looking through some letters and discovered that I had not replied to a letter I received six months ago. When I checked my word processor I found that I had written a reply but had not printed it or sent it. So now I have to change some of the verb tenses because I have already done all the things that I said I was going to do in the letter. The letter was dated 5 January. Now it is

15 June. What changes will I have to make to the verbs and other words in the letter before I can send it?

5 January

Dear Edward

I am really excited because I have just booked my tickets for my trip to Australia. I am leaving on the 15th of this month and will be in Sydney for two weeks. I'll be staying with two old friends, Jim and Cathy, who have a flat on Sydney Harbour and they have promised to take me to all the places of interest in and around Sydney like the Opera House, Bondi Beach and even on a trip into some of the parks and the country outside Sydney. It is summer now in Australia so I will get lots of sun.

It's a long way to go from London and I only have two weeks' holiday but if I don't go this year I may never go at all. So I will just have to be content with two weeks and do as much as possible while I'm there.

You said in your letter that your final exams are at the beginning of February. I hope you do well in them and that you get a chance to take a holiday before you start your new job at the end of February.

You must write and tell me all about the job, your new flat and everything as soon as you are settled in.

Write and give me all your news.

Lots of love,

UNIT 2.7
PAST CONTINUOUS

I was thinking about the test tomorrow.
When we were having supper Peter turned up.
What were you doing when I phoned you yesterday?

It has been calculated that less than five per cent of verb forms are **continuous** and more than ninety-five per cent are **non-continuous**. **Continuous** forms are more frequent in spoken, conversational English and rare in scientific texts.

The **Past Continuous** form is used for **past habits, activities** and **states** just as the **Present Continuous** form is used for the **present time** (see Units 2.3, 2.4). The **Past Continuous** form can convey the following three meanings:

the event or state continued for some time. For example:
Why **weren't** you **taking** notes in the lecture?
I **was thinking** about the test tomorrow.

the time or duration of the state or event is limited. For example:
When we **were having** supper Peter turned up.

the state or event is not necessarily complete or finished. For example:
What **were** you **doing** when I phoned you yesterday?
I **was writing** a letter to Wendy.

There is always an idea of **duration**, that the happening continued for some time, but the other two meanings need not necessarily be present. For example:
When we **were having** supper Peter turned up.
This statement suggests that **having supper** continued for some time and was of limited **duration**, but our knowledge of the context tells us that it is now complete – they are no longer having supper.

On the other hand, the following example doesn't tell us whether or not the letter is written, whether the speaker finished the letter or not:
I **was writing** a letter to Wendy.

Certain verbs (see Unit 2.4) do not normally occur in the **continuous** form, either Present or Past, unless they are used to express a **dynamic** state or take on a meaning connected with an **event**. For example, although the verb **to be** is normally a **state** verb which is not used in the **continuous form**, we could say the following:

The children **were being** very noisy and I couldn't concentrate on the programme.

This suggests that the children's noisiness was a **temporary**, **dynamic** state and **being** is used to replace a word such as **behaving**.

Unit 2.7 Past Continuous

The **Past Continuous** form is often used to express actions that were going on for a period of time when another event occurred. For example:

He **was making** some tea when they arrived.

In this case, the tea-making began **before** they arrived. But if we said the following:

He **made** some tea when they arrived.

then we would mean that he began to make the tea **after** they arrived.

If the two events happen at the same time, then we need to use **as** rather than **when**. For example:

The band **was playing**, the flags **were fluttering** and the crowd **was cheering as** the players ran onto the field.

Unit 2.7 Past Continuous – TASKS

Task one

Look at the following sentences and state which of the two events happened first:

(a) She was talking to her sister on the phone when the doorbell rang.
(b) When I arrived Jim was putting the children to bed.
(c) They were watching the match on television when the police came in.
(d) We were sitting in the garden when I got down on one knee and asked her to marry me.
(e) The neighbours were making such a lot of noise that he banged on the wall to make them stop.
(f) When your letter arrived I was writing a letter to you.

Task two

Ron and Joanne decided to give a Come As You Are party. This is a party to which the guests must come dressed as they were when they received the invitation. Ron phoned the fifteen guests at different times of the day and evening and they all agreed to come to the party.

(a) Barbara arrived in a very old pair of jeans and a T-shirt, carrying a spade.
   What was she doing when she got the invitation to the party?
(b) John arrived in a towel.
   What was he doing when Ron phoned?
(c) Peter arrived in a suit but without any shoes.
   What was he doing when he answered the phone?
(d) Sarah arrived in a swim suit.
   What was she doing when Ron phoned?

With a partner, continue this task, taking turns to ask and answer the question, What was s/he doing when . . . ? Use the following examples:

(e) Robert arrived in an apron.
(f) Edward was carrying a large grammar book.
(g) Anne came in pyjamas.
(h) Bernard was wearing shorts without a shirt.
(j) Sam had old clothes on and was carrying a pair of pliers.
(k) Sally was in overalls and was carrying a paint brush.
(l) Philip brought his dog.
(m) Alan brought his Walkman.
(n) Margaret was in her bare feet and had a bottle of nail varnish.
(p) Sylvia brought a kettle and a tea bag.
(q) Mary brought the telephone.

Task three

Certain events in history have such an impact that people will always remember how they heard the news. President John Kennedy was assassinated in November, 1963 and there are many people today who can still remember what they were doing when they first heard the news.

Think of an important event that many people remember and ask your colleagues what they were doing when they heard the news. Then write down all the things they said they were doing as well as what you yourself were doing at the time you heard the news.

UNIT 2.8
EXPRESSING THE FUTURE IN ENGLISH

English has no **future** tense but there are a number of ways of expressing **future time** in English. We can use any of the following forms:

Will/shall + infinitive
Be going to + infinitive
Will/shall + be + continuous infinitive
Present Simple form
Present Continuous form
Be about to + infinitive
Be to + infinitive

We can also talk about the **future** from a point of time in the **past**. This is often called the **Future in the Past** and five different forms can be used to express this idea.

These different ways of expressing **future** time are not necessarily interchangeable – each one is used to express a particular meaning or idea. Sometimes, although the **meaning** of two forms may be the same, one or the other form may be more appropriate in **informal** speech and the other more acceptable in **formal** situations or in **written** English.

In Units 2.9–2.16 we examine in turn each of these ways of talking about the future.

UNIT 2.9

FUTURE 1: will/shall + infinitive

What will the British education system be like in twenty years' time?
Will the future be any different?
Only time will tell which predictions will turn out to be accurate.
I'll get the book for you. I won't be long.

The most usual way to express the future is by using **will** or **shall** or the contraction **'ll +
infinitive**. Some call this 'the neutral future of prediction'.

Look at these examples:

What **will** the British education system **look** like in twenty years' time?
Only time **will tell** which predictions are accurate.
Will the future **be** any different?

The three sentences above are from a television panel programme discussing the possible
changes in the British education system over the next twenty years. The following sentences
come from a weather forecast in a newspaper:

Parts of the east and south of England **will be** mainly dry at first but rain **will spread** to all
places later.
A low, west of the Hebrides, **will move** east across Scotland.

The next example refers to the British Government's new social security Act:

From April the number of families with children who can get extra benefits **will double**.

And the last example was spoken by someone who was offering to do something for
someone:

I'**ll get** the book for you. I **won't be** long.

This example illustrates the following two further points you need to know about **shall/will**
or **'ll**:

First, only **will/shall** or **'ll** can be used to express decisions that have been made at the
moment of speaking. (It would **not be possible** to use **going to** in this statement.)
Second, it shows the use of the negative contraction **won't** for **will not**.

All of these examples demonstrate that you can use **will/shall** to make a prediction about the
future or to ask a question about something in the future. You must also use **will/shall**, **'ll** or
won't (in the **negative**) when you are stating something you have **just decided to do**.

Will or shall?

One 'rule' you may have learnt is that **shall** is used with the first person (I or we) and **will** is
used with the second and third persons (she, he, it, you, they). In many British schools
children are still taught that this is the correct way to use **shall** and **will** but this distinction is
rapidly disappearing in ordinary speech and writing. In the USA and Canada **shall** is rarely
used at all. The most common form in spoken English all over the world is the contraction **'ll**.

Continued

Another use of **will** is to signal that there is an element of **intention** or **personal involvement** in the statement. If you say, 'I'll be there tomorrow', you are expressing an **intention** or a **promise**.

Shall with the **first person** (I or we) is still used when making an **offer** to do something:

> **Shall** I carry that for you?
> **Shall** I do that for you?

Or to ask for **permission** or **instructions**:

> **Shall** I come to your house or **will** you come to mine?

Will with the **second person** (you) is used to ask for **help**:

> **Will** you hold this for me?

Or to issue an **invitation** or a polite order or **request**:

> **Will** you come into my office, please.

Unit 2.9 Future 1 – TASKS

Task one

(a) *Look at the following headlines and state whether they refer to the future or to something that had already happened when the headline was written:*

Skiing
....
Zurbriggen keeps World Cup

Gadafy to withdraw troops

Troops to guard civilian gaols

World's cities to tackle urban health problems at pioneering Liverpool conference

Whitbread to axe 300 London jobs

BAe calls for shake-up of Airbus

Bell sells TV stations

*How did you decide whether the headlines referred to the present situation or to the future? You probably noticed the difference in the verb form: the Present tense refers to a fact or event that affects the present although it has already happened; the future is signalled by the use of **to**. Newspaper headlines often signal the future by using **to** plus the infinitive. For example, the headline for the article you will be asked to write in Task 4 could be THREE TO BE HONOURED. This means that three distinguished people will receive honorary degrees.*

(b) *All of the headlines in the list above that refer to the future could be re-written using **will**; the ones that refer to past events could be written using a Past form of the verb. Re-write the headlines as the first lines of the newspaper article using **will** for those that refer to the future and using the Present Perfect for those that refer to the past.*

Task two

(a) *Read the following text and fill in the missing words with the correct forms of the verbs in brackets.*

   (i) Today's weather forecast. General outlook: Northern Ireland, Wales and south-west England . . . . . . *(begin)* wet but . . . . . . *(become)* brighter.

   (ii) Western Scotland and the remainder of England . . . . . . *(begin)* dry with some sunshine in extreme eastern parts. Rain . . . . . . *(spread)* with heavy falls especially over southern England.

  (iii) It . . . . . . *(become)* brighter and showery in central, southern and north-western England and western Scotland.

  (iv) Eastern Scotland . . . . . . *(begin)* dry and sunny with a touch of ground frost. It . . . . . . *(be)* cloudy with rain in the afternoon.

(b) *What statements could you make about the weather on this day? Write six statements that are true according to the forecast. An example has been written for you.*

      It probably won't rain in western Scotland.
....

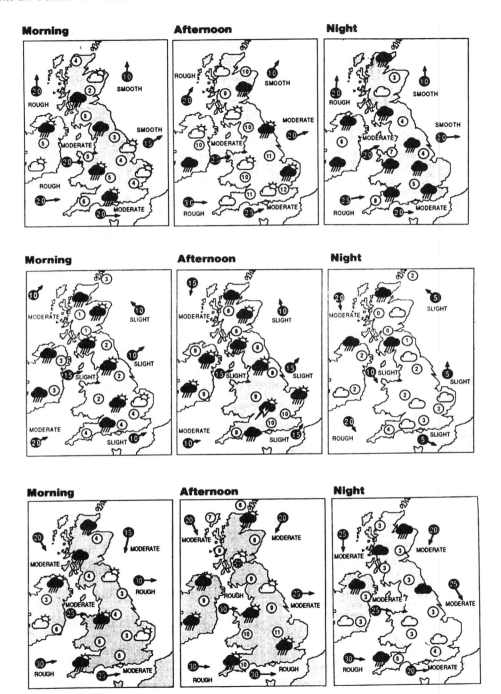

Task three

Most British newspapers and television and radio programmes carry items about the weather. This may be because, as you have probably heard, the British weather is very changeable and the British seem to talk about it a great deal.

Here are three weather forecasts. Match each forecast with the correct picture sequence that illustrates the text.

(a) A depression will move south-east across Scotland. Another low will affect south-west England. There will be showery conditions elsewhere. It will be mainly cloudy over Scotland and Northern Ireland, with outbreaks of rain, heavy in places and snow on some hills. Wales and south-west England will be mostly cloudy with occasional rain.

(b) A changeable westerly airstream covers the British Isles. Eastern Britain will start dry and quite sunny, with just a few rural fog patches. Western areas will be more cloudy with some showery rain and these cloudier skies will reach all areas by mid-afternoon. Most of the rain will be in the north-west. Brighter weather will follow, but during the evening further rain is expected.

(c) There is a depression off eastern Scotland with a showery airstream over most of the country. In northern and eastern Scotland there will be showers or longer periods of rain. There will be snow over the mountains at times. Elsewhere there will be sunny periods and showers, confined to western districts at first, becoming more widespread later with only well-sheltered eastern or southeastern parts remaining dry. It will remain windy everywhere with gales over southern and western parts of England and Wales. Although temperatures will be near normal for mid-March the winds will make it feel much colder.

Task four

Read the following notes that were made by the secretary at a meeting of the Senate of the University of Lancaster. Imagine that you are a reporter for the local Lancaster newspaper and have been asked to write up the notes into a short article. The article will appear one week before the ceremony.

The Chancellor, HRH Princess Alexandra – preside at a ceremony for the conferment of higher and honorary degrees on Thursday, 3 December.
Sir Ronald Halstead – receive the honorary degree of Doctor of Science.
M. Maurice Lévy – receive the honorary degree of Doctor of Science.
Dr Derek Whiteside – receive the honorary degree of Doctor of Letters.

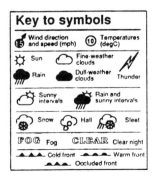

UNIT 2.10
FUTURE 2: be going to + infinitive

We are going to get the report out early next week.
What are they going to do now?
Jason Donovan is going to be on the programme next week.
The last episode of *Crossroads* was on last night. Is there going to be another series?

Be going to + infinitive is commonly used to express the future in informal speech. There are two basic meanings of this form and both depend on the situation in the present time.

The first meaning expresses the **future fulfilment** of a **present intention** or plan.

Look at these examples:

We **are going to get** the report out early next week.
What **are they going to do** now?
Jason Donovan **is going to be** on the programme next week.
The last episode of *Crossroads*, the soap opera, was on last night. **Is** there **going to be** another series?
You**'re going to be** very surprised when you see the house.
He**'s going to give** a talk at the conference in Berlin next month.

All of these statements are spoken utterances which tell the hearer what is **going to happen** as a result of a plan which has already been made.

The second meaning of this form is to express the **future result** of a **cause in the present**.

Look at these examples:

It**'s going to rain**. (The sky has become very dark.)
He**'s going to win** the race. (He is well ahead of all the other contestants.)
She**'s going to have** a baby next month. (She is pregnant now.)

In this use of **be going to + infinitive**, there is a sense that the result is **almost immediate**. In the first two utterances this is certainly true. If, however, as in the third utterance, the result is not going to be immediate, then you must use a **time phrase** such as **next month, next year, in March**, etc.

WARNING BOX

We do not use **be going to + infinitive** to make an **offer**. If, for example, you are at home with your family and the phone rings, you would say:

'I**'ll get** it'
'I**'ll answer** it'

and **not**

'I*'m going to answer* it'.

'I*'m going to answer* it' would suggest that you had a **definite intention** and that you thought someone would **prevent** you from doing what you wanted to do. It would not be an offer to do something.

If we are talking about the future, we do not usually continue to repeat **be going to + infinitive** throughout the text. So, if you were talking about the weather, for example, you might say:

It**'s going to rain** tomorrow morning but then in the afternoon it**'ll clear** and **be** sunny and much warmer. So it**'ll be** nice for the barbeque in the evening.

Unit 2.10 Future 2 – TASKS

Task one

Read the following text and fill in the missing words with the correct form of the verb in brackets. It is a conversation between a television interviewer and an actress in the television soap opera, Crossroads. *The last episode has just been screened.*

Interviewer: Now that you've finished *Crossroads*, what . . . . . . *(do)* next?

Actress: I've been very busy. I don't know what I . . . . . . *(do)* next but I have quite a few plans.

Interviewer: Is there . . . . . . *(be)* another series?

Actress: Possibly. But I don't know. I keep meeting people in shops who tell me 'My wife . . . . . . *(miss)* you' and I think quite a lot of people . . . . . . *(feel)* like that.

Interviewer: We're . . . . . . *(see)* a clip from *Crossroads* now and one of your co-stars . . . . . . *(watch)* this with us.

Task two

Geoff and Ellen Scott have just returned from a time management course run by a college of further education in a town near their offices. They are very enthusiastic about what they have learned and have persuaded their two children to make some plans for managing their time more efficiently. Everyone has written down how they plan to be more efficient and manage their time better and Geoff has pinned their notes to a bulletin board in the hall to remind them of their plans.

Geoff	**Ellen**
Buy a personal organiser and use it.	Start a time log to see how I spend my time.
Delegate more to my staff.	Keep an up-to-date shopping list.
Set aside regular times for meetings with my staff.	Make a schedule of household chores and assign something to everyone.
Hold fewer meetings.	Get to the office half-an-hour earlier so I can sort things out before my staff arrive.

Anne	**Charles**
Buy a filing cabinet to keep my notes from college in so I can find what I need quickly.	Make a weekly study schedule. Do my homework every evening.
Put my books in alphabetical order on the shelves.	Limit my phone calls to twenty minutes each.
Practise typing for thirty minutes a day.	Get Anne to take the dog for a walk every other day.

Continued

(a) *Look at the notes above and write down what each member of the family would say about his or her own ideas for time management. An example has been written for you.*

Example:

I'm going to buy a personal organiser and use it.

(b) *When Ellen went to work the next day, she told some of her friends what had happened. After she had told them what she was planning to do, she told them about the others' plans. Write what she said. An example has been written for you.*

Example:

Anne is going to buy a filing cabinet to keep her notes in

Task three

Look at the cartoons below and, using **be going to + infinitive**, *say what you think is going to happen next.*

(a)

(b)

(c)

(d)

(e)   SHOP-LIFTING IS A CRIME!   LATEST VIDEOS

(f)   NO PARKING

(g)

(h)   RING-RING!

Task four

Think of seven things you plan to do next week and decide when you can do each one. Then fill in the following page from the diary with the seven things. If you have a friend who is studying with you or you are in a class, ask your partner to do the same and then ask her/him questions about what s/he is going to do, buy, see, watch, etc., next week. Then get your partner to do the same. If you are working on your own or if you want to get some more practice with this form, you can write down the questions and answers. Some examples have been written for you.

Examples:

Q: What are you going to buy next week ?

A: I'm going to buy a record.

Q: What are you going to watch on TV tonight ?

A: I'm going to watch the film.

Monday 5

Tuesday 6

Wednesday 7

Thursday 8

Friday 9

Saturday 10

Sunday 11

UNIT 2.11

FUTURE 3: will/shall + be + continuous infinitive

I'll be moving to London in August.
Will you be selling your house in Switzerland?
I'll be starting another book very soon.
I'll be doing plenty of exercises and getting fit for the race.

We can use **will/shall** or **'ll + be + continuous infinitive** to talk about the future when we want to put the event or state into the **continuous time** frame.

Look at these examples:

More than 300 million people **will be watching** the Grand National tomorrow.
They're wondering whether he**'ll be running** in the marathon next week.
I**'ll be doing** plenty of exercises and **getting** fit for the race.
I**'ll be starting** another book very soon.

In these statements, the speaker is thinking about an event or experience in the **near future** which will continue for a **specific** period of **time**, with a definite **beginning** and **end**.

Another purpose of this form is to indicate that the future event or experience will happen as **a matter of course**, without the implication that there is any human intention, planning or promise involved.

Look at these examples:

Brian **will be handing in** the keys to the flat and he**'ll be moving in** with his son next month.
Now that we've won this award I think we**'ll** probably **be getting** a bigger audience for our performances.
I**'ll be moving** to London in August.
Will you **be selling** your house in Switzerland?
I**'ll be starting** another book very soon.

Brian has been working as a lighthouse keeper and is about to retire. He will, of course, leave the lighthouse and go to live somewhere else.

The spokesman for the singing group who made the second statement sees a bigger audience as a natural result of the publicity they have received by winning the award.

The last three statements come from an interview on television with Sally Burton, Richard Burton's widow. The rest of the interview was as follows:

Interviewer: **Are** you **coming** back to London?
Burton: Yes. I**'ll be moving** to London in August.
Interviewer: Does that mean you**'ll be selling** your house in Switzerland?
Burton: Yes.
Interviewer: What do you think might happen in the next ten years? **Will** you **write** another book?
Burton: I**'ll be starting** another one very soon.

From this exchange we can see that Sally Burton considers these events as following, as a matter of course, one on the other. By using **will/shall + continuous infinitive** she gives them a sense of **inevitability** or **routine**. This meaning explains the following expression:

I'll **be seeing** you.

This example is a very casual way of saying that I'll see you some time because we will certainly meet again soon but neither of us has a definite plan to meet or any fixed meeting time. The same construction is useful when we want to remind someone tactfully of an **obligation** or **duty** and do not want to seem as if we are ordering them to do anything. For example,

When **will** you **be paying** this bill?

When **will** you **be clearing** your overdraft?

In both cases, the suggestion is that there is no question of your not paying, the person is simply asking **when** you will pay your debts.

If there is no human involvement, however, there is no difference in meaning between the **continuous** and **non-continuous** forms. For example:

The next train to Glasgow **will arrive/will be arriving** on platform 2.

The continuous form, however, is more informal.

Sometimes we use **will + be + continuous infinitive** as a roundabout way of **asking someone for something** or **asking someone to do something** for us..

Look at these examples:

Will you **be using** your lawn mower tomorrow?

Will you **be going** to the library today?

Will you **be seeing** Richard this evening?

Will you **be using** the word processor this afternoon?

All of these 'questions' are indirect ways of **asking someone to do something** for you. You would not expect a simple Yes or No answer to any of them because the person you addressed would know that you were not asking simply out of curiosity or interest but that you had another reason for asking. So the exchange might go something like this:

Will you **be using** your lawn mower tomorrow?

No, do you want to borrow it?

Will you **be going** to the library today?

Yes, do you want me to take your book back for you?

Will you **be seeing** Richard this evening?

Yes. Why? Do you have a message for him?

Will you **be using** the word processor this afternoon?

Yes I will. Sorry. You can use it this evening though.

Unit 2.11 Future 3 – TASKS

Task one

(a) *After the spring break, Barbara and John will be going back to university and getting back into the same routine as before the holidays. Write some sentences, using **will/shall** or **'ll + be + continuous infinitive**, about what they will be doing when they get back. Use the cues to help you or think up your own activities.*

(b) *If you rewrote the sentences using* **be going to + infinitive** *how would the meaning of the statements change?*

Task two

A radio newsreader has been given the following notes for his next sports broadcast. All the events are in the future. What will he say when he reads the news?

The Grand National – 300 million people watch; thirty-six horses; at Aintree.

The London Marathon – one million spectators; over 25,000 runners.

British versus Brazilian Schoolboys football – 60,000 spectators at Wembley Stadium.

Severiano Ballesteros, Sandy Lyle, Greg Norman – 20,000 viewers; US Masters Golf Championship at Augusta, Georgia.

Task three

(a) *Practise a dialogue with your partner using* **will/'ll + be + continuous infinitive** *to indirectly ask her/him to do something for you.*

Your partner is going shopping and you want some aspirin from the chemist's, some bread from the baker's and a computer magazine from the newsagent's.

(b) *Now change roles and have your partner make the indirect requests.*

Your partner wants to borrow your bicycle, use your computer and watch *Dallas* on television in the evening.

UNIT 2.12
FUTURE 4: Present Simple form

Tomorrow is Friday.
The flight doesn't leave at 16.45; it leaves at 18.45.
The Money Programme **returns at 5 o'clock on Wednesday.**
The big race tomorrow is The Grand National at Aintree.

The **Present Simple** form is used to talk about the **future** when the event is seen as a definite **fact**, just as the **Present Simple** form is used to express a **fact** in the **present time**.

Look at these examples:
> Tomorrow **is** Friday.
> The flight **doesn't leave** at 16.45; it **leaves** at 18.45.
> *The Money Programme* **returns** at 5 o'clock on Wednesday.
> A new comedy series **starts** on Channel 4 at the end of the week.
> The big race tomorrow **is** the Grand National at Aintree.
> In England, Luton **take** on Portsmouth tomorrow and in Scotland, Hearts **face** Celtic.

The calendar is fixed and one day follows another in the same order. Similarly, airline and television schedules and sports events are decided many months in advance and are not subject to change in the normal course of events. We see these events, therefore, as **facts** and not as possible events in the future.

Now look at this example:
> The wedding **is** next month and it**'s** a white wedding.

Again, the woman who made this statement did not consider that there was any doubt that the wedding would take place or that the bride would be wearing a long white dress.

The **Present Simple** form is used to express the **future** very often but this is usually in dependent clauses after conditionals such as **if** or **unless** (see Units 2.35–2.39) or after time conjunctions such as **when, as soon as, until**, etc. The main clause is usually in the **will/shall** or **'ll** form or the **be going to + infinitive** form but the verb in the dependent clause which is introduced by a conditional or time conjunction is in the **Present Simple** form. For example:
> What will happen if it **rains**?
> I'll let you have a copy of the report as soon as I **finish** it.
> I'm going to work on this when I **have** more time.

Unit 2.12 Future 4 – TASKS

Task one

(a) *Look at the following British Rail timetables for trains from Lancaster to London and back, then answer the questions below.*

London → Lancaster

Mondays to Saturdays	London Euston depart	Lancaster arrive
▲ ® ⊘	0730	1035
B ® ⊡ SO	0840	1259B
▲ ® ⊘ SX	0855	1259
A ® ⊡ SO	0900	1159A
® ⊡	0930c	1259
® ⊘	1030	1319
® ⊘	1130c	1515
® ⊘	1300	1604
® ⊘	1400	1733
▼ ® ⊘	1530	1841
▲ F ® ⊘ SX	1630p	2006
■ ® ⊘	1730	2023
⊡ SO	1825	2156
® ⊘ SX	1830	2156
⊘ SX	1930p	2309
B ② ® SO	2200	0204B
② ® SX	2300	0246
A ② ® SO	2300	0422A

Sundays	London Euston depart	Lancaster arrive
H ⊡	1000b	1500H
E ® ⊡	1000	1502E
G ⊡	1000p	1543G
® ⊡	1300	1653
⊡	1450c	1829
® ⊡	1530	1854
® ⊘	1630	1953
® ⊡	1730	2033
⊡	1830	2150
② ®	2300	0252

Lancaster → London

Mondays to Saturdays	Lancaster depart	London Euston arrive
② ®	0225	0635
② ®	0337	0733
▲ F ® ⊘ SX	0620p	0948
⊡ SO	0620p	0948
® ⊘	0703	1034
® ⊘	0827	1157
⊡	0949p	1336
® ⊘	1036	1356
® ⊘ SX	1128p	1517
A ® ⊡ SO	1142	1453A
® ⊘	1330	1652
® ⊘	1418p	1731
® ⊘	1554	1924
® ⊘	1627	1940
F ⊡ SO	1717c	2049
® ⊡ SX	1717c	2105
® ⊘	1717	2131
® ⊘	1931	2253
② ⊷ SX	2301f	0448

Sundays	Lancaster depart	London Euston arrive
C ② ®	0224	0748C
B ② ®	0224	0834B
D ⊡	0856p	1525D
E ⊡	0930b	1525E
G ⊡	1000b	1525G
D ⊡	1208	1727D
E	1245b	1831E
D	1311	1831D
G	1325b	1831G
D ® ⊡	1403	1845D
D ® ⊡	1609	1926D
⊡	1633	1952
H	1710	2040H
® ⊡	1728	2101
® ⊡	1905p	2244
② ⊷	2301f	0443

   (i) Anne is going to London on Sunday. Her train leaves at 12.08. What time does it arrive in London?

  (ii) Sally's train arrives in London at 10.34. What time does it leave Lancaster?

 (iii) What time does the first train leave Lancaster on Sundays?

 (iv) What time does the last train leave Lancaster on Mondays to Saturdays?

  (v) What time does the first train arrive from Lancaster on Mondays?

(b) *With a partner think of your own questions like the ones above and work together to ask and answer them.*

Task two

Susan and Joan are discussing what they plan to watch on television in the evening. Look at the following television schedule and fill in the missing words, using the correct forms of the verbs in brackets.

TODAY AT A GLANCE

BBC1

6.00	Six O'Clock News
6.35	Regional magazines
7.00	Top of the Pops
7.30	EastEnders
8.00	Tomorrow's World
8.30	Mastermind
9.00	Nine O'Clock News
9.30	Crimewatch UK
10.10	Black and White
10.40	Question Time
11.40	Crimewatch Update
11.50-11.55	Weather

BBC2

6.50	Cartoon Two
7.00	Cover to Cover
7.30	Call My Bluff
8.00	Top Gear
8.30	Nature
9.00	Blackadder II
9.30	40 Minutes
10.10	Have Footlights – Will Travel
10.40	Newsnight
11.25	Weather
11.30	Weekend Outlook
11.35-12.05	Open University

Susan: I'm going to study until 7.00 and then I'll watch some television. What ...... *(be)* on tonight?

Joan: Well, *Top of the Pops* ...... *(start)* at 7.00. It ...... *(be)* a pop music programme. Then there ...... *(be) Eastenders* at 7.30.

Susan: When ...... *(finish)*?

Joan: At 8.00. *40 Minutes* ...... *(start)* at 9.30.

Susan: So it ...... *(not finish)* until 10.10.

Joan: No. But that's all right.. *Black and White* ...... *(not start)* until 10.10.

Susan: Oh. Well nothing ...... *(sound)* very interesting. What ...... *(be)* on ITV and Channel 4?

Task three

How many correct and sensible sentences can you make by choosing one word from each of the following columns? The verbs are in the infinitive form so you will have to put them in the correct form. You can use the words in any order and you may add other words such as nouns, prepositions, adjectives, adverbs if you like. Statements, questions and negative statements or questions each count as one sentence. Give yourself or your group a time limit and, if you can, have a competition with another group or pair. When the time is up, check each other's sentences to make sure they are correct and make sense. Some examples have been written for you.

Examples:

I'll telephone him when I arrive.
....
I'll ask her as soon as I speak to her.
....
When you leave I'll play the record you don't like.
....
Will you stay if I go?
....
If it rains she won't come.
....

I	do	me	if	speak
you	come	you	when	tell
she	ask	her	as soon as	go
he	play	him	after	see
it	have	it	before	rain
we	arrive	us	until	leave
they	stay	them	unless	telephone
your name	get	partner's name	till	finish

UNIT 2.13
FUTURE 5: Present Continuous form

They're meeting at 4.30 this afternoon.
Manchester is playing Liverpool next Saturday.
We're having fish for dinner.
Sanyo are opening a new shop in Lancaster next month.
Where are you going for your honeymoon?

We can talk about the **future** by using the **Present Continuous** form. The meaning is similar to the meaning with **be going to** + **infinitive** in that it suggests something that is going to happen fairly soon, unless there is a time phrase that gives a later time. Like **be going to** + **infinitive**, the **Present Continuous** form is usually used in **informal** speech and is less commonly used in writing.

Look at these examples:
Manchester **is playing** Liverpool next Saturday.
They**'re meeting** at 4.30 this afternoon.
We**'re having** fish for dinner.
We**'re getting married** in Portsmouth in June.
Where **are you going** for your honeymoon?
Sanyo **are opening** a new shop in Lancaster next month.
This film **is coming** to a cinema near you very soon.

All of these statements have one basic meaning: they refer to a **future event** which arises from a **present arrangement** or **plan**.

One important point to note is that the **future arrangement** or **plan** must involve **human beings**. You **cannot** say the following:

It is raining tomorrow.
The birds are building their nests next month.

With domestic **pets**, however, which many people consider to have human qualities, we can use the **Present Continuous** form to indicate the future. For example:

My cat**'s having** kittens next week.

WARNING BOX

The **Present Continuous** form can be used to indicate the **future** only with **event** or **dynamic verbs**, not with **state verbs** (see Unit 2.4) which cannot take the **-ing** form. With **state verbs**, we have to use **will/shall** or **'ll** + **infinitive** or **be going to** + **infinitive**. *For example:*

There **will be** no programme tomorrow.
It**'s going to seem** very quiet when all the students have left.

Unit 2.13 Future 5 – TASKS

Task one

(a) *Read the following text and underline the Present Continuous forms of the verbs.*

I'm having a party tomorrow night. I'm putting all the living room furniture upstairs so there'll be lots of room for everyone to stand and move around. I'm putting all the food on the dining-room table and everybody can just mill around and help themselves. I'm having a huge turkey, fried chicken, plenty of bread, salads and little things like pickled onions and olives and cheeses. I'm having all the drinks on the sideboard. And I'm getting an entertainer to play the guitar.

(b) *Which verbs are not in the Present Continuous form? Why are they not?*

(c) *The person who was speaking about the party was definitely planning to have a party and was telling a friend what she planned to do for it. If she had begun with 'I think', what form would she have put each of the verbs in?*

(d) *Rewrite the passage beginning with 'I think . . .' and change all the verb forms that need to be changed.*

Task two

Peter and Lisa Owen are taking a one-week holiday from work next week. They aren't going away because they are planning to redecorate the kitchen and they are going to use the time to get it all done. Here is a list of all the things they are planning to do. Look at the list and then complete the letter to Peter's friend Bill, telling him what they are planning to do.

paint the kitchen ceiling;
tile the wall above the sink;
paint the other walls;
put two new shelves on the wall over the counter;

replace the floor tiles;
put up new curtains;
install a new cooker.

Dear Bill

Lisa and I are planning to completely re-do the kitchen next week. Perhaps you'd like to come and help with some of the work?

We're . . .

All the best,

Task three

Write a letter to a friend telling them about a plan you have to do something in your house or garden.

UNIT 2.14

**FUTURE 6: be about to +
infinitive**

The programme's about to begin.
They're about to leave for Rome.
He's about to make the dinner.
I'm about to leave.
If you're about to buy a new television,
check our prices first.

Be about to + infinitive indicates the **very near future**. It has almost the same meaning as **just going to** or **going to in a very short time**. Like **be going to + infinitive**, it is used in **informal**, colloquial English.

Look at these examples:
The programme's **about to begin**.
They**'re about to leave** for Rome.
He**'s about to make** the dinner.
I**'m about to leave**.
If you**'re about to buy** a new television, check our prices first.

The same meaning could be expressed by the following:
The programme's **just going to** begin.
They're **just going to** leave for Rome.
He's **just going to** make the dinner.
I'm **just going to** leave.
If you**'re going to** buy a new television **soon**, check our prices first.

Unit 2.14 Future 6 – TASKS

Task one

Read the following questions and write replies that make excuses for not doing what they ask you to do. (You can use the suggested cues in brackets if you like.) An example has been written for you.

Example:
I'm going out now. If Philip phones, would you tell him I'll be back at 4.00.

Sorry. I'm about to leave myself.

(a) Do you want to watch the film on television? *(Start the dinner.)*
(b) Would you help me hang these pictures? *(Wash the car.)*
(c) Do you want to go shopping with me? *(Go to the cinema.)*
(d) Would you give me a hand with the washing up? *(Hang up the clothes.)*
(e) Can you go and see who's at the door? *(Take a shower.)*

UNIT 2.15
FUTURE 7: be to + infinitive

The government are to make changes that will make motorway travel safer.
Speed limits at road works are to be mandatory.
Cars behind slow-moving traffic are to put on hazard lights.

Be to + infinitive can be used to refer to a **future plan** or **programme**. This is a fairly **formal** way of expressing the future and is used more often in written than in spoken English.

Look at these examples:
The government **are to make** changes that will make motorway travel safer.
Speed limits at road works **are to be** mandatory.
Cars behind slow-moving traffic **are to put on** hazard lights.

This form is often used to suggest that it is a requirement. For example:
You **are to report** to the District Office tomorrow.
Passengers **are to clear** their hand baggage through Security after checking in.

It is often used in the passive. For example:
Postage stamp prices **are to be frozen** until the end of the summer.

Be to + infinitive is often used in the first sentence of a report. After that, the writer usually continues by using **will/shall + infinitive**. For example:

THE BBC is to screen a new series for young people produced by Janet Street Porter as part of its £50 million summer schedules, announced yesterday. Its plans include 600 hours of original material.

The series, called DEF2, will start on May 9 and include music, factual programmes and repeats of classics.

A weekly series, Rough Guide, will look at life for the young in European cities, including Dublin, Milan, Madrid and Copenhagen.

Unit 2.15 Future 7 – TASKS

Task one

Read the following sentences and fill in the missing words with the correct form of **be to + infinitive** *of the verb in brackets.*

(a) Activists from the Green Party and the Social and Liberal Democrats . . . . . . *(join)* forces in campaigning on a range of issues.

(b) Mr Willis . . . . . . *(address)* representatives of manual workers at Ford's twenty-two UK plants.

(c) British Airways and other international airlines . . . . . . *(begin)* detailed negotiations with the New Zealand government for the purchase of a large shareholding in Air New Zealand.

(d) France . . . . . . *(transfer)* underground nuclear tests from Mururoa to an island twenty-five miles away.

(e) *Debrett's Peerage*, the 210-year-old *Who's Who* of the aristocracy, ... *(become)* a stablemate of books on computers, technology and management.

UNIT 2.16

FUTURE 8: the future in the past

You were going to phone me yesterday.
I was going to tell you all about it.
She was going to get her degree and then get a job in Japan but she went to Madrid instead.
She was leaving for Singapore the next day.
He was about to go out when I arrived.

Many of the **future** forms we have studied in Units 2.9–2.15 can be used in the **Past** form to talk about something which is in the **future** when looked at from a point in the **past**.

Be going to + infinitive and **be about to + infinitive** often have the meaning of **unfulfilled intention** or of plans that did not come about. If there is nothing to contradict this interpretation, then we usually assume that whatever was planned did not take place.

Look at these examples:
   (a) You **were going to phone** me yesterday.
   (b) I **was going to tell** you all about it.
   (c) He **was about to go** out when I arrived.
   (d) We **were about to have** dinner when the lights went out.
   (e) She **was going to get** her degree and then get a job in Japan but she went to Madrid instead.

Example (a) was said by someone, possibly as a complaint, who is asking for an explanation for the other person's behaviour in not telephoning. The answer could be, for example:
   Sorry. I **was going** to phone you but I went out and couldn't find a phone I could use.

Example (b) was said by someone whose friend has heard some news from other people. The conversation could be as follows:
   Anne: I've just heard that you are coming to London for a holiday.
   Sally: Yes, I'm sorry. I **was going to tell** you all about it but I've been so busy I never got around to writing to you.

Example (c) suggests that he didn't go out because I arrived.

Example (d) suggests that we couldn't have dinner right away because we had to spend time looking for torches and candles.

Example (e) means that she did get the degree but changed her mind about going to Japan.

The **Past Continuous** form is used to talk about a **plan** or **arrangement** that was decided in the **past** and that would take place in the **future** when looked at from that point in the **past**. For example:
   She **was leaving** for Singapore the next day.

Be to + infinitive is used in **formal** writing or speech and is most common in literary works. It suggests **fulfilment of an arrangement** or of someone's **destiny** or **fate**. For example:
   They **were** eventually **to be sentenced** to ten years' imprisonment each.
   The decision she made that day **was to have** unforeseen consequences.

The form using the modal **would** is also found in **formal**, literary styles. For example:
   The young boy **would grow up** to become President of France.

All of the above forms differ in **meaning** from the same forms used in **reported** speech. (See Units 2.43, 2.44.)

Unit 2.16 Future 8 – TASKS

Task one

Look back to Unit 2.10 Task 2. The Scott family made lots of plans for the future but they did not do all the things they planned to do. One month after they sat down and made those plans, they are talking about them and explaining why they didn't manage to stick to their original plans.

Read the following conversation and fill in the missing words with the **be going to + infinitive** *form of the verbs in brackets. Then continue the conversation, giving each member of the family excuses for not doing what they planned to do. If you have a partner you can do this orally and write down the verb forms only for practice.*

Geoff: Well, it's been a month since we decided to organise ourselves more efficiently. Let's see what has happened to those plans. I'll start and then the rest of you can tell us what has happened.

First, I . . . . . . *(buy)* a personal organiser and use it. I bought it and I used it for two weeks but then I stopped because it was taking a lot of time to fill things in and I wasn't really using it very efficiently.

Then I . . . . . . *(delegate)* more to my staff. Well, I've done that, so that's one thing that I said I . . . . . . *(do)* and I've done.

Task two

Think of some of the things you were about to do in the past few weeks that were interrupted and that you weren't able to do. Write six sentences about them using **about to + infinitive.** *Some examples have been written for you.*

Examples:

I was about to read the newspaper when the fire started.

They were about to start the race when a starting block collapsed.

Task three

Use the Past Continuous form to write about what happened one day two weeks ago. Choose one day and recount your activities that day using, where possible, the Past Continuous form to indicate the future. (Remember that you cannot use the continuous form with state verbs and that you must use the Simple Past for those verbs.) An example has been written for you.

Two weeks ago on Monday I got up early. I was meeting Tony and Dianne at 9·00 and we were planning our work for the following week.

UNIT 2.17
PRESENT PERFECT

The University has revealed plans to make massive changes in the structuring of some departments.
Over the past fifty years many urban trees have been lost through disease, drought, development and neglect.

The **Present Perfect** is formed with **has/have ('s/'ve) + past participle**. In English, the **Present Perfect** can cause problems for learners because, in other languages, the **Present Simple** or **Past Simple** is used to express the meaning that the **Present Perfect** has in English.

Look at these examples:
    I**'ve been** here for an hour.
    They**'ve lived** in Lancaster since 1985.
In these two cases, many languages would use the **Present Simple** to express the idea. But this is not possible in English.

Look at these examples:
    I **am** here for an hour.
    They **live** in Lancaster.
The first example refers to the time from now to the future; in other words, I will be here for an hour from now. The second is a simple statement of fact but we are not able to refer to the time in the past (i.e. 1985) when they first started living in Lancaster.

1. Uses of the Present Perfect

There are three main uses or meanings of the **Present Perfect**:

1. A state **continuing** from the past up to the present time. For example:
    How long **has** he **been** ill?
    The road **has been closed** for two weeks.

2. Events in a period **leading up to** the present time. For example:
    The Barclayshare Personal Equity Plan **has been designed** to make life really easy.
    The University **has revealed** plans to make massive changes in the structuring of some departments.
    Have you **seen** Clive?

This use of the **Present Perfect** form implies:
    that the time leads up to the present time;
    that the event is recent;
    that the result of the action is still present.
but not all of the three necessarily apply in every case.

In American English, the **Simple Past** is often used instead of the **Present Perfect**, especially with such adverbials as **just, yet, already** and **recently**. For example:
    American: I **just arrived**
            He didn't do it yet.
    British: I**'ve just arrived**.
            He **hasn't done** it yet.

65

3. **Habits** or **recurrent events** in a period **leading up to** the present time, for example:
> Over the past fifty years many urban trees **have been lost** through disease, drought, development and neglect.
> British Telecom **has spent** £1 million a month to improve the payphone service.
> **Have** you ever **eaten** snails?

The important thing to remember about the use of the **Present Perfect** is that the speaker or writer is **focusing** on **now**.

In the units on the **Past Simple** (Units 2.5, 2.6), we said that this form refers to events or states that are distant or remote in some way such as **time** or **probability**. But the **Present Perfect** form is not distant in this way. Although it refers to **events** or **states** which **started** in past time, these events or states are either **still present** now or have some effect on or give some meaning to the present time.

Look at these examples again:
> I**'ve been** here for an hour.
> They**'ve lived** in Lancaster since 1985.

The first means that I am still here and I arrived an hour ago (in the past time); the second means that we can infer that they still live in Lancaster.

2. Using adverbs and prepositions with the Present Perfect

Certain **adverbs** and **prepositions** are commonly used with the **Present Perfect**. These include: **since, up to, so far.**

Look at this example:
> The European drinking water directive **has been** in force **since** 1985.
> There **has been** no proof **up to now** that nitrates in drinking water do you any harm (except in a few rare cases).
> The only response the authorities **have produced so far** is a statement that there is no need for people on a public water supply to buy water filters.

Ever is another **adverbial** that is commonly used with the **Present Perfect** but it is never used with the **Past Simple**. It means **at any time** and, when used with the **Present Perfect**, refers to **all time** up to and including the present time. For example:
> **Have** you **ever been** to Thailand?
> I don't think I **have ever seen** her looking so upset before.

Ever is used only in **questions** or **negative** statements. It **cannot** be used with a **positive** statement.

Never is commonly used with the **Present Perfect** but it can also be used with the **Simple Past**. For example:
> I**'ve never been** to Hungary.
> I **never liked** going to the cinema on my own when I was a teenager.

For can be used with either the **Present Perfect** or the **Past Simple**. For example:
> **For** the past few years, a new approach **has been adopted** by conservationists.
> Pete **lived** in Cambridge **for** five years before he moved to Stirling.

If a **definite time** in the past is given, then the **Past Simple** should be used. For example:
> Geoffrey Berry, who devoted much of his life to the conservation of the Lake District, **died on 29 January**, aged 75.
> Four pages of scribblings by Beatle John Lennon in a school exercise book **were sold** for £12,000 at Sotheby's in London **yesterday**.

If, however, the time mentioned is a period which includes the **present time**, then either the **Past Simple** or the **Present Perfect** can be used. The form you choose depends on whether you are thinking of a present or past time; in other words, whether you are thinking of something that **happened** or **was true in the past** or whether you are thinking of the **effect** of the event or state **on the present time** of speaking.

Look at these examples:

> Researchers **have shown** that expert and novice teachers **differ** in their recall and analyses of problem situations.

The writer here is **focusing** on the **implications** of the finding and not on the time when the research was carried out.

> This study **investigated** whether these differences **existed** during actual teaching sessions.

But here the **focus** is on the **study** which took place in the past.

Adverbs and **prepositions** which can be used with either the **Past Simple** or the **Present Perfect** include the following:

today, this morning, this year, recently, for, already, before, this month, once, just, yet.

3. For or since?

For and **since** sometimes cause problems for learners. **For** can be used with either the **Past Simple** or one of the **Perfect** forms but **since** can be used only with one of the **Perfect** forms.

For means **during** or **for a period of time**. For example:

> She **lived** in Rio de Janeiro **for** thirteen years.
> We've **been** here **for** eight months.
> **For** decades some proportion of the nitrate fertilisers used on cereal crops to increase yields **has been washed** into the soil by rain.

Since means **from a point in time** in the **past**. For example:

> They **have lived** in Madrid **since** 1986.
> We've **been** here **since** March.
> **Since** 1985 the European drinking water directive **has been** in force with standards for sixty-six parameters covering taste and appearance as well as the safety of drinking water.

WARNING BOX

> Remember that you **cannot** use **ago** with the **Present Perfect**. **Ago** can be used only with the **Past Simple**.
>
> Remember that **ever cannot** be used in **positive** statements. You **cannot** say:
> *I have ever been to Jamaica.*

Unit 2.17 Present Perfect – TASKS

Task one

Read the following text and fill in the missing words with either the Present Perfect or the Past Simple form of the verb in brackets. Then discuss your choices with a partner before you check your answers. You should be prepared to explain why you have chosen each form.

(a) For the past three years, Prince Charles . . . . *(work)* for a renaissance of Britain's inner cities. He . . . . . . *(give)* his royal seal of approval to the relatively new phenomenon of 'community architecture' and . . . . . . *(visit)* dozens of projects throughout the country. He . . . . . . *(host)* dinner parties at Kensington Palace for those involved and . . . . . . *(make)* powerful speeches in its support. Community architecture . . . . . . *(start)* with an explosion of protest by residents in the 1960s against insensitive official development plans. The protests . . . . . . *(lead)* to growing involvement by the people in the development of their own communities.

(b) This is what attracted the attention of Prince Charles, whose participation in the inner city debate . . . . . . *(be)* one of the most welcome and remarkable events of the 1980s. It is also why community architecture . . . . . . *(steal)* the headlines.

Task two

Read the following sentences and complete the second one. Put the verb in the Present Perfect form. An example has been written for you.

Example:

He doesn't study very much.

In fact, he hasn't done any homework for three weeks.

(a) I don't own a car. In fact I . . .
(b) The standard of public water supplies in England and Wales is high. The Water Authorities Association . . .
(c) Roger is going to Naples for the Conference. He is looking forward to going because . . .
(d) A band of astronomers in the USA hopes to raise enough money to reopen the Hooker telescope on Mount Wilson. Supporters of the scheme . . .
(e) Film director Willie Christie once had a job on the Burton's yacht, feeding Elizabeth Taylor's dogs. But . . .

Task three

Most newspaper articles deal with bad news of disasters, scandals, problems etc. It has been said that this is because good news is boring and people will not buy papers unless they can find exciting or stimulating news stories.

However, it should be possible to make good news just as exciting and interesting as bad news. Think of six newspaper headlines for good news that you would like to have happen. Then join with another person and discuss what the story might be. Choose one of your partner's headlines and write the story. Since you want to concentrate on the effects of the news on the present time, you should use the Present Perfect for most of the verbs and use the Simple Past only for statements that refer specifically to a particular time in the past, and one of the future forms for the future. Some examples have been written for you.

Examples:

NEW VACCINE ELIMINATES ALL VIRUSES

WAR ABOLISHED

FREE BOOKS FOR E.F.L. LEARNERS

And here is an example of one of the stories:

The EEC has announced that all charges for books for registered EFL learners have been abolished. The publishers have agreed to supply free books to anyone who has enrolled in a full- or part-time English course and the EEC members have promised to subsidise this enterprise. Commenting on the announcement, Ralph Marsh of the British Council said 'I think they have made a very wise decision'. A student in Kuala Lumpur said, 'I have spent many hundreds of ringgit on books for my studies. Last month I spent fifty ringgit on a new dictionary and my teacher has told me that I need a new grammar book. Now I can get all the books I want.'

UNIT 2.18
PRESENT PERFECT CONTINUOUS

The Canadian government has been putting pressure on the administration for some time to reduce the USA's emissions of sulphur dioxide and nitrogen oxides.
The National Council for Voluntary Organisations has been publishing its annual directory of agencies for many years.

The **Present Perfect Continuous** is made up as follows:

has/have ('s/'ve) +	been +	present participle
have	been	working
has	been	putting

The **Present Perfect Continuous** has a similar meaning to the **Present Perfect** but there are two important differences, as follows:

1. When we use the **Present Perfect Continuous** form we are thinking of the event or action as having **limited duration**. For example:

    The number of active organisations **has been increasing** at an extraordinary rate.

    In this case we understand that the number began to increase fairly recently. If the action has been going on for a **long period** of time, then we have to indicate **how long** that period is. For example:

    The National Council for Voluntary Organisations **has been publishing** its annual directory of agencies for many years.

    The Canadian government **has been putting** pressure on the administration for some time to reduce the USA's emissions of sulphur dioxide and nitrogen oxides.

2. The **Present Perfect Continuous** usually shows that an action is **continuing** into the present. For example:

    Hundreds of airline passengers **have been waiting** for hours for their flights to take off.

    The implication is that they are still waiting now.

Like the **Present Perfect**, the **Present Perfect Continuous** can be used to refer to **actions** that happened in the **recent past** but that have **consequences** or **results** in the **present** time. For example:

    You're looking very tired. **Haven't** you **been sleeping** well?

    I think he**'s been crying**. His eyes are all red and swollen.

There are certain verbs such as **learn, live, rain, sit, sleep, study, wait, work**, which suggest actions that **continue** over a **period** of time. With these verbs either the **Present Perfect** or the **Present Perfect Continuous** can be used. In both cases, the action **continues** over a period of time. For example:

    She **has worked** for British Airways for six years.

    She **has been working** for British Airways for six years.

WARNING BOX

> Certain verbs, known as **state** verbs, are not normally used in the **Continuous** form. (See Unit 2.4 for a list of these verbs and an explanation of when they can be used in the **Continuous** form).

Unit 2.18 Present Perfect Continuous – TASKS

Task one

Read the following passage and fill in the missing words with either the Present Perfect, the Present Perfect Continuous or the Past Simple form of the verb in brackets. Then discuss your choices with a partner before you check your answers. You should be prepared to explain why you have chosen each form.

(a) The United Nations Environment Programme last week . . . . . . *(renew)* its call for a tough international treaty to control international shipments and disposals of toxic wastes.

(b) The call . . . . . . *(come)* after a number of reports that companies based in Europe and North America . . . . . . *(dump)* their toxic waste cheaply in poorer countries where controls . . . . . . *(be)* more lax.

(c) The executive director of the UNEP . . . . . . *(say)* last week in Nairobi that he would not settle for a watered-down treaty even though other governments . . . . . . *(press)* him to produce one by next January. 'The convention must be action-orientated' he . . . . . . *(say)*.

(d) At a meeting this month in Caracas, however, delegates from rich and poor nations . . . . . . *(disagree)* on several fundamental points in the treaty, including the definition of toxic waste. Although the EEC . . . . . . *(have)* a directive in force since 1987 that . . . . . . *(ban)* exports of toxic waste unless the importing country could handle the material, only Belgium and Denmark . . . . . . *(pass)* laws enacting the directive.

Task two

Look at each of the drawings below and imagine that someone comes to the house and rings the doorbell. Write the dialogue, under the drawing, that could have taken place between A, the caller, and B, the person in the drawing. An example has been written for you.

A: Have you been crying ?

B: No, I have been chopping onions.

(a)

A: Have . . . . . .
B: Yes/no, I . . . . . .

(b)

A: Have . . . . . .
B: Yes/no, I . . . . . .

(c)

A: Have . . . . . .
B: Yes/no, I . . . . . .

(d)

A: Have . . . . .
B: Yes/no, I . . . . . .

(e)

A: Have . . . . . .
B: Yes/no, I . . . . . .

(f)

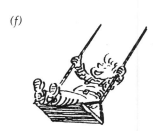

A: Have . . . . . .
B: Yes/no, I . . . . . .

(g)

A: Have . . . . . .
B: Yes/no, I . . . . . .

(h)

A: Have . . . . . .
B: Yes/no, I . . . . . .

(i)

A: Have . . . . . .
B: Yes/no, I . . . .

(j)

A: Have . . . . . .
B: Yes/no, I . . . . . .

UNIT 2.19
PAST PERFECT

When Edward Frankland announced his discovery in 1849, it was the first time that anyone had identified a compound that was organic but also contained a metal.
We had tried dinghies and windsurfing and now we thought we would try a sailing holiday. It wasn't quite what I had expected.

The **Past Perfect** is made up of **had + past participle**. For example:
   had identified.

The **passive** form is made up of **had + been + past participle**. For example:
   had been burgled.

The **Past Perfect** is sometimes called the **Past in the Past**. It is used when we want to refer to **events** or **states** in a time **before a point of time** which is already in the **past time**. In other words, if you are speaking about **yesterday**, then everything that happened **before yesterday** can be seen as happening in the time **before the past time** you are thinking about.

Look at this example:
   When Edward Frankland announced his discovery in 1849, it was the first time that anyone **had identified** a compound that was organic but also contained a metal.
The discovery was made before the announcement.

Now look at this chart:

Before then (time before a point in the past)	Then (time at a point in the past)	Now (time now)
Past Perfect had identified compound	announced 1849	article written in magazine 1988

Now look at this example:
   We **had tried** dinghies and windsurfing and now we thought we would try a sailing holiday. It wasn't quite what I **had expected**.
This passage refers to a time in the past when they decided to try a sailing holiday. Before that time, they had taken holidays that involved sailing in dinghies and windsurfing.

The **Past Perfect** can refer to **events, states** or **habits**. For example:
   The businessman who **had** just **lost** his job said that he thought too many executives wasted too much time going to meetings.
   The workers **had been** on strike for three weeks when the agreement on pay was reached.
   Residents on the estate **had complained** about the state of the roads for two years before any action was taken.

The main purpose of the **Past Perfect** is to put events into a **chronological order** and to make it clear which event occurred first. Sometimes the context can tell you which event or state occurred first and it is then not necessary to use the **Past Perfect**. For example:

The survey conducted last month showed that of people who **had been burgled** in the past two years, two-thirds **were** burgled on a weekday.

In this context, the second verb, **were**, is in the **Past Simple** because it is clear that the burglaries took place before the survey was conducted. It would also be correct to put **had been burgled** in the **Past Simple**.

Similarly, when we include the words **before** or **after**, the use of the **Past Perfect** is optional because the meaning of the words makes it clear which event or state came first in chronological sequence. For example:

Edward Heath, the former British Prime Minister, learnt to play the organ after his voice **broke** at 14 and he stopped singing in the choir.

John was a policeman for six years before he **went** to Lancaster University to do research for a PhD.

In these two cases, it would be possible to use the **Past Perfect** forms **had broken** and **had been** but it is not necessary because the sequence of events is clear without the **Past Perfect**.

Unit 2.19 Past Perfect – TASKS

Task one

Study the following pairs and decide which came first. Then write a sentence indicating the sequence of events by using the Past Perfect form for the earlier event or state and the Past Simple form for the second and later ones. An example has been written for you.

Example:
Go out and post a letter/write a letter.

When he had written the letter he went out and posted it.

(a) Gather data on crime/write a report.
(b) Go on holiday/take an exam.
(c) Save money/buy a video recorder.
(d) Arrange a loan/go into business.
(e) Be interviewed by the BBC/win a gold medal.
(f) Learn to type/go to university.
(g) Get a visa for Senegal/fill in the forms.
(h) Buy a used car/consult a mechanic.
(j) Discover serious faults/buy a house.

Task two

Read the following text and fill in the missing words with the Past Simple, the Present Perfect or the Past Perfect form of the verb in brackets.

A British zoologist . . . . . . *(discover)* a new species of monkey in the rainforests of Gabon in central Africa. The animal . . . . . . *(call)* a sun-tailed guenon. Mike Harrison, of Edinburgh University, ... *(find)* the monkey during an expedition with a forestry prospector to count trees. Hunters . . . . . . *(bring)* an adult male guenon, which . . . . . . *(shoot)*, into the foresters' camp. Harrison . . . . . . *(confirm)* that it . . . . . . *(be)* a new species after he . . . . . . *(examine)* skins and other captured individuals.

UNIT 2.20
PAST PERFECT CONTINUOUS

When the results of her medical tests arrived she realised she had been feeling ill since she had been on holiday.

I had been doing *The Guardian* crossword puzzle for three years before I managed to do one in less than fifteen minutes.

The **Past Perfect Continuous** is made up of **had been + present participle (-ing)**. For example: **had been feeling**.

Had is often contracted to **'d**. For example:
I**'d** been doing; She**'d** been running.

The **Past Perfect Continuous** is used when we want to refer to **events, habits** or **states** in a time **before** a particular time in the **past** and when we want to stress the **duration**. For this reason, we often include a **time expression** with **for** or **since**.

Look at these examples:
When the results of her medical tests arrived she realised she **had been feeling** ill **since she had been on holiday**.
I **had been doing** *The Guardian* crossword puzzle **for three years** before I managed to do one in less than fifteen minutes.
He **had been teaching** English **for twenty-two years** when he retired from Skerton Secondary School.

Like the **Present Perfect Continuous**, the **Past Perfect Continuous** can be used to explain a state or event. For example:

Present Perfect Continuous	Past Perfect Continuous
Your eyes are all red. **Have** you **been crying**?	Your eyes were all red yesterday. **Had** you **been crying** when I saw you?

Unit 2.20 Past Perfect Continuous – TASKS

Task one

Below are some of the things that have happened in the last year. Tell your partner what had been happening before the events or what conclusions you have made about the events that caused them. Use the Past Perfect Continuous form to report the facts or your explanations. An example has been written for you:

Example:
The road was flooded when you got up one morning. *(Heavy rain; all night.)*

You could say to your friend:

> ### The road was flooded last week . It had been raining heavily all night.

(a) Hundreds of passengers waited for hours at the airports in Britain last month. *(Air traffic controllers strike; two weeks.)*
(b) You were very tired when you arrived in London at 2 a.m. *(Drive; ten hours.)*
(c) Scientists announced a new discovery last month. *(Experiment; six years.)*
(d) The builders finished the house last week. *(Work; eighteen months.)*
(e) Joan bought a dishwasher and a microwave oven last week. *(Save; six months.)*
(f) Edward went to Baghdad last week. *(Plan; three months.)*
(g) Edward and Nicki published a book last year. *(Write; eighteen months.)*
(h) Brendan passed his driving test last month. *(Take lessons; six months.)*
(j) Hywel finished his thesis in June. *(Do research; three years.)*
(k) James retired in January. *(Work; twenty-five years.)*

UNIT 2.21
FUTURE PERFECT, FUTURE PERFECT CONTINUOUS

In six weeks' time the bricklayers will have laid 90,000 bricks.
By the end of the summer fifty conductors will have taken the rostrum in this year's Proms in London.

1. Future Perfect

The **Future Perfect** is made up of **will/shall/'ll + have + past participle**. For example:
will have finished.
I **will have finished** by six o'clock.

The **Future Perfect** expresses the idea that an **action** will be **completed** or a particular **state** will be **reached** by a specific time in the **future**.

Look at these examples:

In six weeks' time the bricklayers **will have laid** 90,000 bricks and they **will have built** five walls up to thirty feet high inside a tram shed for Peter Brook's *The Mahabharata* in Glasgow.

By the end of the summer fifty conductors **will have taken** the rostrum in this year's Proms in London.

Economists predict that by the end of the year the prices of houses in London **will have risen** by a further five per cent.

The **Future Perfect** is often used for **predictions**. So it is often used after an **If** clause. For example:

If I stop smoking now, in three months' time I**'ll have saved** enough to buy a new jacket.

2. Future Perfect Continuous

The **Future Perfect Continuous** is formed with **will/shall/'ll + have been + present participle**. For example:
will have been studying.

The **Future Perfect Continuous** can be used to show that an **action** or **state** will be **completed** by a certain time in the **future** if you want to emphasise the **duration** of the action or state. For example:

By the end of the month we**'ll have been working** on this book for eight months.

Although this form exists in English, it is rarely used as it is an awkward construction. People usually find another way of expressing the idea. For example:

By the end of the month it**'ll be** eight months since we **started working** on this book.

Unit 2.21 Future Perfect,
Future Perfect Continuous – TASKS

Task one

Look at the following predictions and make statements, using the Future Perfect form of the verb in brackets, to express the ideas. An example has been written for you:

Example:
Interest Rates – January ten per cent. Interest Rates – December eleven per cent *(Rise).*

By the end of the year interest rates will have risen by one per cent.

(a) World Population 1988 5 billion. World Population 2000 10 billion. *(Increase).*
(b) Mike and Joan: married 1957. 1997. *(Married).*
(c) Edward bought a house in 1988. 1998. *(Own).*
(d) Lisette saves £30 a month. Twelve months. *(Save).*
(e) Nicki: new car 1 July drives 20 miles a day. 31 July. *(Drive).*

Task two

Conduct a survey among your friends or classmates to find out some facts about their habits and actions. Then calculate how many times something will have been done or how much time or money will have been spent by the end of the month. Write your conclusions, using the Future Perfect to express your calculations.

For example, you may find that three people each spend thirty minutes getting to class or to the office every day by bus. You could then write the following:

By the end of the month those three people will have spent a total of sixty hours on buses.

Task three

Write down some facts about yourself, such as how many hours a day you watch television, how many books you read a week, how long you spend studying, how much you spend on food every week, etc. Then join your partner and ask and answer questions about how many hours, how many books, etc., you will have spent/read, etc., by a specific time in the future. Use the Future Perfect and the Future Perfect Continuous. An example has been written for you.

A: How many soft drinks do you drink in a week?

B: Four or five.

A: So how many will you have drunk by the end of the month?

UNIT 2.22
USED TO, BE USED TO

Ercole Pasquali used to be the chef at Chez Vito, a small pizzeria in Montreal.
Teachers used to think that learners had to avoid making errors because the errors would be 'learned'.
Susan used to sit in her room and play the cello for hours every evening.

Used to refers to a **habit, action** or **state** in the **past**. It is always followed by the **infinitive** and can be used only for **past** time. Also it can be used only to refer to a **habit, action** or **state** that was **true in the past** but is **no longer true**.

Look at these examples:

Ercole Pasquali **used to** be the chef at Chez Vito, a small pizzeria in Montreal.
But Pasquali is no longer at Chez Vito; he is now one of the owners of a first-class Italian restaurant called Vespucci.

Dr Robert Peter **used to** be a professor of art at the University of British Columbia.
Dr Peter is now retired and a full-time writer.

Susan **used to** sit in her room and play the cello for hours every evening.
Susan no longer lives in the same place and no longer practises the cello in the evening as she used to do.

Teachers **used to** think that learners had to avoid making errors because the errors would be 'learned'.
Now they realise that making errors is a necessary part of learning.

There are different ways of forming the **negative** and **interrogative** of **used to**. For example:

(a) She **usen't to** like learning English. ⎫ More common in
(b) She **used not to** like learning English. ⎭ British English.

(c) She **didn't use to** like learning English. ⎫ Used in both British
(d) She **didn't used to** like learning English ⎭ and American English.

She **didn't use to** (examples (c) and (d)) is preferred but most people avoid the problem altogether by using **never**. For example:

He **never used to** watch television.
They **never used to** do any homework.

For questions, there is only one form, as follows:

Did you **use to** take piano lessons?

WARNING BOX

> **Used to** which refers to past habits, states and actions that are no longer true should not be confused with **be + used to + noun phrases or present participle**. For example:
>
>   Most Indonesians **are used to eating** rice at least once a day.
>   But they **aren't used to** a cold climate.
>
> **Be used to + noun phrase or present participle** is another way of saying **accustomed to**. It means that someone is **familiar** with something or someone else.
>
> This form can also be used with **get** instead of **be**, to say that someone has **become accustomed to** or familiar with someone or something. For example:
>
>   After my first winter in a cold climate, I **got used to** feeling cold most of the time.
>   You can **get used to** almost anything if you have to.

Unit 2.22 Used to/be used to – TASKS

Task one

Explain the difference between the following pairs of statements:

(a) (i) She's used to hard work.
    (ii) She used to work hard.

(b) (i) They're used to eating fish for dinner.
    (ii) They used to eat fish for dinner.

(c) (i) He used to live alone.
    (ii) He's used to living alone.

(d) (i) I used to drive a car.
    (ii) I'm used to driving a car.

Task two

(a) *Think of the time when you were a child and write some sentences, using* **used to**, *about the following:*

what you did, thought, liked, wanted, ate, drank, said, etc.

but that you no longer do, think, like, etc. One example has been written for you.

Example:

I used to walk to school and I used to think it was very
unfair that some of my friends could go by bus.

(b) *Discuss the things you have written down with your partner and see how many things you both used to do that you no longer do.*

UNIT 2.23
PASSIVE 1: form

Lonsdale was followed from his flat to the Midland Bank.
Penicillin was discovered by Alexander Fleming.
The hospital will be opened by Princess Alexandra.
The city has been attacked.

Look at these examples:

On 27 August, they followed Lonsdale from his flat to the Midland Bank

On 27 August, Lonsdale was followed from his flat to the Midland Bank

Alexander Fleming discovered Penicillin

Penicillin was discovered by Alexander Fleming

Princess Alexandra will open the hospital

The hospital will be opened by Princess Alexandra

We have attacked the city

The city has been attacked

In the above examples, the **active** sentences contain **transitive** verbs, i.e. in each case the verb is followed by an **object**. In each sentence, there is **subject** + **verb** + **direct object**. For example:

They followed Lonsdale.

Sentences were the verb is used **transitively** can be re-formed in the **passive**. When this happens, the original **object** becomes the **subject** and the verb is made up of the auxiliary **be** and the **past participle** of the original verb; when the original **subject** is maintained as an **agent**, it is preceded by **by**, as follows:

Active: subject + verb + object.

Passive: subject + verb (be + past participle) (+ by + agent).

Look at these examples:

Princess Alexandra **will open** the new hospital on 19 May.
The new hospital **will be opened by** Princess Alexandra on 19 May.

It isn't always necessary to complete the sentence with the **by** phrase, if the original subject is unimportant. For example:

We **have attacked** the city.
The city **has been attacked**.

WARNING BOX

Where there is an **indirect object**, this can also be made the subject of the **passive** sentence, for example:

The manager **gave** the secretary a pay rise.

This can be transformed as either of the following:

A pay rise **was given to the secretary**.

The secretary was given a pay rise.

Unit 2.23 Passive 1 – TASKS

Task one

Where possible, change the following sentences into the passive:

(a) John Fuller unearthed Stephen Spender's novel *The Temple* at Texas University.
(b) You can buy peaches there for 10p each.
(c) They laughed at Jim as he fell into the water.
(d) On Friday morning, we all met at Alex's flat.
(e) They had been drinking all night.
(f) Someone heard the cuckoo very early this year.
(g) You can park cars in the street behind the hotel.
(h) We cannot accept bookings after 30 September.
(j) The party continued until breakfast.
(k) The Queen has given the title of Princess Royal to her daughter, the Princess Anne.

Task two

Rewrite the following texts in the passive.

(a) A report yesterday cleared the weathermen in general and the BBC's Mr Michael Fish in particular of irresponsible forecasting before last October's storms, which killed ten people and destroyed 15 million trees across the south of England.
(b) They have shot dead a candidate in next week's election. They threw bombs and fired shots at the candidate from close range. The main opposition parties are boycotting next Wednesday's elections.
(c) They hired no extra staff. Instead they transferred a hundred workers from other duties, and transferred some of the workload to Liverpool.
(d) Mrs Thatcher has given two women politicians new posts after the resignation of Lord Stoddart, following a heart attack. Baroness Nicol has taken his job as Energy Spokesman, while the Prime Minister has made Baroness Ewart-Biggs a Whip.

UNIT 2.24
PASSIVE 2: use

Look at the following newspaper report (the names of the criminal and hotel are fictitious):
Police searching for a man in connection with . . . were last night questioning a man arrested at a West London hotel.

Armed detectives surrounded the London Visitors Hotel on Holland Road shortly before 8 p.m. after a member of the public told them that the man they were seeking was there.

Mr Nat Handworth, aged 35, offered no resistance and was taken to Paddington Green police station after his arrest.

Note that this report uses the **active** voice and focuses on the **police** until the final paragraph, when we find out who the criminal was.

Now look at the following report of the same event:
. . . Nat Handworth – the most wanted man in Britain – was captured last night after a dramatic swoop by armed police.

Handworth, 35, was seized in an early evening raid in West London – nearly thirty hours after a massive police hunt was mounted for him following . . .

Last night he was being questioned by senior officers at the high-security Paddington Green police station in London.

This report focuses on the **criminal**, and in order to do this, the writer has had to use the **passive** voice. Look again at the first paragraph in the first report and the last paragraph in the second report. These report exactly the same event, but with a different **focus**.

The **subject** of a sentence very often tells us what the sentence is about (see Unit 5.9). In the first example, the writer is talking about the **police** and what they were doing, so he uses the **active** voice; for example:

Police . . . **were** last night **questioning** a man . . .

Whereas in the second example, the writer is talking about the **criminal** and what was happening to him, so he uses the **passive** voice; for example:

Last night he **was being questioned** by senior officers . . .

Continued

Unit 2.24 Passive 2

Many reasons are given for using the **passive** voice rather than the **active**; essentially, however, the writer/speaker makes use of the **active** or **passive** to **focus** what is being said.

In an article about a new hospital, the writer says:

The hospital **will be opened** by Princess Alexandra . . .

This is done because the writer is focusing on the **hospital**. If the writer had said, Princess Alexandra **will open** the hospital, then the focus would have been on **Princess Alexandra**.

It is often said that the **passive** is used a lot in scientific reports. This is an over-generalisation. It is used when the writer wishes to focus on the **process** that is being reported. For example, the writer is more likely to say:

It was discovered that the virus could be controlled by . . .

rather than:

Dr Robertson discovered that the virus could be controlled by . . .

This is because he wishes to focus on the **discovery** about the virus. Note also that very often the sentence begins with the anticipatory **It** (see Unit 5.2). To say, for example:

That the virus could be controlled by . . . was discovered.

would place too much in the subject when there is nothing following the verb, and this would unbalance the sentence. It is not wrong, but stylistically, it feels ugly (see Unit 2.40). If, however, the writer of the report is Dr Robertson himself and he wishes to focus on **what he has done**, he might write the report in the **active**, as follows:

I discovered that the virus could be controlled by . . .

Unit 2.24 Passive 2 – TASKS

Task one

Add a second sentence to each of the sentences below, using the words in brackets. Make the word in bold type the focus of the second sentence. Two examples have been written for you.

Example:
The concert finished with a father and child act. (**child**, *sing, song.*)

   The child sang a song .

....

(*child, sing,* **song**.)

   A song was sung by the child.

....

(a) Everest is the highest mountain in the world. (*it, climb,* **Hilary**, *in 1953.*)
(b) It is a beautiful fireplace. (**it**, *design, Adam.*)
(c) He liked to start the day going over the news. (**secretary**, *always buy, every newspaper.*)
(d) The school day always began with prayers. (*headteacher, say,* **prayers**.)
(e) The day ended tragically with an accident. (**other car**, *drive, somebody drunk.*)

Task two

Rewrite the following text so that **Nick** *is the focus of each sentence in the paragraph.*

The police had followed Nick all day. They had seen him leave his flat at 7.30 in the morning, take a bus to Regent Street and enter the airline office by a side door. He came out again at 1.00 and they tailed him to the language school where he usually worked. He stayed in the school until 8.00 that evening and then went with Maria in her car for a drink. At about 11.30 she drove him home. The police were still following him, but they had been exhausted by him.

Task three

Write a report on some event/activity you have been involved in recently. For example:

a scientific experiment, a day out with friends, a party, a holiday, a special presentation at school or at work, etc.

When talking about what you did, make **yourself** *the focus; when talking about what other people did, make the* **activity** *the focus.*

UNIT 2.25
MODAL VERBS 1: form
can, could, may, might,
must, ought to, should, will,
need, be able to, have to

This **COULD** be worse than school.
Applications **MAY NOT** be withdrawn.
You **NEEDN'T** tell him.
I'M NOT ABLE to see him tomorrow.

There are many verbs which are used to express **modality** in English. These verbs are used to express different **attitudes** to an event or situation. In the way they are used structurally, i.e. the way they are used to form sentences, they can be divided into three types, as follows:

Central modals	Marginal modals	Semi-auxiliaries
can could may might must ought to should will would etc.	need etc.	be able to have to etc.

1. Central modals

The characteristics of **central modals** are as follows:
(a) There are **no non-finite** forms. For example, there is **no form**:
    *maying, mayed, to may
    *musting, musted, to must, etc.
There is only the bare **infinite** form **may, must, should**, etc.
(b) They **combine** with other verbs in a sentence in the following way:
    modal + bare infinitive

Look at these examples:
    A separate cheque **must accompany** each application.
    This **could be** worse than school.
    Medical costs **can be** expensive.
(c) The **negative** is formed by placing **not** after the modal. For example:
    You **cannot/can't** be serious.
    Applications **may not** be withdrawn.
    People **must not/mustn't** approach the wild animals.
(d) The interrogative is formed by subject-modal **inversion**. For example:
    Could you close the window?
    Must we finish it tonight?
(e) There are **no complete tense** forms.

On some occasions an action involving **can** in the past can be expressed with **could** (see Unit 2.27).

2. Marginal modals

The term **marginal** is used as these verbs share some characteristics of **central modals** and also characteristics of **main verbs**. The most often used **marginal modal** is **need**.

The characteristics of **marginal modals** are as follows:
(a) They display the characteristics of the central modals. For example:
>   You **needn't** tell him.
>   **Need** I go there today?
(b) They sometimes display the characteristics of main verbs. For example:
>   You **don't need** to tell him.
>   **Do** I **need** to go there today?

WARNING BOX

> **Need** also exists as a lexical verb in its own right. For example:
>   This car **needs** a new engine.

3. Semi-auxiliaries

The characteristics of **semi-auxiliaries** are as follows:
(a) They can behave like main verbs in the following ways:
>   They have **non-finite** forms. For example:
>   **To have to.**
>   **Being able to.**
>   They form the **negative** with auxiliary **do**. For example:
>   He **doesn't have to.**
>   They can make an **interrogative** form. For example:
>   **Do you have to?**
>   **Was he** able to?
>   They have **all** tense forms.
(b) They can be preceded by another **modal verb**. For example:
>   They **must be able to**.
>   You **might have to**.
>   He **shouldn't have to**.
(c) Because **to** is contained in the **semi-auxiliary modal**, these modals are followed by the **bare infinitive** form. For example:
>   **I'm not able to see** him tomorrow.
>   They **have to be** here by nightfall.

For the use of **past** forms and the use of the **modal + perfect infinitive (have + past participle)**, **must have been**, see the units for each modal.

Unit 2.25 Modal verbs 1 – TASKS

Task one

Read the following sentences and then complete the chart below by identifying the type of modal in each of the sentences. Say which characteristic of each modal is shown. An example has been written for you.

Example:
It **may** be difficult to convince the rest.

(a) Cigarettes **can** seriously damage your health.
(b) You **may** choose a Mercedes-Benz.
(c) Dishwashers **won't** (will not) wash everything.
(d) You don't **need** to buy a sleeping-bag.
(e) They won't **be able to** go there next week.
(f) Children under 14 **cannot** be admitted.
(g) You don't **have to** pay the earth to be warm.
(h) **Are you able to** pass our test?
(j) **Need** he know about it?
(k) **Must** you do that?

	Type of modal	Characteristic
Example	central	combination with other verb MODAL + BARE INFINITIVE
(a)		
(b)		
(c)		
(d)		
(e)		
(f)		
(g)		
(h)		
(j)		
(k)		

Task two

Complete the sentences below by choosing an appropriate modal verb from the following list:

can, could, will, be able to, ought to, should, can, might, may, could

(a) Holidays abroad . . . . . . be wonderful.
(b) In twelve weeks you will . . . . . . speak another language.
(c) You . . . . . . not like what you see.
(d) The airport . . . . . . be developed to take the larger planes.
(e) You . . . . . . not walk around the town late at night.
(f) You . . . . . . buy only second-hand books in that shop.
(g) He . . . . . . run the marathon in three hours.
(h) People . . . . . . always pay for good service.
(j) It's very unlikely, but he . . . . . . be prepared to help you.
(k) It's not certain, but he . . . . . . be a millionaire in two years' time.

UNIT 2.26
MODAL VERBS 2: meaning
can, could, may, might,
must, ought to, should, will,
need, be able to, have to

You SHOULD use first-class post.
Dishwashers WON'T wash everything.
It really COULDN'T be easier.
This MAY be worse than school.

Modal verbs are used in two ways to express various attitudes towards a situation or event. These are known as the **primary use** and the **secondary use**. Many of the verbs are used to express more than one meaning.

1. Primary use

Primary use is concerned with **fact** or **reality** and expresses the following moods:

(a) **Ability** (says what you are **able to do**). For example:
> You **can't** hypnotise anyone who doesn't want to co-operate.
> You miss a lot, if you **can't** speak the language.
> They reach out to people they **couldn't** reach before.
> There are many ways you **are able to** help.

(b) **Advisability** (expresses what it is **best to do**). For example:
> You **should** use first-class post.
> You **ought to** follow the instructions for agents.

(c) **Certainty** (expresses a **general certainty**). For example:
> Take the form to your doctor, who **will** complete it.
> Dishwashers **won't** wash everything.

(d) **Exemption** (indicates what is **not necessary**). For example:
> You **needn't** pay in advance.
> You **don't have to** book early, but it helps.

(e) **Necessity** (indicates what is **necessary**, but not obligatory). For example:
> You **need** to earn at least £20,000 a year.

(f) **Obligation** (tells you what is **obligatory**). For example:
> Applications **must** be received by 15 October.
> You **have to** complete this form for membership.
> Relatives **should** complete and sign box 7.

(g) **Permission** (expresses what you are **allowed to do**). For example:
> Applications **may** be made only by persons over 18.
> You **can** withdraw £200 whenever you wish.
> **May** I check the answers?
> **Can** we stay longer?

(h) **Prohibition** (expresses what you are **not allowed to do**). For example:
> Once made, applications **may not** be withdrawn.
> You **must not** leave your car for any reason.
> Can we stay longer? No, you **can't**. There's work to be done.

(j) **Request** (when you ask somebody to do something). For example:
> **Can** you lend me some money, please?
> **Could** you close the window, please?
> **Would** you mind handing me that cup?

2. Secondary use

Secondary use is concerned with **beliefs** based on **facts**. The speaker is saying that the conditions exist for this situation or event, but it may not occur.

Look at these examples:

Holidays abroad **can** be fun.

Here the speaker is saying that it is possible to enjoy a holiday abroad, but it is not always the case.

So begins seven days alone on a desert island with my parents. This **could** be worse than school.

Here the speaker is saying it is possible for this period of seven days to be unpleasant, but he's not certain.

Secondary use expresses the following moods:

(a) **Certainty/likelihood** (when you are **certain** that you have guessed correctly). For example:

From the sound of the footsteps, that'**ll (will)** be Valerie.

That picture **would** look nice in your room.

(b) **Near certainty** (when you are **almost certain**, but not quite sure). For example:

She's coming by train and **should/could/might** arrive just after midday.

(c) **Possibility** (when it is **possible theoretically**). For example:

Holidays abroad **can/may/might** be fun.

This **may/might/could** be worse than school.

(d) **Impossiblity** (when the evidence makes you believe it is **not true**). For example:

Mrs Chevely, you **cannot (can't)** be serious!

It really **couldn't** be easier.

(e) **Probability** (when you think something is **very likely** from what you know of the situation). For example:

As you're a doctor, you **must/should** know such a lot about viruses.

That's a loud knock on the door. It **could** be Jim.

Unit 2.26 Modal verbs 2 – TASKS

Task one

Summarise the information in Unit 2.26 by listing the appropriate modals after the following headings:

(a) **Ability:**	
(b) **Advisability:**	
(c) **Certainty (primary use):**	
(d) **Exemption:**	
(e) **Necessity:**	
(f) **Obligation:**	
(g) **Permission:**	
(h) **Prohibition:**	
(j) **Request:**	
(k) **Certainty (secondary use):**	
(l) **Near certainty:**	
(m) **Possibility:**	
(n) **Impossibility:**	
(o) **Probability:**	

Task two

Read the following and make grammatically correct statements, using the chart below, to describe **vertical people** *and* **horizontal people.**

Mark your statements V for vertical people and H for horizontal people. Choose only statements that you believe to be true from the information you have in the text. You will not need to use all the sentences possible from the chart. An example has been written for you.

Example:

They need to learn Russian. (V.)

Jill Tweedie divides the world into two types of people – vertical people and horizontal people. Vertical people are those who feel pressure to do things and need things to change. What's new? they ask. What's next? They're always planning to do things. Their lives are full of 'needs' and 'musts'. Having another baby; writing a new book; travelling to a new country: they're always trying to get involved in new things. Horizontal people, on the other hand, feel none of these pressures. They are content with a comfortable life. What's your next step? Where do you plan to go? you ask them. Nowhere, they reply. We just want more of the same.

They	must don't have to should couldn't could need needn't can mustn't can't don't need have to	lose weight get a new partner to learn Russian be content own a house look at the garden to have a baby have nice children cut the grass change jobs

UNIT 2.27
MODAL VERBS 3: ability, permission, request, prohibition/refusal, possibility, impossibility

These are the ways in which you CAN help.
COULD you lend me £200?
Holidays abroad CAN be fun.

1. Primary use

Primary use expresses the following moods:

Ability (see also Unit 2.36)
Can is used to express **ability (or inability)** to do something. For example:
> These are ways in which you **can** help.
> We have found a hotel you and your boss **can** agree on.
> Because of his illness, he **can't** work anymore.
> You miss a lot, if you **can't** speak the language.

In this case it is possible to replace **can** by **be able to**. For example:
> These are ways in which you **are able to** help.
> You miss a lot, if you **aren't able to (are unable to)** speak the language.
> After some time and experience, you **will be able to** judge mountain conditions when you go climbing.

The **Past** form is expressed by **could** or **was able to**. For example:
> These were the ways in which you **could (were able to)** help at the hospital.
> Last year we found a hotel you and your boss **could (were able to)** agree on.
> Because of an illness, in the last years of his life, he **couldn't (was unable to)** work anymore.
> You missed a lot in Italy, if you **couldn't (weren't able to)** speak the language.

Permission (see also **may**, Unit 2.29)
Can and **could** are both used to ask **permission**. For example:
> **Can** I borrow £200?
> **Could** I borrow £200?

Can is more direct, whereas **could** is more tentative.

In granting **permission**, only **can** is used. For example:
> Can I go now? – Yes, you **can**.
> Could I go now? – Yes, you **can**.

May is also possible in granting **permission** (see Unit 2.29), but **could** is inappropriate.

Request

The same rules apply when a **request** is made to a second person. For example:
> **Can** you lend me £200? – Yes, I **can**. – No, I **can't**.
> **Could** you lend me £200? – Yes, I **can**. – No, I **can't**.

May is not possible for making **requests** of this nature, but a possible alternative form is **would** (see Unit 2.31).

Prohibition/refusal (see also **may**, Unit 2.29)

Can't is used to express strong **prohibition** (see Unit 2.32). The same rules apply as with granting permission. For example:

Can I borrow £200? – No, you **can't**.

Could I borrow £200? – No, you **can't**.

You **can't** enter without a tie.

Children over 5 **can't** be members of the playgroup.

2. Secondary use

Secondary use expresses the following moods:

General possibility (see also Unit 2.29)

Look at this example:

Holidays abroad **can** be fun.

Here the speaker is talking about holidays in **general** and not about a specific holiday. There is **no prediction** that the next holiday abroad will be fun. As this is a **general** statement, there is **no Past** or **Future** form.

Specific possibility

Look at these examples:

Ten days alone on a desert island with my parents. This **could** be worse than school.

That's a loud knock on the door. It **could** be Jim.

In each case the speakers are talking about one **specific** occasion, and making a **prediction** about what the situation will be. There is **no certainty**, however. Because the speaker is talking about one occasion, it is possible to discuss this with reference to the **past**. For example:

Last year, I spent seven days alone on a desert island with my parents. That **could have been** worse than school.

The implication is that in fact it wasn't worse than school and it was a good holiday.

Specific possiblity in the **Past** is formed with **modal + have + past participle**.

For example: **could have been**.

Impossibility

In the following examples each speaker is making a deduction based on the information available:

Mrs Cheveley, you **can't** be serious!

That knock's too loud. It **can't** be John.

In the first example, the speaker is suggesting that what Mrs Cheveley has said is too absurd to be a serious statement. In the second, the speaker is suggesting that John does not knock the door so loudly.

Couldn't is sometimes used, but it is not so definite as **can't**. There's more doubt with the use of **couldn't**.

It is possible to use both **can't have been** and **couldn't have been** when the event or situation is in the **past.**

3. Summary

Primary use

	Ability	Permission	Request	Prohibition/refusal
Present Past	**can** **be able to** **could** **was able to**	**can** **could**	**can** **could**	**can't**

Secondary use

	Possibility		Impossibility	
Present Past	*general* **can**	*specific* **could** **could have** **+ past participle**	*more certain* **can't** **can't have** **+ past participle**	*less certain* **couldn't** **couldn't have** **+ past participle**

Unit 2.27 Modal verbs 3 – TASKS

Task one

Using the chart below, identify the meanings expressed by the use of the modals in the following sentences:

(a) I can't imagine any of our best writers agreeing to work for such people.
(b) This page could put you on the map.
(c) Hostellers camping in the grounds can do their own cooking.
(d) You will be unable to avoid cancellations this week.
(e) All you are able to see is a mountain.
(f) Forty mothers and their babies can stay in this hospital.
(g) You could say cheap cars made Henry Ford's fortune.
(h) Before he came here, he couldn't even write his name.
(j) You can have your salary monthly or weekly, whichever is more convenient for you.
(k) Could you drive me to work tomorrow?

Ability	
Permission	
Request	
Prohibition/refusal	
Possibility	
Impossibility	

Task two

Where possible rewrite the sentences below in the Past form. After each sentence, state what meaning of modality is expressed.

(a) You can't see that film because you're not 18.
(b) Medical fees can be expensive.
(c) The baby is already able to say a few words, even though it's only 9 months.
(d) You could become very famous with that work.
(e) Can you tell me the way to the town hall?
(f) Surely that can't be Jack. It's far too early.

Task three

Think of a place you know well and would like to invite a friend to visit with you.

(a) *Make lists of the following:*
  (i) **five things that are prohibited;**
  (ii) **five things that are possible – general;**
  (iii) **five things that are possible – predictable.**
(b) *Write the letter to your friend persuading him/her to accompany you.*

UNIT 2.28
MODAL VERBS 4:
obligation, necessity,
exemption, prohibition,
probability

There MUST be at least ten per cent real
orange juice in it.
I HAVE TO finish this book tonight.
All you NEED to do is attach a recent
photograph.

1. Primary use

Primary use expresses the following moods:

Obligation (see also **should**, Unit 2.30)
Obligation is expressed with **must**. For example:
   The cheque **must** be made payable to 'Eurotunnel UK offer'.
   There **must** be at least ten per cent real orange juice in it.
   Each hosteller **must** use an approved sheet sleeping bag.

These **rules** are almost like laws and it is unlikely that **have to** would be used here in the
Present. **Must** expresses an **obligation** imposed by an **outside authority**. **Have to** is more
informal. For example:
   I **have to** finish this book tonight.
   You **have to** arrive before nine o'clock.

With a **past obligation**, only **had to** can be used. For example:
   The cheque **had to** be made payable to . . .
   Each hosteller **had to** use . . .
These are just statements about an obligation in the past.

Necessity
Necessity is expressed with **need** or **have to**. For example:
   All you **have to** do is cut out this voucher.
   All you **need** do is cut out this voucher.
   All you **need** to do is attach a recent photograph.

The **Past** is formed with both verbs. Again there are two **Past** forms, as follows:

(i) To express the necessity of doing something. For example:
   All you **had to** do was cut out the voucher.
   All you **needed** to do was attach a recent photograph.

(ii) To imply that the action wasn't done. For example:
   All you **had to have done** was cut out the voucher.
   All you **needed to have done** was attach a recent photograph.

Exemption
Exemption (shows that it is **not necessary** for you to do something or that you are **not
obliged** to do something). It is expressed through **need not** or **don't have to**. For example:
   Only the group leader needs to be a member. The other people in the group **need not/
   don't have to** have membership.

Prohibition (see also **cannot**, Unit 2.27 and **may not**, Unit 2.29)

Prohibition can be expressed by using **must not (mustn't)**. For example:

Hostellers who have contracted an infectious disease **must not** use hostels.

> With **must not** the obligation is on the **person addressed**, whereas with **cannot** or **may not** the obligation is an **imposed duty**.

2. Secondary use

Probability

Must used to express **probability** means that we are not certain about something, but we express what we expect to be the outcome. For example:

But as you're his doctor, you **must** know everything about him.

The **Past** is expressed through **must have + past participle**. For example:

As Raymond is in France and Richard is in Germany, it **must have been** Robert who telephoned.

In the examples above, the speaker is not certain, but from what is known about the situation, this is the **probable** outcome.

3. Summary

Primary use

	Obligation	Necessity	Exemption	Prohibition
Present Past	must have to had to	need have to needed had to	needn't don't have to didn't need to didn't have to	mustn't

Secondary use

	Probability
Present Past	must must have + past participle

WARNING BOX

> Although **have to** can replace **must** in the **positive** form, this is not possible in the **negative**. In the **negative** form **have to** expresses the same idea as **need**, i.e. **exemption**.
>
> So **don't have to** means **needn't**.

Unit 2.28 Modal verbs 4 – TASKS

Task one

(a) *Using the chart below, identify the meanings expressed by the use of the modals in the following sentences.*

(b) *Where possible, rewrite the sentences in the* **Past**.

    (i) You don't have to pay the whole amount in advance.

    (ii) That must be Charlie. He said he would be here about now.

    (iii) A separate cheque must accompany each application.

    (iv) You need to add some more sugar to that.

    (v) You mustn't walk on the grass!

    (vi) You'll have to be there by 9.00, if you want to be sure of a seat.

    (vii) As a senior official, you must have great influence over the committee's decisions on appointments.

    (viii) You needn't wait for me.

    (ix) You don't need smallpox vaccinations any more for anywhere.

    (x) Books must be returned on or before the date stamped below.

Obligation	
Necessity	
Exemption	
Prohibition	
Probability	

Task two

Rewrite the following instructions and slogans using **must, need** *or* **have to**. *An example has been written for you.*

Example:
No bathing or canoeing when red flag is flying.

You mustn't bathe or canoe when the red flag is flying.

(a) No children under 18 admitted.

(b) Keep your dog on a lead.

(c) Cheques accepted only with a bank card.

(d) With Visa, waiting is unnecessary.

(e) Seventy-five tokens gets the coffee-pot!

Task three

With a friend, plan to set up a club and design the rules for membership. Think in terms of **obligation, necessity, prohibition** *and* **exemption**.

UNIT 2.29
MODAL VERBS 5:
permission, prohibition, possibility

Only members MAY use the lounge.
Holiday insurance MIGHT be obtained
from . . .

1. Primary use

Permission (see also **can**, Unit 2.27)

Both asking and granting **permission** can be expressed using **may**. For example:

May I have more time to complete the work? – Yes, you **may**.
Only members **may** use the lounge.

Prohibition (see also **can't**, Unit 2.27 and **mustn't**, Unit 2.28)

Prohibition or refusing permission is expressed through **may not**. For example:

May I keep the book a week longer? – No, you **may not**.
Once made, applications **may not** be withdrawn.

Sometimes the negation is contained in another part of the utterance or statement. The following two examples have the same meaning:

No hosteller **may** bring an animal into any hostel.
A hosteller **may not** bring an animal into any hostel.

2. Secondary use

Possibility (see also **can** and **could**, Unit 2.27)

Both **general** and **specific possibility** can be expressed through **may** and **might**.

Look at these examples:

Holiday insurance **may be** obtained from . . .
Holiday insurance **might be** obtained from . . .

These are examples of **general possibility**.

The different means for expressing **possibility** are graded on a scale as follows:

might	may	can

less   more
possibility   possibility

As with **could**, the reference to a **specific** action or event tries to **predict** what will happen. For example:

The sea around Denmark **may** be cool for bathing, but the beaches are there for lazing in the sun.
What you **may not** be aware of is that we sell works of art of every kind.
That **may** be Jim at the door. It sounds like his knock.

The first signs are those you **might** easily overlook.

It **might** be better to get your visas from the London embassy rather than face delays on the spot.

The different means for expressing **predicting** and **specific possibility** can be graded on the following scale:

could	might	may

less possibility		more possibility

3. Past forms

There is no **Past** form for the uses that express **permission** or **prohibition**, as these represent immediate attitudes or moods. To report a **past prohibition** or **permission** that was given it is necessary to use **to be allowed to** or some similar verb. For example:

May I go out?

No, Margaret, you may not.

The report on this is, Margaret **was not allowed** to go out.

But compare the following example:

Margaret **could not** go out.

This might mean that she **wasn't able to** go out, because she was ill or for some other reason.

WARNING BOX

Might is **not** a Past form of **may**.

You must be careful how you interpret the meaning of the form. For example:

You may withdraw £500.

Here, **may** can be interpreted in the following two ways:

You **have permission** to withdraw £500.

It is **possible** for you to withdraw £500.

When speaking about the past, however, only the interpretation about **possibility** is acceptable. For example:

You **may have withdrawn** £500.

This can only be interpreted as follows:

It is **possible** that you withdrew £500.

---

4. Summary

Permission	Prohibition	Possibility
may	may not	may might

Unit 2.29 Modal verbs 5 – TASKS

Task one

(a) *Using the chart below, identify the meanings expressed by the use of the modals in the following sentences:*

(b) *Where possible, put the sentences into the Past.*

    (i) May I have longer to complete the assignment?
    (ii) It might be Rosalie, but I doubt it.
    (iii) The house repairs may cost more than the house is worth.
    (iv) The sea may be cool for bathing, but the beaches are warm with the sun.
    (v) You might not be aware of the advantages of this scheme.
    (vi) Nobody may leave the hall before the exam has finished.
    (vii) They may have what you want, but I doubt it. They only stock torches in small numbers.
    (viii) That tree looks dangerous. It might fall down.
    (ix) You may withdraw up to £250 at any time.
    (x) There might be a heavy frost during the night.

Permission	
Prohibition	
Possibility	

Task two

Look at the illustrations below and write an appropriate caption for each one using **may** *or* **might**. *One example has been written for you.*

Example: **It might rain.** ....

UNIT 2.30
MODAL VERBS 6:
obligation, advisory, near certainty

Beds SHOULD be prepared one hour before closing time.
Cycles SHOULD be locked.
Your doctor OUGHT to be able to help you.

1. Primary use

Obligation

Should is sometimes used to express a duty where the **obligation** is a **moral** one rather than one that can be **imposed**. For example:

> Either (a) each member must use a sheet sleeping-bag of the approved type, or (b) if a down sleeping-bag is used, a sheet sleeping-bag must also be used to protect blankets. Beds **should** be prepared one hour before closing time.

In this example, the rule about sleeping-bags is **imposed** on the members. It is impossible, however, to impose the rule about preparing beds, because some people may arrive late. Thus it becomes a **moral obligation** for the members.

WARNING BOX

> **Ought to** is rarely used in this way.
>
> There is no **Past** form to express a **past moral obligation**. The **Past** form + past participle implies a moral obligation that wasn't carried out. For example:
>
> > Beds **should have been prepared** one hour before closing time.
>
> This example suggests that the beds weren't prepared and they still aren't.

Advisory

The **advisory** mood is a means for giving advice. For example:

> You **should** use first-class post and allow two days. (If you don't, the letter may arrive late.)
> Cycles **should** be locked. (Otherwise they may be stolen.)

Ought to can replace **should** in the above examples.

The **Past** here is expressed with **should have/ought to have**. For example:

> The bicycle **should have been** locked.

This implies that the bicycle wasn't locked and now it has been stolen.

2. Secondary use

Near certainty

When you are predicting an event that you believe is almost certain to take place, you use **should**. For example:

> It's nearly seven o'clock. Jack **should** be here in a few minutes.

Your doctor **should** be able to help you.
Ought to can replace **should** here.

The **Past** is expressed as in the advisory mood, with **should have/ought to have**. For example:

Your doctor **should have been** able to help you. (But he wasn't.)

The **negative** form of **ought to** is **ought not to**.

3. Summary

	Obligation	Advisory	Near certainty
Present Past	**should**	**should** **ought to** **should have** **ought to have**	**should** **ought to** **should have** **ought to have**

Should is also used in **conditional** clauses (see Unit 2.35) where it suggests something that might happen by chance. For example:

If you should meet him . . .

It is also used as an alternative form of conditional. For example:

Should you meet him . . .

Unit 2.30 Modal verbs 6 – TASKS

Task one

Complete the chart below to show the use of **should** *or* **ought to** *in each of the following sentences:*

(a) Children under 14 should have parental permission to see this film.
(b) It's twelve o'clock, and the President's plane should be coming into view at any moment.
(c) He ought to have been more diplomatic in his approach.
(d) As you'll be in Japan at New Year, you ought to visit Nara.
(e) If he's the leader, he should lead.
(f) The oil should be changed every 5,000 kilometers.
(g) This book should be made compulsory reading for anyone who has thought of going into business on their own.
(h) A child ought to be able to speak by the age of 3.
(j) Members ought to support the party whatever happens.
(k) People in glass houses shouldn't throw stones.

Obligation	Advisory	Near certainty

Task two

What advice would you give in the following situations? An example has been written for you.
Example:
A child runs across the street and is nearly run over.

Advice: *You should stop and look both ways before crossing the road.* ....

(a) You friend is always having difficulty starting his car.
(b) A friend has complained of having headaches and not sleeping.
(c) There's a very popular play which you and your friend want to see.
(d) The train a colleague plans to travel on is known to be crowded on every journey and she wants a seat.
(e) A friend who is very lazy has criticised colleagues for their work. The friend is now under attack.
(f) A colleague has lost some very important documents, which he fears may have been stolen.
(g) A friend who doesn't like violence plans to see a film, which you know is very violent.
(h) Your friend is interested in India. There is a new book about India, which has been highly praised.
(j) Your child always gets up late and is late for school.
(k) A friend needs to pass an examination to get promotion in her job, but she goes out a lot and does little work for the exam.

UNIT 2.31
MODAL VERBS 7: certainty (primary and secondary use)

> You then take the form to your doctor, who
> WILL complete it.
> That book WOULD make a good film.

We usually think of **will** as an auxiliary used to express a future event (see Unit 2.9). It is also used, however, to show **certainty** about some **general situation** or **event**, or about a **deduction** or **prediction** we are making.

This use is often linked with the conditional (see Units 2.35–2.38).

1. Primary use

Will is used to show **certainty** about a **general situation** or **event**. In these cases, **will** contains the idea of **volition**, i.e. a willingness or unwillingness to do something. This is unusual with inanimate objects, but there are times when the writer or speaker wants to give the object a personality.

Look at these examples:
The example below is from a government leaflet giving advice when travelling:
> You then take the form to your doctor, who **will** complete it.

Here the doctor has a duty to sign the form, but s/he must also be willing to do so.

The following is from an advertisement:
> Dishwashers **won't (will not)** wash everything.

The advertisement has made the dishwasher like a person. The dishwasher is in control of doing the washing and deciding which things to wash.

Will is sometimes used to indicate a **habit**, which the speaker finds irritating or frustrating. For example:
> He **will** come late!
> She **will** use the most expensive way to post mail!

In these cases, **will** always carries the stress in the sentence.

As well as the idea of habit, there is also a sense of **volition** on the part of the subject. Sometimes **always** is also used. For example:
> He**'ll always** come late!

Here the stress is on **always**.

When we talk about the **past** here, we use **would**. It has the same meaning as **used to** (see Unit 2.22). In such cases, the implication is that nowadays things have changed: now your doctor won't sign the form; now dishwashers will wash everything. For example:
> In the past you took the form to your doctor who **would** complete it. (But he won't now).
> In the past dishwashers **wouldn't** wash everything (But they will now).

2. Secondary use

Will is used when the speaker makes an **educated guess** about an immediate situation from the evidence available. If it is six o'clock in the evening and the telephone rings, Anne might say, for example:

That'**ll** be Marilyn. She said she would ring at six.

Anne is guessing. But from all the evidence she has, she is certain that the person phoning is Marilyn. And if a letter has just arrived, she might say, for example:

That'**ll** be from John.

Anne hasn't opened the letter. From the evidence, she has (the handwriting or expecting a letter), she is certain John has written the letter.

With the expression of **certainty** in the **secondary** use there is also the idea of a **vague future possibility**, connected to the conditional. For example:

It's a beautiful book. It'**ll** make a good film. (If somebody decides to film it.)

This can also be interpreted as a suggestion for someone to make the film.

It is possible for **would** to replace **will**. **Will** is often used, when the speaker is making a **suggestion**, rather than expressing a certainty. For example:

A car at that price **will/would** be a Jaguar.
That picture **will/would** look nice in your room.

The **Past** can be expressed in the two following ways, depending on the situation.

(a) When the speaker is making an educated **guess**. For example:

A: The 'phone range about six. But I was too late to answer it.
B: That **will/would have been** Marilyn. She wanted to speak to you.

Now look at this example:

A car at that price **will/would have been** a Jaguar.

Here the speaker is still only guessing; but now there is no possibility of finding out if the guess was right. Both forms carry the same meaning.

(b) When there is a vague **possibility** and **suggestion**.

Look at these examples:

That book **would have made** a good film.

This means that it's now too late to make the film.

That picture **would have looked** nice in your room.

This means the picture is no longer available.

For other uses of **will** and **would** see Unit 2.35.

Unit 2.31 Modal verbs 7 – TASKS

Task one

*Where it is possible, rewrite the following sentences using **would** or **will**. Indicate the meaning of the form you have chosen (changed situation, no past expression, polite form, advice or guess). Vary the forms you use. An example has been written for you.*

Example:
This car will go for miles on only a few gallons of petrol.

> **This car would go for miles on only a few gallons**
>
> **(The situation has changed.)**

(a) Photocopies will not be accepted.
(b) At that price, it'll be a BMW they're offering.
(c) Will you post this for me, please?
(d) Tourist offices will give you all the information you need.
(e) It's a big dog. It'll be a Alsatian.

Task two

Make certainty statements from the information given below. An example has been written for you.

Example:
Building for sale/very expensive.

> **At that price, it'll be a mansion.**

(a) Curtains for sale/very cheap.
(b) Restaurant/good, cheap Oriental food.
(c) Visitor/late/accident.
(d) Telephone rings/no reply/Tom at cinema.
(e) Big shop/sells many things/supermarket.

Task three

Your friends have just bought a house. You are with them planning where to put everything. Make suggestions to help them. First make a list of the furniture, etc., and then think of the rooms that are available. It may help you to draw a plan of the house. Two examples have been written for you.

Examples:

> **That bookcase will fit well against that wall.**
>
> **That carpet would look nice in the dining room.**

UNIT 2.32
MODAL VERBS 8: requests

Could I keep the book you lent me?
Would you mind opening the window?
Will you open the window?
Can Johnny come out to play?

We can divide **requests** into the two following types:
  requests for permission
  requests for the addressee to do something.

1. Requests for permission

The request
We make requests for permission in the following way:

Could I keep the book you lent me?

Can I pay by cheque?

May I use your typewriter?

Would you mind if I were a little late for the meeting?

Of these, **Could I? . . . May I? . . .** and **Can I?** are the most common. It is difficult to list them in order of politeness, as a lot depends on the **manner** in which they are spoken and the **context** in which they are used. Most people would probably rate **Could I?** or **May I?** as the most polite. **Would you mind if I?** is used only for special requests.

WARNING BOX

> **Might I?** is very rarely used. When it is, it is usually in a **formal** sense, when the speaker is interrupting a discussion or formal meeting. For example:
>   **Might I** suggest a break for coffee?

The response

Look at these examples:

Could I keep the book . . . ? – **Of course.**

Can I pay by cheque? – **Certainly.**

May I use your typewriter? – **Yes.**

Would you mind if I . . . ? – **Not at all./No, of course not.**

112

These are all neutral, polite responses. There are other forms. You should note the **negative** response with **would you mind if . . . ?** which, in fact gives permission.

If a refusal is given, the response can be pleasant and apologetic, as follows:
I'm sorry, but . . .
I'm afraid not.
These would normally be followed by a reason for the refusal.

WARNING BOX

> The refusal for **would you mind if . . . ?** is **I'm afraid I do** or something positive. However, **I'm sorry but . . .** would be acceptable.

A more aggressive and angry refusal would be one of the following:
Could I . . . ? **No, you couldn't.**
May I . . . ? **No, you may not.**
Can I . . . ? **No, you can't.**
Would you mind if I . . . ? **Yes, I do.**

WARNING BOX

> **Will** is not used in seeking **permission**.

Children often use the following form of request in asking **permission** for a friend to be allowed to do something:
Please, **can Mary** come and play with me?
Could Johnny come to the park with us?
The same pattern is followed in the third person. It is also used when a third person has authority over another, such as the head of a group of workers. For example:
Could Mr Johnson take this letter to the despatch department?

2. Requests for the addressee to do something

The request
Look at these examples:
Could you open the window?
Can you open the window?
Would you open the window?
Will you open the window?
Would you mind opening the window?
Once again, there is no easy way of deciding which is the more appropriate, as this will depend on the **situation** and the **context** in which the request is made. Some people might say that the **will** form is the least likely to be used, as it suggests irritation and frustration on the part of the speaker, especially if **will** is stressed.

Please can be added to any of these requests. It usually comes in the middle or end position. For example:

>**Would you** open the window, **please?**
>**Could you, please,** open the window?

In the middle position it is a little more forceful than in the end position.

WARNING BOX

> Note the **-ing** form after **would you mind . . . ?** for example:
>> Would you mind open**ing** the window?

The response

The polite response is one of the following examples:

> Could you open the window?
> Would you open the window?   – Yes, of course/Certainly.
> Can you open the window?
> Will you open the window?

> Would you mind opening the window?   – **Not at all.**

Note once again, the **negative** response with **Would you mind . . . ?** which is an agreement to carry out the request.

If a refusal is given, it follows the same pattern as the refusal in **1** above. For a polite refusal, you can say, **I'm sorry but . . .** and follow it with a reason for the refusal. For example:

> **I'm sorry, but** I find it rather warm in here.

An aggressive impolite refusal, can be any of the following:

> **No, I couldn't.**
> **No, I can't.**
> **No, I won't.**

WARNING BOX

> *No, I wouldn't* is **not possible**.

If the form of the request is **Would you mind?** the refusal is likely to be, **Yes, I would.**

Unit 2.32 Modal verbs 8 – TASKS

Task one

Below are five situations where you need to ask permission to do something. How would you ask? What would the reply be? An example has been written for you.

Example:
You have borrowed a friend's typewriter and kept it for nearly two months. But you still want to keep it.

Request: Would you mind if I kept your typewriter?

Reply: No, not at all.

(a) You are staying in a friend's house. You came for two weeks, but you have been there for nearly six months. You need to stay for another month.
(b) You want to borrow your friend's car to be able to bring some heavy cases from the town.
(c) You are making some furniture and your friend has some tools that you need.
(d) You want to watch a special programme on television.
(e) You want a day's holiday from work to see an old friend.

Task two

Below are five situations, where the person involved needs help. Indicate how the person might request help and suggest possible responses agreeing to help. An example has been written for you.

Example:
Your house needs painting – you want to do it at the weekend.

Request: Could you help me paint the house at the weekend?

Reply: Yes, of course.

(a) A lot of furniture to be moved.
(b) One more person needed for a football team.
(c) Some documents needed urgently in another town.
(d) Car not starting.
(e) Someone hurt by the roadside.

Task three

Give both a polite and an impolite response to the following requests:

(a) Could you post this letter for me, please?
(b) Would you help me carry this case to the station?
(c) Would you mind moving that box, so I could get past?
(d) Could you, please, return that book I lent you?
(e) Would you mind giving me a lift to work in your car tomorrow morning?

UNIT 2.33
MODAL VERBS 9: modal idioms

> I'd rather be a hammer than nail.
> You'd better check that your employer is willing to contribute.

Both of the modal idioms **would rather** and **had better** behave like the central modals (see Unit 2.25). Their characteristics are as follows:

(a) They have **no non-finite** forms. For example, you **cannot** say:
to rather/to have better
rathering/having better.

(b) They are followed by the **infinitive** without **to**. For example:
I'd rather **be** (*not* *I'd rather to be*)
You'd better **check** (*not* *you'd better to check*).

(c) There are **no other tense** forms.
In the example, I'd rather **have been**, the change in tense is with the infinitive **be**.

(d) On only two occasions (see below) do they have a **negative** form:
You **must** say: **I'd rather not be**. (Here the negative **not** belongs to **be**.)
You **cannot** say: *I wouldn't rather be.*
You **must** say: **You had better not check**. (Here the negative **not** belongs to **check**.)
You **cannot** say: *I hadn't better check.*

1. Would rather

The idiom **would rather** expresses a **preference** and has the same meaning as **would prefer**.

Look at this example:
I'd **rather** be a hammer than nail.
In this popular song, the singer is saying what he **would prefer** to be.

Would rather can be used to express a **choice** about plans or ideas. For example:
The British people have said they **would rather** have a good Health Service than get back money in lower taxes.

The **interrogative** form is also used to show what **choices** there are for the person being asked. For example:
Would you rather have a government that raised taxes to pay for services you might not want, or a government that cut taxes and let you decide what you want?

Both the **interrogative** and **negative** forms are used to make **suggestions**. For example:
Would you rather stay home tonight?
Wouldn't you rather stay home tonight?

The **negative** form strengthens the suggestion, almost as if the speaker were trying to persuade the other person being asked. It is often used when the other person has planned to do something different. For example:
Let's go to the cinema!
Oh, **wouldn't you rather** stay home tonight?

When the idiom is followed by a clause, it follows the same pattern as **wish** and the verb in the clause is in a Past tense (see Unit 2.39). For example:

I'd rather **you did it**.

2. Had better

Had better is similar in meaning to **should** (see Unit 2.30). It is used to give **advice**. For example:

If you are thinking of changing from the government pension scheme to a personal one, you**'d better** check that your employer is willing to contribute more than the minimum.

The idiom is often used to convey a **warning** or **threat**. For example:

You**'d better** get the report finished before you leave.

The implication here is that if the report isn't finished, the person spoken to will be in trouble.

In an informal situation, the **interrogative** form is usually used, not to ask a question but as a means of giving **advice**. Usually the **negative interrogative** form is used. In this case, the advice is very strong and may be considered a **warning**. For example:

Hadn't you better check that your employer is willing to contribute more than the minimum?

Here the speaker isn't asking a question, but giving strong **advice**.

Unit 2.33 Modal verbs 9 – TASKS

Task one

Read the following sentences and fill in the missing words with the appropriate modal idiom – **had better** *or* **would rather**.

(a) ...... you ...... book the taxi early? They may be busy.
(b) The government .... you had a personal pension.
(c) You .... invest that money in something safe. You might lose it if you speculate.
(d) Although it's not comfortable and often very cold, Yousoufa .... live in Canada than in his own country.
(e) I .... have good health than a small fortune.
(f) The Football League .... do something about the hooligans, or England won't play any more World Cup games.
(g) ...... you ...... travel by train? Such a long journey is exhausting by car.
(h) He .... not know the truth about the accident. He's afraid it will upset him.
(j) He .... improve unless he wants to lose his job.
(k) .... you ...... agree to their plan? They could be very difficult people.

Task two

Imagine you are organising one of the following:
(a) **a holiday**.
(b) **a business trip**.
(c) **a plan to develop a part of the place where you live**.
(d) **a research scheme on something that interests you**

State the choices available and your preferences. Explain to your associates/colleagues what should be done – this should be strongly asserted, almost as a warning.

Unit 2.34 Modal verbs 10 – REVIEW TASKS

Task one

The following passage is taken from an official leaflet about some government welfare payments. Read through the text, and state which of the following meanings applies to each modal verb:

Ability, advisability, certainty (primary use), certainty (secondary use), exemption, necessity, obligation, permission, prohibition, request, near certainty, possibility, impossibility, probability.

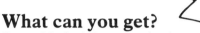

What can you get?

You <u>can</u> claim for the items or services that you <u>need</u> to help you.

There is no list, but grants <u>can</u> include things like furniture, removal costs, connection charges, clothing, laundry costs for a disabled child, essential repairs, bedding and re-decoration. The DHSS <u>will</u> not pay less than £30, unless it is for travel costs.

If you have savings over £500 the amount over £500 <u>will</u> be taken off the grant.

The amount of the grant <u>will</u> be the amount you need for the items you have claimed. You can ask for the actual cost of the items and it <u>will</u> be paid up to a reasonable amount. You <u>will</u> not normally be asked to provide an estimate. There is also a list of items which you are not allowed to claim for. This list includes things like court expenses, work-related expenses, telephone charges, educational or medical needs.

But remember that the social fund for community care grants is strictly cash limited. This means that your claim <u>will</u> be looked at along with all the other claims that DHSS receive. So although you <u>might</u> have claimed for something that you need urgently, you <u>might</u> not get any help because someone else's claim <u>might</u> be treated as being more important.

If you get turned down for a grant, you <u>might</u> be offered a loan instead. Think very carefully before accepting a loan. It <u>will</u> commit you to repayments which you <u>might</u> not be able to afford.

If you claim and are turned down, you <u>will</u> have to wait another six months before putting in for the same thing again unless your situation has changed.

How to claim

You <u>should</u> claim a community care grant by asking for an application form from the DHSS. The form to ask for is Form SF300 'Help for people with exceptional expenses'.

Unhappy with a decision?

Decisions about your claim are made by a DHSS official called the Social Fund Officer. If you are unhappy with any decision which this officer makes about your claim, you <u>can</u> ask for a review of the decision. A review is basically just another chance to put your case.

If you are turned down you do not have any right of appeal to the Social Security Appeal Tribunal.

Advice and more information

You <u>might</u> want advice about community care grants or <u>help</u> with filling in the form.

You <u>might</u> disagree with a DHSS decision and want an explanation or want help with a review.

You <u>can</u> get advice and help from an Advice Centre, Citizens Advice Bureau, or Welfare Rights Officer. To find their addresses call at your local library, or write for the 'Where To Go For Advice' leaflet to:
Lancashire County Council,
Welfare Rights Service,
FREEPOST, Preston PR1 3BR.
(You don't need a stamp.)
For general advice about benefits, telephone DHSS free of charge on 0800 666 555.

Your local Social Services Department <u>may</u> be able to help you if you are in one of the situations covered by community care grants.

Task two

In the following text, which is from a booklet giving advice to people travelling abroad, the modal verbs have been deleted. Complete the text by adding an appropriate modal verb and state which meaning the modal verb has in the context. An example has been written for you.

Example:

Can (ability).

PLAN WELL AHEAD

Check the requirements for your destination
Find out about the health risks in the country you are visiting, and the precautions you ____ take, by reading the chart on page 5. And check on the vaccinations you need, using the advice on pages 9-14. You ____ get more information from your travel agent and the Embassy or High Commission in London of the country concerned.

Consult your doctor at least 2 months before departure
He ____ advise you and arrange vaccinations. Some of these take time to become effective and ____ be given at the same time as other vaccinations. Tell your doctor where you are going and if you are taking your children with you. This is particularly important if they have not had their full course of childhood vaccinations. Rather earlier arrangements ____ be needed if you require vaccination against tuberculosis (see page 9).

Paying for vaccinations and anti-malarial tablets
Some vaccinations are free under the NHS; for others there ____ be a charge. Doctors charge for signing or filling in a certificate. Although you ____ seek your doctor's advice on anti-malarial tablets, some of these are available from a pharmacist without prescription.

Get your doctor's advice if you to take any medicines with you
But you ____ only ____ to get a small supply of medication under the NHS for use while you are away.

Paying for medical treatment abroad
How much you ____ to pay depends on the country you are visiting and the existence of any special arrangements for free or reduced cost medical treatment:

■ If you are visiting a European Community country you ____ need form E111. Read pages 15-22. You ____ need medical insurance as well.

■ If you are visiting a country which has a reciprocal health care agreement with the UK, read pages 23-26. Consider the need for supplementary medical insurance.

■ If you are visiting any other country medical insurance is **essential.** Check with your travel agent on the amount of insurance you ____ need and include enough cover to allow for the extra cost of travelling home in an emergency.

Task three

Using a modal expression, explain what the following texts mean.

Example:
No through road for motor vehicles.

Motor vehicles must not use this road.

(a) Turn left only.
(b) Hotel – open to non-residents for luncheons.
(c) Please place your purchases on this platform.
(d) Kodak film – developing – printing.
(e) Riding by permit only.
(f) No camping beyond this point.
(g) Admission free.
(h) Newcastle Utd. versus Derby County on Wed. 28 Feb.
(j) Road liable to subsidence.
(k) Cold and influenza mixture – not recommended for children under 5 years.

UNIT 2.35
CONDITIONAL 1: form

If it rains on Saturday, we won't go to the fair.
If he came home after seven, he always brought flowers.
If my father were alive, he would be 90 now.

It is often suggested that there are three types of **conditional sentence**. This hypothesis is based on the fact that three different verb forms can be used after **if** in **conditional sentences**. Thus, the supposition is concerned with the **way** the **conditional** is formed and not with the underlying **meanings** of the forms used.

When we base our hypothesis on underlying **meanings**, there are basically the two following types of **conditional sentence**:
1. the **possible conditional**;
2. the **impossible conditional**.

1. The possible conditional

The **possible conditional** expresses a 'real' possibility that an event or action might occur in the present or future or could have occurred in the past. (See Unit 2.36 for further explanation of use and meaning.)

Look at these examples:
   (a) **If it rains** on Saturday, we **won't go** to the fair.
       (We don't know what the weather will be like on Saturday, but rain is possible.)
   (b) **If he comes** home after seven, he always **brings** some flowers.
       (He doesn't always come home after seven, but there are occasions when he does; and these are when he brings flowers.)
   (c) **If it rained** on Saturday, we **wouldn't go** to the fair.
       (As in **(a)**, but more unlikely.)
   (d) **If he came** home after seven, he always **brought** some flowers.
       (As in **(b)**, but an event which happened in the past.)

The **form** is shown in the following chart:

Subordinate clause	Main clause
(a) **If + present**	modal (usually **will**) + main verb (infinitive without **to**)
(b) **If + present**	main verb, present tense
(c) **If + past**	modal (usually **would**) + main verb (infinitive without **to**)
(d) **If + past**	main verb, past tense

2. The impossible conditional

The **impossible conditional** expresses an imaginary situation which is impossible. For example:

(a) With reference to the present, the situation can't occur now or in the future.
(b) With reference to the present, the situation didn't occur in the past.
(c) With reference to the past, the situation didn't occur.
    (See Unit 2.37 for further explanation of use and meaning.)

Look at these examples:
(a) reference to the present, but can't occur:
    (i) **If you had** a video, you **could record** it yourself.
        (But you haven't, so you won't be able to.)
    (ii) If my father **were alive**, he **would be** 90 now.
        (He isn't; he died ten years ago.)
(b) reference to present, but didn't occur:
    (i) **If you had** a video, you **could have recorded** it yourself last night.
        (You don't have a video, so you didn't record it.)
    (ii) **If my father were alive**, he **would have been** 90 last week.
        (But he died ten years ago.)
(c) reference to the past, and didn't occur:
    (i) **If you had had** a video, you **could have recorded** it yourself last night.
        (You didn't have a video last night, so you didn't record it.)

The **form** is shown in the following chart:

Subordinate clause	Main clause
(a) **If + past**	past modal + main verb (infinitive without **to**)
(b) **If + past**	past modal + main verb (past infinitive without **to**)
(c) **If + past perfect**	past modal + main verb (past infinitive without **to**)

3. Alternative forms (see also Units 2.36–2.38)

A **conditional** is not always expressed with an **if** clause. On some occasions (especially more formal ones) an **inversion** form can be used.

Look at these examples:
If + present can be replaced by **should + inversion**:
    Should he come home after seven, he always **brings** some flowers.
If + past can be replaced by **were + inversion**:
    Were it to rain on Saturday, we **wouldn't go** to the fair.
    Were my father alive, he **would be** 90 now.
If + past perfect can be replaced by **inversion** with the auxiliary **had**:
    Had you had a video, you **could have recorded** it yourself.

The clauses can go in **either order**. For example:
> **If my father were alive**, he **would be** 90 now.
> My father **would be** 90 now, **if he were alive**.

Note that when speaking of a **future possibility, will** is rarely used in the **if** clause. In the following example the **will** is used to emphasise a determination and possible habit on the part of the subject:
> **If** you **will arrive** late, you must expect to miss the food.

The following example expresses the same meaning, but lacks the emphasis (this is more common):
> **If** you **arrive** late, you must expect to miss the food.

Would is used similarly to express a past habit.
> **If** you **would arrive** late you must have expected to miss the food.

For use of was *and* were *after if, see Unit 2.37.*

Unit 2.35 Conditional 1 – TASKS

Task one

Complete the following sentences with the appropriate form for the type of conditional indicated in brackets. Some examples have been written for you.

Examples:

If you *(have)* a computer, you *(can produce)* beautiful handouts. *(Impossible)*

If you HAD a computer, you COULD HAVE PRODUCED beautiful handouts. or **If you HAD HAD a computer, you COULD HAVE PRODUCED beautiful handouts**

If the money *(arrive)*, we *(can arrange)* the holiday. *(Possible)*

If the money arrives, we can arrange the holiday.

(a) If the treaty *(be)* signed, we *(will get rid of)* the bombs. *(Impossible)*
(b) If the workers *(go)* on strike now, they *(will lose)* a lot of money. *(Impossible)*
(c) If I *(learn)* to read and write, I *(would be)* a rich business man by now. *(Impossible)*
(d) If the sails of the ship *(be)* black, that *(will mean)* we've lost the battle. *(Possible)*
(e) If they *(cut)* taxes next year, we *(will buy)* a new car. *(Possible)*
(f) If you *(receive)* information about retirement schemes, you *(should ask)* several cautious questions. *(Possible)*
(g) If she *(wake)* early, she *(would be)* on the plane that crashed. *(Impossible)*
(h) If you *(hear)* a rapid series of bleeps, it *(mean)* the line is engaged. *(Possible)*
(j) If they *(not hear)* the bell, they *(drown)*. *(Possible)*
(k) I *(have)* a cup of tea, if you *(make)* some. *(Possible)*

Task two

Make complete sentences from the ideas below. The section in bold type is the condition. State whether you have made a possible or impossible condition. An example has been written for you.

Example:

/**give – £10**/clothe – starving child/

If you give £10, that will clothe a starving child. Possible.

(a) /**not sell – house**/not have to – pay commission/
(b) /**invest – £1,000 – in 1974**/worth £20,000 today/
(c) /**start – early**/see – wonderful sunrise/
(d) /**Jane – stay on**/be – Director of Studies – now/
(e) /**believe that**/believe anything/
(f) /cassettes – only – return/**postage – not enclose**/
(g) /awards – withhold/**sufficiently high standards – not attain**/
(h) /**you – successful – second-stage**/join – semi-final/
(j) /**receive form – before 26 March**/we – send – special free gift/
(k) /**not contact – us tomorrow**/contact you – day after/

UNIT 2.36
CONDITIONAL 2: possible

If he arrives at the office late, everyone knows it's going to be a difficult day.
If he wins there, he stands a good chance of being selected.
If she agrees, they can go ahead from next week.

The **possible conditional** expresses a 'real' possibility that an action or event could occur in the present or in the future, or could have occurred in the past. There are three main types of **possible conditional**.

1. Present and past habit

Look at these examples:

If he arrives at the office late, everyone **knows** it's going to be a difficult day.
If she saw even the smallest fly trapped in a jar, she **would be** upset.

Here **if** can be replaced by **whenever**. It indicates a **habit** or **continually repeated** situation that may occur at any time, or that used to occur regularly in the past.

2. Deductions

Look at these examples:

If he wins today, he **stands** a good chance of being selected.
If the rains don't come again this year, then the country **will not have** enough water.
If it rains next month, there **should be** enough water to last until the monsoon comes.
If you wanted to control your finances, you**'d welcome** a Home-owners Loan plan.

Here the speaker is making a **deduction** about **future possibilities** or **attitudes**. Both the Present and Past tenses may be used. The use of the **Past**, however, usually reflects a **greater uncertainty**.

3. Future possibilities

Look at these examples:

If two more people join, we **can run** the course.
If two more people joined, we **could run** the course.
If you're thinking of buying your first home, **send** for your free Home-buying kit.
If you undercharge, you **could** quickly **go** out of business.

Here the speaker is talking about **possible events** or **actions** in the **future**. Once again, the use of the **Past** tense shows the speaker is **less certain**.

Alternative form

The **conditional** is not always expressed through the use of an **if** clause, but may be shown through the use of **inversion** (see Unit 2.35) or with the **Imperative** and a co-ordinating clause. For example:

Start a savings account now and we**'ll give** you £50.
(If you start a savings account now, we'll give you £50.)
Don't undercharge or you **could** quickly go out of business.
(If you undercharge, you could quickly go out of business.)

Unit 2.36 Conditional 2 – TASKS

Task one

Indicate the type of possible conditional exemplified in the sentences below. Put the number of the sentence in the appropriate column in the following chart.

(a) If he goes out on a cold day, he often wears a knitted white scarf.
(b) If he wrote to his nephew, he always enclosed some money.
(c) If she posts it today, you will get it by Saturday.
(d) If income tax is reduced, the government could win the next election.
(e) If Brownlow is made Minister for Transport, we can expect a lot of changes in the law.
(f) If it snows, then we won't go to Manchester.
(g) If you've got some money to invest, contact Chapman's for advice.
(h) If you buy that painting, you'll be making a good investment.

Past habit	Present habit	Deduction	Future Possibilities

Task two

All the sentences below may be considered possible conditionals. Rewrite them, using another form for expressing this conditional. Some examples have been written for you.

Example:
Read The Guardian and get the best financial advice.

Alternative:

If you read the Guardian, you'll get the best financial advice.

If you published that book, you'd be sued for libel.

Alternative:

Should you publish that book, you'd be sued for libel.

Publish that book and you'd be sued for libel.

(a) Keep the lights on all night and burglars will know you're not at home.

(b) If the price of that house gets any higher, I won't be able to afford it.

(c) Go, and I won't ask you again.

(d) Were he to arrive after dark, he might not find the house easily.

(e) We must leave now or we'll be late.

(f) If you bother him now, he'll forget the time he started cooking the meat.

(g) Should you see Sally, give her my love.

(h) Read that paper tonight, or you'll fail the exam.

(j) If you elect me, I shall bring about changes in the social welfare system.

(k) Return this form within seven days, and you'll get a free gift.

Task three

Imagine that you are organising a party with two friends.

    (a) *Make a list of ten people you want to invite;*

    (b) *Against each guest, note something about their character. For example:*

        Jonathan – argumentative; noisy eater; drinks a lot;

        Mrs Robin – quiet old lady; doesn't like drinking.

    (c) *Decide how you arrange them around the table, so that most of the guests will be happy with their companions.*

Some examples have been written for you.

Example:

If we put Mary next to Patricia they'll certainly quarrel.

Sit David next to Anne and they'll dominate the evening.

You can't sit Mrs Robin next to Jonathan; he'll upset her.

UNIT 2.37
CONDITIONAL 3:
impossible

If you had a video, you could record it yourself.
If my father were alive, he would have been 90 last birthday.
If the car had started, I would have been on time.

The **impossible conditional** expresses an **imagined** situation which **could not occur** or **did not occur**. There are three types of **impossible conditional**.

1. Impossible now (or improbable future)

Look at these examples:
   (a) **If you had video**, you **could record** it yourself tonight.
       (But you haven't got a video, so you won't be able to.)
   (b) **If she had the time**, she **would do** it.
       (But she hasn't got the time.)
   (c) **If my father were alive**, he'**d be** 90 now.
       (But he's dead, so he isn't.)

2. Non-existent past (referring to the present)

Look at these examples:
   (a) If you **had** a video, you **could have recorded** it yourself last night.
       (But you haven't, so you weren't able to do it.)
   (b) If my father **were** alive, he **would have been** 90 last birthday.
       (But he's dead, so he wasn't.)

Compare the different tenses used in **1(a)** and **2(a)**; and also the tenses used in **1(c)** and **2(b)**.

3. Non-existent past (referring to the past)

Look at these examples:
   (a) If you **had had** a video, you **could have recorded** it yourself last night.
       (But you didn't, so you didn't record the programme.)
   (b) if the car **had started**, I **would have been** on time.
       (But the car didn't start.)
   (c) If it **had rained**, the performance **would have been cancelled**.
       (But it didn't rain.)

In all these examples we are looking at events or situations which cannot occur or didn't occur.

WARNING BOX

With the past form of the verb **to be**, **were** is sometimes used instead of **was** in the **if** clause. The form **were** is considered more correct grammatically, but **was** is frequently used in less formal situations. For example:

If he **were** here now . . . *or* If he **was** here now . . .

If I **were** rich . . . *or* If I **was** rich . . .

In the fixed phrase **If I were you**, the use of **was** is not acceptable.

In the **inversion** alternative form, only **were** is acceptable.

With the **impossible conditional**, the only acceptable alternative form is the **inversion** (see Unit 2.35). For example:

Were my father alive, he would be 90 now.

Had you had a video, you could have recorded it yourself last night.

Unit 2.37 Conditional 3 – TASKS

Task one

Read through the sentences below and identify which type of impossible conditional they exemplify. Indicate your choice in the following chart. The first one has been done for you.

(a) If you hadn't read the instructions carefully, you could have made a lot of mistakes.
(b) If they had really been to the Gambia, they would know that the people speak English and not French.
(c) If the university had been open that day, there wouldn't have been the trouble with the Italian students.
(d) If I was going to London by car, I could take the package with me.
(e) If the corner shop were open, I could buy some bread right now.
(f) If I'd got the right lottery number, I'd be a rich man by now.
(g) If the film had been here last week, I could have seen it.
(h) I'd be drinking tea by the Spanish Steps if I were in Rome at this moment.
(j) There'd be no droughts anywhere, if it rained like this in Africa.
(k) If the government had supported the pay award for the miners, it wouldn't have been defeated.

Impossible now *or* Improbable future	Non-existent past (present reference)	Non-existent past (past reference)
		(a.)

Task two

There are several things John wants to do, but can't. From the information given below, express these in terms of the impossible conditional. Use both forms. An example has been written for you.

Example:
He wants to record the television pop concert, but he hasn't got a video.

Conditional:

If he had a video, he could record the television pop concert.

Had he a video, he could record the television pop concert.

(a) He wants to drive to Edinburgh, but he's got to see his mother in London.
(b) He needs to buy some new shirts, but he hasn't got any money.
(c) He wants to attend the dance class, but it's full.

(d) He'd like to go skating on the river, but the ice has melted.
(e) He wants to study at the university, but he failed his exams.

Task three

Mary is now very old. Looking back on her life, there are many things she regrets she didn't do. From the information given below make impossible conditionals about the past. Use both forms. An example has been written for you.

Example:
She wanted to be an explorer, but she didn't keep fit and do any exercise.

Conditional:

If she had kept fit and done some exercise, she could have been an explorer. Had she kept fit and done some exercise, she could have been an explorer.

(a) She thought of being a writer, but she wasn't very good with words.
(b) She planned to buy a large house in London, but didn't save hard enough.
(c) She wanted to be the Prime Minister, but she wasn't seriously interested in politics.
(d) She tried to be a pilot, but they wanted only men in those days.
(e) She imagined being a trapeze artiste, but she didn't like heights.

Task four

Imagine you have just lost a game. (Choose your favourite game – it can be a team game such as football or a board game such as chess.) You are thinking about all the things that went wrong and what should have been done. Write down as many sentences as you can, using the impossible conditional. Some examples have been written for you.

Example:

If he had passed the ball to Roberts, Roberts would have scored.
If she hadn't taken my knight then, I would have got her queen and bishop.

UNIT 2.38
CONDITIONAL 4: unless

Stamford will be dropped from the team, unless he improves his performance.
She always comes, unless she's ill.

Unless is known as the **negative conditional**. It stands in place of **except if/except on condition that**.

Look at these examples:
Stamford will be dropped from the team, **unless** he improves his performance.
(The only way Stamford can stay in the team is to improve his performance. He's playing very badly at the moment.)
She always comes, **unless** she's ill.
(The only reason she wouldn't come would be if she were ill.)

It is used only for **possible conditionals** (see Unit 2.36). For example:
The government will sue, if the book isn't withdrawn. **(Possible)**
The government will sue, **unless** the book is withdrawn.

With the **impossible conditional**, we must use **if . . . not . . . .** For example:
The government would have sued, **if** the book **hadn't** been withdrawn. **(Impossible)**

The version with **unless** is **unacceptable**. For example:
*The government would have sued, *unless the book had been withdrawn.*

Alternative form

As with other conditionals, there are alternative ways of expressing the **unless** form.

Look at these examples:
Stamford should improve, **otherwise/or** he will be dropped.
(Unless Stamford improves, he'll be dropped.)
The book must be withdrawn, **otherwise/or** the government will sue.
Withdraw the book **otherwise/or** the government will sue.
(Unless the book is withdrawn, the government will sue.)

Note from the examples above that in the alternative forms, the obligation is stressed by the use of **should, must** or the **imperative** form in the clause originally governed by **unless**.

Unit 2.38 Conditional 4 – TASKS

Task one

Rewrite the following sentences, using **unless** *or* **otherwise/or***. Some examples have been written for you.*

Examples:
Fulham football team must improve, or they'll be at the bottom.

Rewrite:
Unless Fulham football team improves, they'll be at the bottom.

Unless you get a television licence, you'll be fined £500.

Rewrite:
You must get a television licence or/otherwise you'll be fined £500.

(a) You should wait until next week to change your money, otherwise you'll lose on the exchange rate.
(b) You must take that book back to the library, or you'll have to pay a heavy fine.
(c) Unless the candidate gets 75%, she doesn't stand a chance of being admitted to the course.
(d) Unless they hurry, we'll miss the train.
(e) Drive more slowly, or you'll have an accident.
(f) Unless you order that magazine, you can never get it. It's so popular.
(g) Unless you have a lot of money, you shouldn't think of living in London.
(h) Start early, or you'll get held up in the traffic.
(j) He must attend the next meeting, otherwise they'll ask him to resign.
(k) How can you hope to get better, unless you do what the doctor tells you?

Task two

In the left hand column of the chart over the page are listed John's dreams for the future. In the right hand column, there are the difficulties he has to face. Put the information from the two columns together in one sentence. The first has been done for you as an example.

Example:
John won't be a world-famous film-star, unless he goes to Hollywood.
John must go to Hollywood, otherwise/or he won't be a world-famous film-star.

John's dreams	Difficulties
Example:	
be a world-famous filmstar	go to Hollywood
(a) see the Prime Minister	Private Secretary agrees
(b) go to the theatre	wife book tickets
(c) fly in Concorde	win a lot of money
(d) become very rich	successful songwriter
(e) buy a house	borrow some money
(f) go to the moon	do a lot of hard training
(g) race at Le Mans	find a sponsor
(h) be chairman of his company	get support from the committee
(j) travel round the world	build a strong boat
(k) be a sailor	learn to swim

Task three

(a) *With a friend, think of a sports club or social club that you would like to form.*
(b) *Set down the conditions of membership of the club.*
(c) *Write these conditions down using* **unless** *or its alternative forms. An example has been written for you.*

Example:

You can't join this club, unless you are over 18 years of age.

UNIT 2.39
CONDITIONAL 5: wishing

I wish I were at home now.
If only they would sign the treaty soon.
I wish I had bought that coat after all.
If only he had said so at the time.

Wishing is very close to expressing a **condition**. There is often a second part to a wish, which is either spoken or unspoken. For example:

I **wish** I were at home now, then I could have something refreshing to drink.

This could be rewritten as a **conditional sentence**:

If I **were** at home now, I could have something refreshing to drink.

The difference is that the **conditional** is **neutral** and doesn't express the stronger 'wish'. With **wishing** there is a feeling of **regret** for something.

When you **wish**, the situation is **impossible**. For example, when you say, I wish I had bought that coat after all, the reality is that you didn't buy the coat. But there is the sense of **regret** that you didn't buy it.

I wish I were at home now.

Wishing can be expressed through either the verb **to wish** or the conditional reference **if only**. They both express the sense of **regret** for something that is not, will not be or was not.

The sentence structure to express **wishing** is similar to that expressing the **impossible** or hypothetical conditional (see Unit 2.37). The act of **wishing** is normally in the **present**, but the **impossibility** of the wish is expressed by the use of **Past** tenses.

Unit 2.39 Conditional 5

There are three types of **wishing**:

1. Impossible now

I **wish** **If only**	I **was** at home now. I **lived** by the sea. I **could** paint like that. they **didn't ask** so many questions. she **wasn't** so poor.

In this group, the **wish** is a **regret** for a situation that is **present**. This is expressed in the second part of the structure with the **Past Simple**. **Could** here is the Past form of **can** (see Unit 2.27).

2. Improbable future

I **wish** **If only**	**they would** sign the treaty soon. the sun **would shine**. she **wouldn't** always **argue**. he**'d make up** his mind. they **were coming** here tomorrow.

Here the **wisher** is **regretting** something that **will** or **will not happen**, or something that **continually happens**. The **wish** is expressed through the use of **would** or **could** or the **Past Continuous**.

3. Non-existent past

I **wish** **If only**	I **had bought** that coat after all. he **had said** so at the time. that shop **hadn't closed**. they **hadn't driven** so fast. there**'d been** some good dance music.

In this case, the **wish** is a **regret** for something that has **already taken place**, and is expressed through the use of the **Past Perfect**.

Unit 2.39 Conditional 5 – TASKS

Task one

Identify to which group the following expressions of wishing belong: impossible now, improbable future or non-existent past.

(a) She wishes she hadn't married him.
(b) They wish they were going to Australia with them.
(c) I only wish I had just a little bit more money.
(d) If only she'd seen that dangerous corner sooner.
(e) If only they would arrive on time.
(f) If only I'd posted it on Tuesday instead of on Wednesday.
(g) If only Caesar hadn't gone to the Forum on 15 March.
(h) I wish India wasn't so far from England.
(j) She wishes she was going to see the Queen.
(k) I wish I'd written that.

Task two

*Devise a caption for the cartoons below, using **wish** or **if only** for each one. An example has been written for you.*

Example:

I wish I had an elephant.
Then I could travel through the jungle.

(a)

(b)

(c)

(d)

Task three

(a) *Think of someone progressing through a career and write down all the things s/he has done to be successful in that career.*

(b) *Consider someone who is retiring and hasn't been successful. Make a list of the things s/he wishes had or had not happened. Some examples have been written for you.*

Example:

I wish I had passed that exam.

I wish I hadn't taken that job tranfer.

UNIT 2.40
GERUND and INFINITIVE PHRASES 1

Hall has always enjoyed challenging the established code.
She hopes to change old attitudes.

1. Gerund versus participle

In Unit 1.3, we discussed the use of the **-ing** form of the verb. In the examples there, the **-ing** form was called the **participle** because it was a reduced form of the **verb** and could be expanded into the full form. For example:

Wanting something cheap, they . . .

could become:

Because they wanted something cheap . . .

There is another use of the **-ing** form, where it acts more as a **noun** than a verb. It is not a reduced form and cannot be expanded. This form is known as the **gerund**.

Look at this example:

(a) Hall has always enjoyed **challenging** the established code.

Here, **challenging the established code** is the **object** of **enjoyed**. So the whole phrase acts as a **noun**. It answers the question WHAT? after the main verb.

There are many verbs like **enjoy** which are followed by **gerunds** alone or phrases such as the one above.

2. Use of infinitive

Other verbs which are followed by noun phrases for their **objects**, however, use the **infinitive** form and **not** the **gerund**.

Look at this example:

(a) She hopes **to change** the old attitudes towards women in engineering.

As in **1(a)** above, the phrase after the main verb, **to change old attitudes towards women in engineering,** answers the question WHAT? This construction can be seen clearly in the chart below.

Subject فاعل	Verb فعل	Object مفعول
Hall She	has (always) enjoyed hopes	challenging the established code. to change the old attitudes towards women in engineering.

The choice of whether to use the **infinitive** or the **gerund** depends on the main lexical verb. Some verbs are followed by the **gerund**, such as **enjoy** in **1(a)**, while others are followed by the **infinitive**, such as **hope** in **2(a)**.

Unit 2.40 Gerund and infinitive phrases 1

There are some verbs which can be followed by either form, but very often the selection affects the meaning (see Units 2.41, 2.42).

In the chart below are the common verbs which are always followed by the **gerund**, those that are followed by the **infinitive**, and those which can be followed by the either the **gerund** or the **infinitive**, where the meaning is the same.

Always followed by gerund		Always followed by infinitive	
admit	find	afford	offer
appreciate	finish	agree	plan
avoid	forgive	appear	pretend
celebrate	mention	decide	promise
consider	mind	expect	refuse
defer	miss	hope	seem
delay	pardon	intend	want
deny	postpone	need	
detest	practise		
dislike	prevent	**Followed by either**	
dispute	recall		
enjoy	risk	begin	
escape	suggest	continue	
excuse	understand	prefer	
explain		start	

3. Gerund and infinitive as subject

It is also possible to use noun phrases beginning with the **gerund** or **infinitive** as the **subject** of the sentence. For example:

Providing holidays for handicapped children means fun for all.

To go by train from London to Glasgow 1st class costs £126.

The selection of either the **gerund** or the **infinitive** depends on the category of the verb (see Unit 1.1). It is more usual for **transitive** verbs to use the **gerund** form only, whereas with **intransitive** verbs either the **gerund** or **infinitive** form can be used.

Generally we tend to transfer the **infinitive subject** to the end of the sentence and begin with the introductory **It** (see Unit 5.2). For example:

It costs £126 to go by train from London to Glasgow.

This is not usually done with the **gerund subject**.

Unit 2.40 Gerund and infinitive phrases 1 – TASKS

Task one

Read the following text and then put the verbs in brackets into the correct form, i.e. the gerund or the infinitive. An example has been written for you.

Example:

Joan doesn't want *(go)* to Iraq, but she doesn't mind *(meet)* the teachers from there.

Joan doesn't want TO GO to Iraq, but she doesn't mind MEETING the teachers from there.

Politicians often seem *(get)* angry with their opponents; but this is really a lot of play-acting. Most politicians are people who enjoy *(debate)* their views and they would miss not *(have)* someone to argue with. Look at Mrs Thatcher and Mr Gorbachev. They didn't want *(finish)* *(talk)* to each other, although they disagreed most of the time. Even now, they hope *(see)* each other again soon. If you want *(become)* a politician, you mustn't mind *(be)* attacked very personally on any occasion. From the moment you have celebrated *(win)* your seat in parliament, you risk *(suffer)* a lot of personal and often unfair criticism. The ambitious politician, however, must avoid *(appear)* upset at any time.

Task two

(a) *Think of ten things that are fun to do and write them down. Some examples have been written for you.*

Example:

To go swimming in winter.

Riding a motor-bike.

(b) *Now make up sentences which show why they are fun.*

Example:

To go swimming in winter makes you feel very healthy.

Riding a motor bike is very exciting.

(c) *In which of your sentences are you most likely to use the introductory It?*

UNIT 2.41
GERUND and INFINITIVE PHRASES 2

I remember buying the ginger.
I remembered to buy the ginger.
He regrets playing badly in the last game.
He regrets living in Berlin.
She regrets to say she can't come.
When I stopped feeling angry, I realised a lot of the problem was my own fault.

Some verbs are followed by the **gerund** or by the **infinitive**. For example:

I remember **buying** the ginger.
I remembered **to buy** the ginger.

These should not be seen as alternative forms, however. The use of the **gerund** form conveys a different **meaning** to the use of the **infinitive**. The difference in **meaning** varies according to the **finite lexical verb**.

1. Remember, forget

Look at this example:

I **remember buying** the ginger.

In this example, the situation is that now I remember that I bought the ginger when I was shopping. The order of events is:

(i) buying the ginger;
(ii) remembering.

We could rephrase the sentence as follows:

I remember now that I bought the ginger.

Now look at this example:

I **remembered to buy** the ginger.

In this example, it is the act of remembering that comes first. While I was out shopping, I remembered that I wanted some ginger and then I bought it. The order is:

(i) remembering;
(ii) buying the ginger.

Now look at these examples:

Lord Ballantrae **remembered to bow** when he met Queen Victoria.
Lord Ballantrae **remembered bowing** when he met Queen Victoria.

In the first example, the scene is in 1897. Lord Ballantrae is a small child and he meets Queen Victoria. He remembers that he must bow to her.

In the second example, the scene is 1956. Lord Ballantrae is recalling the time when he met Queen Victoria in 1897.

The **infinitive** form is used in the same way with **forget**. For example:

I **forgot to buy** the ginger.

While I was out shopping, I forgot, so I didn't buy the ginger. The order of the activity is:

(i) I forgot;
(ii) I didn't buy.

With the **gerund** form, however, it is more common to use **remember** with the **negative**.

For example:

    Instead of saying:

        I *forget locking* the door last night.

    we are more likely to say:

        I **don't remember** locking the door last night.

WARNING BOX

> The exception to this is the phrase **I'll never forget**. For example:
> **I'll never forget visiting** Borobodur at sunrise.

2. Regret

Look at these examples:

    (a) He **regrets playing** badly in the last game.

The verb **regret** is usually followed by the **gerund** form. In this example, the reference to **the last game** makes it clear that the event is past.

    (b) He regrets **living** in Berlin.

The context is not clear here. It could mean either of the following:

    (i) that he is no longer in Berlin and regrets the time he spent there;

    (ii) that he is still living there, but doesn't like living there.

In **(i)** the event is **past**, as in the example **(a)**; in **(ii)**, the event is **begun** in the **past** but is still **continuing**.

Regret + gerund can be represented in two ways, in the following diagrams:

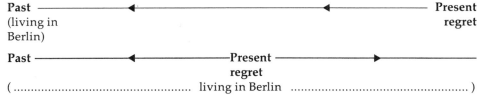

The verbs **say, inform, tell** sometimes occur in the **infinitive** after **regret**. For example:

    She **regrets to say** she can't come.

This refers to a **present** event. The information that the woman can't come to the party is being given at that moment.

When the reference is to a **past** event, the usual form of **regret + gerund** is taken by these verbs. For example:

    He **regrets telling** you that lie about Scott.

This means that he is sorry now that he told you a lie about Scott in the **past**.

It is **unusual** for the **infinitive** form to be used with verbs other than **say, inform** and **tell**.

3. Stop

Many people think that **stop** can be followed by the **gerund** form or the **infinitive**. In fact, only the **gerund** form can be considered as an **object** after **stop**.

Look at this example:

When I **stopped feeling angry**, I realised a lot of the problem was my own fault.
In this case, **feeling angry**, answers the question WHAT? after **stop**. What did I stop?

The **infinitive** form does not answer the question WHAT?

Look at this example:

He **stopped to reconsider** what he'd said.

The **infinitive** form answers the question WHY? Why did he stop? Some people think that the **infinitive** is an abbreviated form where the **object** (the **gerund** form) has been left out. For example:

He **stopped (speaking) to reconsider** what he'd said.

Unit 2.41 Gerund and infinitive phrases 2 – TASKS

Task one

Read the sentences below and then put a tick against the correct explanation of each sentence.

(a) John remembers locking the door.
    Explanation:
      (i) The door is locked now.
      (ii) John is about to lock the door.

(b) The footballer regretted hitting the referee.
    Explanation:
      (i) He has already hit the referee.
      (ii) He is about to hit the referee.

(c) Mary stopped watching television.
    Explanation:
      (i) This is what she stopped doing.
      (ii) This is why she stopped doing something.

(d) The child forgot to hand over the money.
    Explanation:
      (i) The child still has the money.
      (ii) The child handed over the money, but doesn't remember.

(e) The authority regrets to announce the loss of £20,000.
    Explanation:
      (i) The authority is sorry about an announcement it made some time ago.
      (ii) The announcement is being made now.

(f) He stopped to complain about the noise.
    Explanation:
      (i) The noise upset him.
      (ii) He is no longer making a complaint.

(g) Tony remembered to send the photographs.
    Explanation:
      (i) The first action was 'remembering'.
      (ii) The second action was 'remembering'.

(h) Nelson doesn't remember losing the money.
    Explanation:
      (i) The money is not lost.
      (ii) The money is lost.

Task two

Read the following text and then put the verb in brackets into the correct form, gerund or infinitive.

Dear Mary,

I regret *(say)* that I haven't been able to do many of the things I intended to do while you were away. I forgot *(go)* to the insurance company to renew the insurance until it was too late. I did remember, however, *(send)* the application form for the tickets for the pop concert.

I know you will be pleased when I say that I have stopped *(smoke)*, but now I forget *(buy)* matches to light the fire or I don't remember *(put)* them in the place where I finally find them.

I was sorry to hear that you don't like Mr Lawrence. Though I did warn you! I can't say I regret *(call)* him a devious cheat. Don't forget *(make)* your opinion clear to him before you leave. I suppose I must stop *(attack)* him as I do. It will make him feel important. Meanwhile, you should stop *(help)* him in the ways you do.

All good wishes,

Tom.

Task three

*Using one of the verbs **remember, forget, regret, stop**, write a sentence describing each of the pictures below.*

UNIT 2.42
GERUND and INFINITIVE PHRASES 3

Tate & Lyle is trying to change its image.
If you want to have more money, try reading *The Chronicle*.
London Transport doesn't allow smoking on the underground.
The company doesn't allow you to smoke in the workroom.

1. Try

Look at this example:

Tate & Lyle is **trying to change** its image.

In this case, we are talking about what Tate & Lyle is **attempting** to do. We don't know how the company will do it or how successful it will be.

When the verb **try** is in the past we would think the attempt had been unsuccessful. For example:

Tate & Lyle **tried to change** its image.

Here, the company tried but failed.

Now look at this example with the **gerund** *form:*

If you want to have more money, **try reading** *The Chronicle*.

In this example, the overall attempt is **to have more money**. **Reading** *The Chronicle* is one of many ways of trying. It is an experiment. There are several ways to have more money. This can be seen in the following chart:

Attempt	Methods
You want to have more money, try	reading *The Chronicle*. getting a better job. robbing a bank. marrying someone rich.

2. Permission

With verbs of **permission, forbidding** or **advising**, it is the **form** that affects the use of the **gerund** or **infinitive**, rather than the **meaning**. Compare these two examples:

London Transport **doesn't allow smoking** on the underground.

The company **doesn't allow** you **to smoke** in the workroom.

The first statement is a **general** one, so the **gerund** form is used. When the statement is **personalised**, however, even with the impersonal **you**, the **infinitive** is used. This rule applies to the following verbs:

permit, forbid, allow, advise.

Continued

WARNING BOX

> When these verbs are used in the passive, they are always followed by the **infinitive**.
> For example:
>> You are **advised to take** a packed lunch.
>> It is **forbidden to smoke** in here.
>> You are **allowed to bathe** here.
>> We are **permitted to drive** through here.

3. Like, would like

With **like**, the reference is **general** and the event is one that is **repeated**. The **gerund** is the most common form used after **like**; but now the **infinitive** form is often used and is acceptable. For example:

> Sally **likes going** to meetings.
> Sally **likes to go** to meetings.

With **like + the modal would (would like)** the reference is to a **specific** event. Here the **infinitive** form must be used. For example:

> I'd **like to buy** you a present.

Although the time isn't specified, the speaker is considering buying the present on only **one** occasion.

Sometimes the **infinitive** is in its **Past** form. This is used to express **regret** for an event which didn't take place. For example:

> George **would like to have seen** Jim last week.

But he didn't see him; and now it is no longer possible.

Unit 2.42 Gerund and infinitive phrases 3 – TASKS

Task one

Make up sentences from the situations given below, using the verb in brackets.

(a) Andy wants to get a job in Spain. What can he do – teach English; open a restaurant; sell luxury homes? *(Try)*

(b) Jane doesn't like her children to play loud music at night, so she has made a rule about it. *(Forbid)*

(c) Darek has never been on a plane before and is very excited by the idea. So how does he want to travel to Britain? *(Like)*

(d) Eric Newby has made his living as a travel writer. How does he feel about travelling, do you think? *(Like)*

(e) They didn't appoint Jill to the post of Senior Editor. She is very sorry about it. *(Like)*

(f) Brian told his daughter that she could go to the party. What did he do? *(Allow)*

(g) Paul enjoys a challenge and he likes climbing. He has never climbed Mont Blanc. Now he is planning his holiday. What will he want to do? *(Try)*

Task two

Read the following text and then put the verbs in brackets into the correct form, gerund or infinitive.

If you are going to invest your money, you should try *(consult)* a financial adviser first. There are now new regulations which don't allow advisers *(give)* you any mistaken information – even if it is a genuine mistake. The advisers have to accept full responsibility. The law forbids you *(claim)* ignorance of any facts.

Some people don't like *(invest)* money. They consider it immoral. It's like gambling; and not many of them would like *(gamble)*, even if they were sure of winning. They say that if you've got some extra money, there are other things you can do. For example, you could try *(give)* it to a charity.

Obviously, if you are trying *(make)* more money, you would like *(invest)* it. But if you want to help people in need, then you should give to a charity. A new law allows you *(deduct)* the amount from your tax, if you give to charity.

Task three

Imagine your friends are entering an important race.

(a) *Make a list of the things they should try to do to be successful.*

(b) *Make a list of what they are allowed to do and what they are forbidden to do.*

UNIT 2.43
REPORTING 1: statements

He thought he would ask Richard Leakey to join him.
Members mainly agreed that people work best in comfortable clothes.
Police said they knew of no specific threat to Ms Bhutto.

Indirect reports are usually reports of what someone has **said** or someone has **thought**. The verbs **say** or **think** are very neutral ways of introducing **indirect statements**. There are many other verbs which are used, but these often reflect the reporter's attitude to or interpretation of what the person was saying or thinking (see below).

Look at these examples:
I'll ask Richard Leakey to join me.
Report: He **thought** he would ask Richard Leakey to join him.
We know of no specific threat to Ms Bhutto.
Report: Police **said** they knew of no specific threat to Ms Bhutto.

Note the following changes that have taken place:

I→**he**	will→**would**	me→**him**
we→**they**	know→**knew**	

And there are other changes that can take place when a **time adverbial** is included.

I saw him **yesterday**.
Report: He said he had seen him **the day before**.
We'll come **tomorrow**.
Report: She said they would come **the next day**.

The rules that many people are taught concern the change of **pronoun**, the change of **verb tense** or the change of **time adverbial**, are as follows:

Unless the reporters are talking about themselves or addressing the person they are reporting, the first and second person become third person:

I you }	→	he/she	me you }	→	him/her
we you }	→	they	us you }	→	them

When the reporting verb (**say, think**, etc.) is in the **Past**, there can be a shift to a form that refers to an earlier time. For example:
Present→Past
Past→Past Perfect, etc.
will go→**would go**
is going→**was going**
go→**went**

has gone→**had gone**
went→**had gone**
would go→**would have gone**

When a time is specified (**yesterday, today, tomorrow**) it is replaced by a less specific term. For example:

yesterday→**the day before, the previous day**
today→**that day**
tomorrow→**the day after, the following day.**

But the above rules do not always apply.

1. Verb forms

Look at these examples:

Our policy **is** not to hold customers liable . . .
Report: They said their policy **is** not to hold customers liable . . .
People **work** best in comfortable clothes.
Report: Members agreed that people **work** best in comfortable clothes.

In these examples, the verb in the report has remained unchanged. This is because what is reported is a statement that is **still true**. In these cases, these are **general** statements which are **still true**. It is not wrong, however, if we keep to the general rule and change the tense. For example:

Members agreed that people **worked** best in comfortable clothes.

This shows less involvement in the report on the part of the reporter.

2. Time adverbials

Look at this example:

I'll finish the report by Saturday.
Report 1: She said she**'d finish** the report by Saturday.
Report 2: She said she**'ll finish** the report by Saturday.

Both are acceptable if the report is being made **before** the Saturday in question. The effect of keeping the original tense form in Report 2 is to make the report more immediate.

If the report is made **after** the Saturday in question, then we must make the changes both with the **verb** and the **time phrase**.

For a **specific time** (when the Saturday concerned is only recently past or can be identified) we would say, for example:

She said she**'d finish** the report by **last Saturday/the Saturday before last**.

For a **general time** (when the Saturday concerned is in the distant past or not easily identifiable) we would say the following:

She said she**'d finish** the report by **the following Saturday/the Saturday**.

Other verbs for **reporting** are:
agree, report, suggest, announce, answer, reply, etc.

Unit 2.43 Reporting 1 – TASKS

Task one

Rewrite the following statements as reported speech.

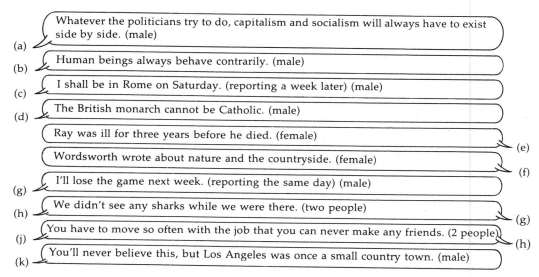

(a) Whatever the politicians try to do, capitalism and socialism will always have to exist side by side. (male)

(b) Human beings always behave contrarily. (male)

(c) I shall be in Rome on Saturday. (reporting a week later) (male)

(d) The British monarch cannot be Catholic. (male)

(e) Ray was ill for three years before he died. (female)

(f) Wordsworth wrote about nature and the countryside. (female)

(g) I'll lose the game next week. (reporting the same day) (male)

(h) We didn't see any sharks while we were there. (two people)

(j) You have to move so often with the job that you can never make any friends. (2 people)

(k) You'll never believe this, but Los Angeles was once a small country town. (male)

Task two

Rewrite the following paragraph as a dialogue between Agnes and Fred, two people in their 70s. Begin like this:

Agnes: I never go out after dark.

Fred: It's dangerous nowadays.

Agnes said that she never went out after dark; and Fred agreed that it was dangerous these days. But Agnes felt that it could make things very difficult. She complained that she never went to the cinema any more. Fred said that he hadn't been to the cinema for ages; and Agnes replied that she didn't miss it. Fred agreed and said that they didn't make films like they used to. Agnes pointed out that everyone had video now and Fred commented that you could watch films at home. Agnes was sad and said she used to like the cinema. Fred agreed that it had made a nice night out. Agnes said that there were no films worth seeing. Fred agreed and said they only made violent films and not the good adventure stories like those when he was young.

Task three

Record or make notes of a speech given by a local celebrity and write a letter to a friend in Britain reporting what was said.

UNIT 2.44
REPORTING 2: questions, requests

We asked people what they thought about the chemical treatment of fruit and vegetables.
He asked Leakey if he would join him in the interview.
He urged them to play a full part in the policy review.

1. Reporting questions

The most common verb used to report **questions** is **ask**. In most cases, **ask** must be followed by a reference to the person(s) asked. For example:

> We asked **people** . . .
> He asked **Leakey** . . .

Look at these examples:

> What do you think about the chemical treatment of fruit and vegetables?
> *Report:* We **asked people what they thought** about the chemical treatment of fruit and vegetables.
> Leakey, will you join me in the interview?
> *Report:* He **asked Leakey if he would join** him in the interview.

Notice what happens to the original question:

> what do you think→**what they think**→**thought**

The question form is replaced by the normal **positive statement** form (see Unit 1.2). The **verb tense** may be changed, as it is in **reporting** statements (see Unit 2.43).

With **yes/no**-type questions we introduce the report with **if** (or **whether**) followed by a positive statement. For example:

> Will you join me in the interview?→ . . . **if he would join him in the interview**.

Here **if** is not introducing a conditional statement (see Unit 2.35), so the rules regarding the use of **will/would**, etc., do not apply.

2. Reporting requests/commands

In reporting **requests** and **commands**, the **imperative** form is replaced by the **infinitive**.

Look at these examples:

> Play a full part in the policy review!
> *Report:* He urged them **to play** a full part in the policy review.
> Please arrange the meeting for Thursday.
> *Report:* She asked them **to arrange** the meeting for Thursday.
> Don't come without the invitation!
> *Report:* He told them not **to come** without the invitation.

Continued

Notice what happens to the verb in the **request/command**:

    play a full part→**to play** a full part

    arrange the meeting→**to arrange** the meeting

    don't come→not **to come**.

The most common verb used for a **question** or a **request** is **ask**, and for **commands** is **tell**. There are, of course, other verbs which can be used and these will reflect the reporter's interpretation of how the request or command was made. Some of them are listed in the chart below.

Request	Command	
urge	**order** (strong)	
wonder (casually request information)	**demand** (strong)	
beg (strong)	**direct**	
implore (strong)	**instruct**	

WARNING BOX

Words such as **please** are omitted in the **report**, because they are merely conversational and show **attitudes** only, not **meaning**. The verb chosen to introduce the **report** will often express the attitude of the speaker.

Unit 2.44 Reporting 2 – TASKS

Task one

Rewrite the following dialogue as a continuous reported paragraph. Begin like this:

Lee heard a noise and wondered what it was.

Juliet didn't know.

Lee: What was that?
Juliet: I don't know.
Lee: Well, what could it have been?
Juliet: It was probably Concorde.
Lee: Does it always go that fast?
Juliet: Yes.
Lee: Have you ever flown in it?
Juliet: Of course not! It's too expensive!
Lee: Would you like to?
Juliet: Not really. I'm not terribly interested. Would you?
Lee: Yes. I reckon it would be an exciting experience.
Juliet: Oh well! Then you'll take me with you when you go, won't you?

Task two

Read through the report below and then rewrite it as a dialogue. Begin like this:

Dr. Robertson: I don't want to continue with my research into the effects of rain on butterflies' wings. It's useless.
Colleague: Why do you feel like that?

Dr Robertson didn't want to continue with her research into the effects of rain on butterflies' wings. She felt it was useless to go on. Her colleague asked her why she felt like that. She replied by asking him why he was interested. She then asked him if his research on the size of worms' eggs had uncovered anything of interest and value to mankind. He felt that it had. She wondered how it was valuable. He thought it could stop some illnesses. Suddenly she became very firm and demanded to know why he thought that. He couldn't answer. He wanted to know what she thought about research generally. She replied that her decision to abandon her research was her answer.

Task three

Watch an interview on television or listen to one on the radio and report what the interviewer asked.

Section 3: Determiners

UNIT 3.1
DETERMINER GROUPS

Section 3 introduces a term, **determiners**, which you may not be familiar with but which is useful to help you understand the role of such words as **the, some, many, all,** etc. **Determiners** are words which come before **nouns** and are used to identify them and give the range of reference of the nouns. For example, **determiners** can make a noun **specific** (**the** child) or **general** (**a** child), indicate **quantity** (**many** children) or **possession** (**my** children), etc.

Determiners always come **before** nouns and, according to their position before a noun, they are classified into three groups: **predeterminers, central determiners** and **postdeterminers**. These groups are examined in detail in Units 3.2–3.11. For reference, below is a chart of the three groups of **determiners** with some examples in each category:

Predeterminers	Central determiners	Postdeterminers
all, both, half, etc. **once, twice, double,** etc.	**Articles:** a, an, the **Demonstratives:** this, these, that, those **Possessives:** my, her, your, etc. **Quantifiers:** some, any, no, every, each, much, either, neither, enough **Wh- determiners:** what, which, whose, whatever, whosever, whichever,	**Cardinal numbers:** one, two, three, etc. **Ordinal numbers:** first, second, etc. **General ordinals:** next, last, further, other, etc. **Quantifiers:** more, many, less, few, little,

There are two things to understand about these lists:

1. **Determiners** always come **before** the noun.
2. If we use more than one **determiner** before a noun, then we must put them in this order:
   (a) **predeterminer**
   (b) **central determiner**
   (c) **postdeterminer.**

Look at these examples:
> **All the** contestants will receive prizes.
> **The first** prize will be a gold medal.
> He trains **once a** day.

WARNING BOX

> It is important to remember that in English every **singular countable noun** must have a **determiner** unless it is in a special idiomatic phrase (see Units 3.3, 3.4 and Appendix 1).

UNIT 3.2
CENTRAL DETERMINERS
1: the use of articles

I'll have two coffees please.
I like Parmesan cheese.

1. Countable and uncountable nouns

Before we look at **articles** in more detail, the first idea that needs to be understood is the concept of **countable** and **uncountable** nouns (sometimes referred to as **mass** and **unit** nouns or **count** and **non-count** nouns).

Countable nouns are those nouns that can be used in the **singular** form to refer to **one** and in the **plural** form to refer to **more than one**. For example:
one book/ten books

Countable nouns always have both a **singular** and a **plural** form.

Uncountable nouns are nouns that refer to things that **cannot** be counted. They are usually **substances** such as gases or liquids, **solids** such as sugar or sand composed of such small units that we would not want to count them even if we could, or **solid masses** such as butter or cheese which form a unit. Or they may be **abstract** nouns that name **qualities** or **concepts** such as beauty or truth. For example:
sugar, butter, water, gold, oxygen.

Uncountable nouns can only be **singular**; they have no plural form when they are used with their common meaning.

Problem words

There are a number of nouns that are considered to be **uncountable** nouns in English which are countable in many other languages and this can cause confusion. For example:

advice	anger	behaviour	clothing	conduct
courage	education	equipment	furniture	homework
information	machinery	news	parking	photography
poetry	progress	publicity	research	safety
scenery	shopping	sunshine	traffic	transportation
violence	weather			

Some nouns can be either **countable** or **uncountable**, depending on what particular meaning they have. Examples of these are:
cheese, wine, tobacco.
Almost all of this type of **uncountable** noun can be used as **countable** nouns when they refer to **kinds** or **types**. For example:

Uncountable	Countable
I like Parmesan **cheese**.	Italian **cheeses** are used in pizzas.
She prefers white **wine**.	White **wines** tend to be more expensive than red ones.
Tobacco is grown in many countries.	Virginia **tobaccos** are milder than some Turkish ones.

159

Now look at these nouns:
difficulty, experience, failure.

Abstract nouns like these are usually **uncountable** but they can be used as **countable** nouns when they refer to an **instance** or **example**. For example:

Uncountable	Countable
You won't have much **difficulty** with this.	He experienced **one difficulty** after another.
Experience is the best teacher.	She told of their **experiences** in the Amazon expedition.
If you work hard you needn't fear **failure**.	He felt he was **a** complete **failure**.

Other nouns can be used as **countable** when they refer to a **unit** or **portion**. For example: **coffee, tea, chocolate.**

Uncountable	Countable
Coffee in the cafeteria is cheap.	I'll have **two coffees** please.
A great deal of **tea** is exported from Sri Lanka.	They ordered **three teas**.
Chocolate is produced from cacao.	Our **chocolates** are made from the finest ingredients.

2. A or an?

The rule about choosing **a** or **an** is that we use **a** before **consonant sounds** and **an** before **vowel sounds**. This means that we use **a** before such words as the following:

boy, cat, dog, fish, garden, year, unit (although **unit** is spelt with an initial vowel, it is pronounced with the same initial **consonant sound** as **year**), **European** (although **European** is spelt with an initial vowel, it is pronounced with an initial **consonant sound**, like **year**).

We use **an** before such words as the following:

egg, X-ray (although X-ray is spelt with an initial consonant, it is pronounced with the same initial **vowel sound** as **egg**), **interruption, outing, hour** (although **hour** is spelt with an initial consonant, it is pronounced with the same initial **vowel sound** as **outing**), **opener, honest** (although **honest** is spelt with an initial consonant, it is pronounced with the same initial **vowel sound** as **offer**), **ultimatum**.

Some words beginning with the letter **h** can be pronounced in two ways. Before these we use **a** or **an** depending on how we pronounce them. For example:
    a hotel *or* **an** hotel.
    a historical novel *or* **an** historical novel.

3. When not to use a determiner

Although we have said that every **singular, countable noun** must have a **determiner**, there are some **idiomatic phrases** that do not have an article or any other determiner when they are used with certain meanings or in certain ways. Examples of this usage include the following:

institutions of life and society, means of transport and communication, times of day and night, seasons, meals, illnesses, fixed phrases with prepositions.

You will find examples of these in Appendix 1 and Appendix 2.

Unit 3.2 Central determiners 1 – TASKS

Task one

Decide whether the following words are countable or uncountable or whether they can be either, depending on the meaning. Then list them under the correct headings. If you think the words can be both countable and uncountable write a short sentence for each that shows how the words can be used in each way.

A clue to help you: There are fifty-two words altogether: thirteen uncountable; eighteen countable; twenty-one both countable and uncountable.

advice	fruit	methane	silk
air	gasket	money	tedium
balance	group	night	thought
bank	history	nodule	ultimatum
brain	hope	office	utensil
canal	independence	option	van
cash	industry	paper	variety
ceramic	joke	peer	water
decision	jump	quality	work
duty	kinetics	quarrel	yawn
electricity	knot	realism	year
engineer	language	right	zeal
flight	logic	scenery	zest

Task two

*Put **a** or **an** in front of the following words:*

honest man	efficient machine	hydroplane	newspaper
unusual event	horror film	example	hovercraft
history book	useful tool	hitchhiker	appointment
hysterical child	wastepaper basket	year	

UNIT 3.3
CENTRAL DETERMINERS
2: a and an

A new technique allows molecular biologists to find one DNA molecule in a million and then multiply the target molecule more than a billion times. A group of physicists has pioneered a new, and potentially more accurate, technique.

1. Non-specific reference

The most common use of **a** or **an** is as the **indefinite article** with **singular countable nouns**. It indicates that the noun is not specified or identified as a particular one. For example:

A group of physicists has pioneered **a** new, and potentially more accurate technique.

We do not know which particular group of physicists this refers to or what particular technique they have used.

Look at these examples:

> IT IS MUCH safer to be underground during a major earthquake than in a building on the surface according to a seismologist from the University of Southern California at Los Angeles.

> PHYSICISTS at Heriot-Watt University have developed a new type of acoustic sensor that is capable of locating the direction of sound sources through 100 metres of granite.

In the first example, any earthquake and any building is referred to, not a specific earthquake or a specific building. In the second example the new type of acoustic sensor is simply one of many types. The scientists are not identified in either sentence.

2. In complement position

A very common use of **a** or **an** is in **noun phrases** in a **complement** position, following such verbs as **to be, to seem, to become**, etc. For example:

The editor of each volume is **a** person of high standing with substantial experience of the discipline.

Each author is **a** specialist in one aspect of the field.

3. Replacing the number one

Another use of **a** or **an** is to represent the **number one**. For example:

a kilo of rice;

a hundred dollars;

a thousand kilometres.

A NEW technique allows molecular biologists to find one DNA molecule in a million and then multiply the target molecule more than a billion times.

4. Replacing per or every

A or **an** can represent the word **per** as in **per cent**; in other words, to say how many units apply to each of the items being measured when we refer to rates, ratios, prices or measurements. For example:

THE POPULATIONS of many of the most poorly nourished nations on Earth are growing at nearly 4 per cent a year.

Here, **a** means **per** or **every**.

5. Class of objects, etc.

Like **the** and the plural form of nouns, **a** and **an** can be used in a general sense to refer to the **whole class** of objects, animals or people named. For example:

A cat is **a** carnivore.

In this use, however, **a** or **an** cannot be used in every way that **the** and the **plural** form can be used. There are certain restrictions on its use. It can be used only in a sentence where it refers to a **representative member** of the class and is therefore a substitute for **any** or **every**.

Like the use of **the** to refer to a **whole class** of objects, animals or people, the use of **a** or **an** in this sense can be difficult for a learner and can often produce ambiguous sentences, even for native speakers. It is much better to use the **plural** form of the noun to refer to a whole class. For example:

Cats are carnivores.

Unit 3.3 Central determiners 2 – TASKS

Task one

*Underline the indefinite articles (**a** or **an**) in the following texts. Then write them, with the nouns they refer to, in the correct column in the chart below. One example has been written for you.*

For decades, physicists have known that the neutron is stable in an atomic nucleus, but unstable on its own. It decays into a proton, an electron and an antineutrino.

In Amsterdam and Brussels it rains, on average, 206 days a year but there are over, 1,550 hours of sunshine a year.

A BRITISH company has come up with a device which destroys used needles and syringes, avoiding the risk of accidental transmission of blood-borne viruses such as HIV. The invention is a box which can contain the fire when its contents are burned.

The box is made of corrugated cardboard, with an insulated lining.

The idea of progress is a fundamental tenet of modern Western thought.

More than a dozen books have been published on the subject in the past two years.

Non specific reference	In complement position	One	Per
an atomic nucleus			

UNIT 3.4
CENTRAL DETERMINERS
3: the

The learner should be given opportunities to use language . . . in a creative way.
We know for certain that 3,500 years ago the cat was already fully domesticated.
I did not care for the camel, nor the camel for me.

The article **the** has two main but distinct functions: it can be used to **generalise** about a noun or to **specify** a particular noun.

1. Generalisation

The can be used to **generalise** about a whole class of objects, animals or, occasionally, people. In this use, the noun is in the **singular**. For example:
   The learner should be given opportunities to use language . . . in a creative way.
   We know for certain that 3,500 years ago **the** cat was already full domesticated.
   Like **the** cat, **the** dog sees its human owners as pseudo-parents.

This use of the definite article is relatively rare and it is more usual to refer to a whole class of objects, animals, or people by using the **plural** form of the noun without an article (without **the**). For example:
   Learners should be given opportunities to use language . . . in a creative way.
   We know for certain that 3,500 years ago **cats** were already full domesticated.
   Like **cats, dogs** see their human owners as pseudo-parents.

Or, with certain restrictions (see Unit 3.3 on **a/an**), we could use the **indefinite article**. For example:
   A learner should be given opportunities to use language . . . in a creative way.
   Like **a** cat, **a** dog sees its human owners as pseudo-parents.

2. Specification

The second use of the article **the** is to **specify** or **identify** a particular noun. It can be used to **specify** a particular object, animal or person or a group of objects, animals or people. This is the most common use and this is why **the** is usually called in traditional grammar books the **definite article**.

If we examine the use of **the** as a **specifying** determiner, we can see that there are three reasons why, in English, we specify a particular noun, as follows:
(a) because the noun has been mentioned before and we want to refer back to that **specific** object, animal or person. For example:
   (i) 'Take my camel, dear,' said my aunt Dot, as she climbed down from this animal on her return from High Mass. . . . I did not care for **the** camel, nor **the** camel for me.
   Here, **the** is used to refer to the camel the second and third time because it is the same camel as the one aunt Dot offered.

(b) because it has been **specified** in the noun group and we are referring to something **specific** or **definite**. In this case, the noun is followed by a phrase beginning with, for example, **of** or **in**.

Look at these examples:

(ii) From **the** heart of London to **the** heart of Paris.

(iii) **The** production of rice in Japan has gradually increased since 1979.

In (ii), it is the **heart of London** and the **heart of Paris** that are being referred to: the phrases **of London** and **of Paris** specify **which** hearts the writer means.

In (iii), of rice specifies what kind of production the writer is referring to. If the writer had written the following:

Rice production in Japan has gradually increased since 1979.

then there would be no need to use a specifying **the** because **production** is **uncountable** and does not need a determiner.

(c) because it is **specified** in the context.

The context can be a **global context** which is known to all people: For example:

(iv) **The** sun rises in **the** east and sets in **the** west.

Here, the writer can assume that everyone who reads the sentence shares his knowledge of which sun he is referring to since there is only one sun in our solar system.

With **superlatives** we need to use **the** because our **global** knowledge tells us that a **superlative** form indicates a **unique**, and therefore, **specific** reference. For example:

(v) Steve Cram decided yesterday that **the** quickest way to recover from losing a race was to win another. . . .

Or it can be a **local context** which is understood by the group of people who are addressed. For example:

(vi) Please clean **the** blackboard.

In a classroom, **the** blackboard, **the** door and **the** windows are all specific objects in the local context and instantly identifiable.

It may seem that there is no need to use any article at all when you are referring to something which is specified in the **local** or **global context**. This is certainly true if the nouns are in the plural. For example:

(vii) **Stars** shine at night.

But in English, every **singular countable** noun must have a determiner – unless it is in one of a group of idiomatic phrases (See Appendix 1, Appendix 2). With **singular** nouns, therefore, the choice is not between using and not using a determiner but (if you do not use any other determiner, such as **my** or **her** or **this**, etc.) between whether to use **a** or **the**. So if you are **specifying** you must remember to use **the** and if you are **not specifying** then you should use **a**.

If you are using **plural** nouns, then the choice is between using **no article** if you are making a **general statement** and using **the** when you mean a **specific group**. For example:

(viii) **Stars** shine at night.

(ix) **The** stars are very bright tonight.

In (ix) the speaker is referring to the **specific** stars that can be seen on that particular night.

3. Summary

Nouns or pronouns are made **specific** in three ways, indicated by the use of the article **the**, as shown in the following chart:

Mentioned before	Specified in the noun group	By context	
		Local	Global
the camel (i)	**the** heart of London (ii) **the** heart of Paris (ii) **the** production of rice (iii)	**the** blackboard (vi) **the** door (vi) **the** window (vi) **the** stars (ix)	**the** sun (iv) **the** east (iv) **the** west (iv) **the** quickest way (v)

*(For the use of **the** with such nouns as personal names, geographical names, public institutions, newspapers, etc., see Appendix 2.)*

Unit 3.4 Central determiners 3 – TASKS

Task one

Fill in the blanks in the following text with **the, a** *or* **an,** *or put Ø if there should be no article.*

(a) ...... National Trust is to spend £12.5m over ...... next four years on ......
(b) conservation and restoration in ...... Lake District, ... national park.
(c) Launching ...... public appeal for £2m recently, ... Trust said that
(d) growing pressures on ...... area posed ...... severe financial problems.
(e) With ...... area of only just over 880 square miles ...... Lake District
(f) attracted ...... 12 million visitors ...... year with inevitable pressures
(g) on ...... parking facilities. ...... woods and hedgerows, ... habitats for
(h) many of ...... rare animals and flora of ...... Lakes, were being lost.
(j) ...... recent report by ...... Nature Conservancy Council revealed that
(k) nearly ...... half of ...... natural broad-leaved woodlands recorded in ......
(l) 1940s have now been lost.
(m) Meanwhile, ... enormous task facing ...... Lake District Planning Board
(n) in looking after ...... area's public rights of way has been outlined by
(p) ...... John Capstick, ... board's head of ...... park management. ...... major
(q) survey has shown that more than ...... £1m would need to be spent on ......
(r) outstanding projects.

Task two

Read the following passages and underline all the examples of **the.** *Then write these examples in the chart opposite. The first one has been written for you.*

Various people have managed to sell *the* Eiffel Tower over the years, but nobody has managed to steal the thing itself. In Uruguay the police are on the trail of the first burglar-engineers who sound capable of going for the big one. They unbolted the 160ft-long iron bridge over the river Santa Lucia Chico in the town of Florida, and removed it overnight. No one is quite sure how, or what they have done with it.

The Smiths are arriving on Sunday.

The world possesses nearly two billion hectares of tropical forest.

Since the turn of the century, over half of the world's tropical rain forests have been lost and as the destruction continues, it brings in its train an increase in floods, droughts and barren land prone to desertification. .... The irony of rain forest clearance is that it is all for nothing. Tropical jungle grows on the poorest land in the world.

Mentioned before	Specified in the noun group	By context	
		Local	Global
			the Eiffel Tower

Task three

*The following passage was copied from a newspaper by a careless student who left out **the** because he thought it wasn't important. Read the passage and decide where he should have put in **the**. Then rewrite the passage correctly. You should add **the** in eight places.*

Jones out of Rome marathon

Steve Jones, world's second-fastest marathon runner, withdrew from British team yesterday because of torn ligaments suffered when he ran in UK 10,000 metres championship seeking selection for a second event at world championships.

Jones had been selected for marathon in Rome after finishing second in Boston marathon but chose to run track race in hope that he might win a second place.

UNIT 3.5
CENTRAL DETERMINERS
4: this, these, that, those

You could be in Barbados this summer.
These conditions are necessary to qualify
for a personal subscription to the journal.
That brand of washing powder is widely
advertised.
Those days are gone.

The demonstratives, **this, these, that** and **those**, are used to indicate either **position** (near or distant) or **place in time** (now or then).

This and **that** are **singular determiners** and can be used with **singular countable** nouns or with **uncountable** nouns. For example:

> **this** booklet/**this** milk.
> **that** section/**that** brand.

These and **those** are **plural determiners** and can be used only with **plural, countable** nouns, not with uncountable nouns. For example:

> **these** conditions/**these** days.
> **those** days/**those** moments.

This and **these** refer to things or people which are **near** in space, position or time.

Look at these examples:

Place	Time
Fill in the application form in **this** booklet and send it to Barclayshare Limited. In **this** section a process-product experiment is described. **This** milk is pasteurised. **These** conditions are necessary to qualify for a personal subscription to the journal.	You could be in Barbados **this** summer. A new drama series starts **this** week on ITV. We get instant news coverage of disasters **these** days.

That and **those** refer to things or people that are distant either in space or position or in time.

Look at these examples:

Place	Time
That brand of washing powder is widely advertised. Pass me **that** hammer.	**Those** days are gone. It was one of **those** moments that make television history.

The choice of **this/these** or **that/those** depends on the speaker's or writer's perception of distance in **space** or **time** from the named object or person. It is quite common for people to relate an experience, informally. For example:

I met **this** engineer at a party, who was . . .

The effect of using **this** is to make the story more immediate and to bring the listener into the action by involving him/her in it.

On the other hand, **that/those** can be used to **create a distance** between the speaker and the subject or to indicate **disapproval**. For example:

That child is impossible.
Those people have terribly noisy parties which go on all night.

Unit 3.5 Central determiners 4 – TASKS

Task one

(a) *Read the following texts and underline the demonstratives.*

(b) *Then write them in the correct columns in the table below. An example has been written for you.*

   (i) This action kit provides simple and clear instructions on how to buy and sell shares.

  (ii) This series is designed to improve the reading performance of students and professionals.

 (iii) These changes come about as new movements grow and others decline.

 (iv) One reason why efforts to transfer technology to Third World countries have often been inept and destructive is an assumption that these countries have no significant technological traditions of their own.

  (v) In that case historical studies served as examples to illustrate a sociological point.

 (vi) During the nineteenth century those principles provided the basis of their historical studies.

Sentence	Time reference	Space reference
Example: (i)		**this action kit**
(ii)		
(iii)		
(iv)		
(v)		
(vi)		

Task two

Draw two plans of an empty room and label them (a) *and* (b).

Imagine you are sitting in the room and mark the spot with an X on plan (a).

Next, imagine you just moved into the house and during the move you slipped and twisted your ankle so you are unable to move around. Two friends have volunteered to help you.

First, draw on plan (a) *where you want the pieces of furniture to go and then tell your friends, John and Andrew, where you want the furniture and other things to be placed in the room.*

Of course, it would be easier just to show them your plan, but the three of you are learning English and you all want to practise using demonstratives, so everything must be done orally.

Decide what you would tell them to do to get the room to end up looking the way you want it.

If you are working with a partner, give him/her your blank plan (b) *and ask him/her to draw your furniture and other things on it in the positions you describe.*

You and your partner should not look at each other's plans until you have finished, when you should check that they are the same.

UNIT 3.6
CENTRAL DETERMINERS
5: possessives: my, your, her, his, its, one's, our, their

Glasgow's International Festival of the Arts is now in its sixth year.
At the age of 16 Carson McCullers wrote her first novel.
Andrew Cruickshank made his debut at the Savoy Theatre in London in 1930 in a production of *Othello*.

Possessive determiners are used to indicate a **relationship** between the **noun** which follows and the subject or person addressed.

Look at these examples:

At the age of 16, Carson McCullers wrote **her** first novel.
Andrew Cruickshank made **his** debut at the Savoy Theatre in London in 1930 in a production of *Othello*.

In the sentences above, we know that it is Carson McCullers' first novel and Andrew Cruickshank's debut that are referred to.

Glasgow's International Festival of the Arts is now in **its** sixth year.

Here, we know that it is the sixth year of the International Festival.

If there are old people living in **your** neighbourhood, try to visit them regularly.

Here, the advice is addressed to the reader and so we know that the neighbourhood referred to is the reader's neighbourhood.

Our company can give you the benefit of **its** many years of experience in building.

In this text, the advertiser is again addressing a reader but referring to the company and the years of experience of the people who work for that company.

Scientists have succeeded in isolating the virus. **Their** success is most welcome.

In this example, **Their** refers to the scientists.

The impersonal **one's** is used in **formal** English. It is much less commonly used today than it used to be.

Look at this example:

Fortunately, in New York, in the upper region, it is impossible to lose **one's** way.
This sentence comes from a novel written by Henry James in 1870. Today, we would be more likely to reword the sentence as follows:

Fortunately, in New York, in the upper region, it is impossible to lose **your** way.

You may have learnt that such words as **each, every, any,** etc. are **singular** determiners and that they must be followed by a **singular possessive** determiner. So the correct form of the **possessive** in older grammars would be **his** in the following sentence:

Everyone who applies will receive . . . own copy of the instruction booklet

However, **his** is considered by many people to be offensive since it has a gender bias. There is a general tendency in English today to avoid sexist language. Two ways of avoiding it are either to use both the feminine and the masculine (**her or his,** or **his/her**) or to use the plural (**their**). In **informal** speech and writing, the second alternative, the use of **their,** is the most usual way to deal with the problem. In **formal** writing, the first alternative is more common. Probably the best way to avoid the problem altogether is to put the subject into the plural. For example:

All applicants will receive **their** own copy of the instruction booklet.

Or you can use a neutral **a**. For example:

Everyone who applies will receive **a** copy of the instruction booklet.

WARNING BOX

Note that the possessive **its** has no apostrophe. **It's** with an apostrophe is a contraction that stands for **It is**. The only possessive determiner to have an apostrophe is **one's**.

Unit 3.6 Central determiners 5 – TASKS

Task one

Read the following texts and fill in the missing words with the most appropriate possessive determiners.

(a) Nowadays many wives continue to work throughout much of . . . . . . marriage and contribute substantially to . . . . . . family finances.

(b) Being a Member of Parliament helps to keep you in touch with . . . . . . constituents because you hear from . . . . . . own people about . . . . . . real problems.

(c) Each household spends about fifteen per cent of . . . . . . weekly income on travel.

(d) Many of the one-way traffic schemes in . . . . . . big cities were installed in the late 1950s and 1960s.

(e) When you invest in a Unit Trust, ... money buys units in the fund of . . . . . . choice. Should you wish to sell . . . . . . units, at . . . . . . request by phone or post on any business day, we will accept . . . . . . instruction to buy back units at the bid price.

(f) It is said there is no substitute for experience. And . . . . . . experience goes back over 180 years.

Task two

(a) *The editors of the career guide that produced the following text have decided to remove the sexual bias by changing the references to **he** and **his**. How would you rewrite it to make it non-sexist?*

The modern professional traffic engineer will need to continue to develop his skills to provide the sound, unprejudiced advice that decision-makers should have. The pattern of work can vary considerably and he will have to attend meetings with clients and make site visits and surveys. He will need to be computer-literate and be able to write clear and concise reports.

(b) *Rewrite the following text to remove the sexual bias:*

An important skill for a teacher is classroom management. She must be able to motivate the learner to achieve his potential and to fulfil his aims. She must exercise patience and adopt a positive attitude towards her learners. This means encouraging the slow learner when he has trouble grasping certain points as well as providing interesting and motivating activities for the fast learner. If the learner who is quick to absorb new materials is not given challenging work, he will rapidly lose interest in the whole process of learning and he will stop paying attention in class. He may even drop out of the course altogether.

Continued

Task three

Study the following advertisements for product and services and note the use of the possessives.

STUDENT BANKING: THE DETAILS

At Barclays we think it's important to help students in the long term, not just the first term.

That's why our student banking package offers more than a useful bonus to tempt you into our branches.

It provides a full range of services that should help to keep your finances in order from the first day of term, right through to graduation day and beyond.

Now write your own advertisement for a product or service that is available in your country (for example: shampoo, herbal remedies, insurance, a restaurant, etc.)

UNIT 3.7

CENTRAL DETERMINERS
6: quantifiers: some, any, no, every, each, much, either, neither, enough

I haven't any idea what you're talking about.
No serious student of English should be without a good grammar book.
I'm going to talk to each student before the exam.
Every essay paper will be double marked.

Quantifiers tell us **how many** or **how much** is being referred to. **Each** and **every** are **singular** and can be used only with **singular countable** nouns. For example:

I'm going to talk to **each** student before the exam.

Every essay paper will be double marked.

Much can be used only with **uncountable** nouns. For example:

There isn't **much** milk left.

In informal, spoken English, **much** is usually used only in **negative** sentences or in questions. For **positive** statements, we usually use **a lot of**.

The remaining quantifiers can be used with either **countable** or **uncountable** nouns and in both the **singular** and the **plural**.

Look at these examples:

Some work on the relationship between science and technology has been based on the assumption that influence always proceeds from science to technology.

I haven't **any** idea what you're talking about.

Some scientists have argued against the theory.

No serious student of English should be without a good grammar book.

You can have **either** cheese or strawberries for dessert.

Neither Philip nor his twin brother was interested in joining the family business.

There isn't **enough** time to go into that subject on this programme.

These **quantifiers** are **central determiners**; that means that they follow **predeterminers** but come before **postdeterminers.** For example:

Once **every** two weeks we have a meeting to decide on the timetable for the rest of the month.

Some or any?

You may have been taught that **some** is used for positive sentences and **any** is used for negative sentences or for questions. This may be a useful rule for beginners but when you get to an intermediate stage you need to re-examine the rule and learn a more accurate one because it doesn't account for a number of uses. For example:

This is an elegant restaurant where good food, reasonable prices and pleasant service will please **any** lover of Italian food.

There are **any** number of good restaurants in Montreal where you can find authentic French food.

He doesn't like **some** modern pop groups.

Would you like **some** coffee?

Instead of calling these examples exceptions, it is better to amend the rule itself to say that **some** is used when we refer to **limited** quantities and **any** is used when we refer to **unlimited** quantities.

Look at these examples:

> **any** lover of Italian food
> **any** number of good restaurants

Each of the above examples refers to an **unlimited** number.

> **some** modern pop groups
> **some** coffee

These two examples refer to a **limited** number or amount. It might be considered rude to suggest to someone you are offering coffee to that he or she might want an unlimited amount. On the other hand, if you wanted to suggest unlimited choice, you might say, Would you like **any**thing else to drink?

Unit 3.7 Central determiners 6 – TASKS

Task one

The following are two lists of goods and services. The first contains some of the things that were available in Britain in 1957 but no longer exist. The second list shows some of the things that did not exist in Britain in 1957 but that have been introduced since. Read the lists, then fill in the sentences below with suitable quantifiers.

1957

Vauxhall Cresta

Strand cigarettes

BBC Home Service

halfpenny coins

1987

credit cards

colour television

Open University

pound coins

self-service petrol stations

motorways

Concorde

windsurfing

digital watches

(a) In 1957 there were . . . . . . motorways and . . . . . . self-service petrol stations but . . . . . . people owned Vauxhall Crestas.

(b) In 1957 . . . . . . people had television sets but there was . . . . . . colour television.

(c) In 1987 you could pay for the things you bought with . . . . . . credit cards or cash; in 1957 people had . . . . . . credit cards nor pound coins.

Now write some more true statements about the differences between 1957 and 1987.

Task two

Make a list of the things you can see in the room you are in or in a cupboard in your kitchen. Then work with a partner to ask and answer questions about the things on your lists. There are nine quantifiers in this unit so try to use each one at least once in a question or an answer.

Remember that you are using these words as determiners, not pronouns, so each one must be followed by a noun. An example has been written for you.

Is there any sugar in the cupboard?

Yes, there's some sugar but there isn't enough milk to have a cup of tea.

UNIT 3.8
CENTRAL DETERMINERS
7: wh-determiners: what, which, whose, whatever, whosever, whichever

What courses are you taking this year?
Which poster did you buy?
Whose newspaper is this?
You can use whatever paper you want in this photocopier.
He buys whichever soap powder is on special offer.

What is the **indefinite wh-determiner** which refers to an **unlimited** number. For example:
    What courses are you taking this year?
The speaker did not have any specific number of courses in mind when he asked that question.

Which on the other hand, implies that there is a **limited** number. For example:
    Which poster did you buy?
In this case, the speaker knew that there were only three posters on sale and she was asking her friend which one she had bought.

Although it is generally true that we tend to use **what** for an **unlimited** number and **which** for a **limited** number, you will find that **what** is the more common form of **wh-determiner** and it is often used even when there is a **limited** choice. For example:
    What television programme are you going to watch tonight?

Whose is a **possessive determiner**. For example:
    Whose newspaper is this?
The speaker here is asking who the newspaper belongs to.

If we add **-ever** to these determiners we are referring to **anything** or **anyone** and it usually does not matter which. For example:

    You can use **whatever** paper you want in this photocopier.
    Whosever theory it is, I don't agree with it.
    He buys **whichever** soap powder is on special offer.

Again, the use of **whichever** suggests that there is a **limited choice**, in this case, of soap powders, but there is no real limit of types of paper that can be used in the photocopier.

Note that all of these determiners can also be used as **pronouns**. For example:

    I'm taking Economics, French and German. **What** are you taking this year?
    I bought Georgia O'Keeffe's poster. **Which** did you buy?
    I haven't seen today's newspaper yet. **Whose** is this?
    Can I use this paper? – You can use **whatever** you want in this photocopier.
    That's Selinker's theory of interlanguage. – **Whosever** it is, I don't agree with it.
    What soap powder does he usually buy? – He buys **whichever** is on special offer.

Unit 3.8 Central determiners 7 – TASKS

Task one

*Use **what, which** or **whose**, to replace the missing words in the following sentences:*

(a) Do you know . . . . . . keys these are?
(b) . . . . . . salary does she earn?
(c) . . . . . . microwave did you decide to buy?
(d) . . . . . . river is longer, the Nile or the Amazon?
(e) . . . . . . section of the newspaper do you read first?
(f) . . . . . . currency do they have in Finland?
(g) I can't decide . . . . . . book to read first.
(h) . . . . . . car is parked in my space?

Task two

Write down some facts about yourself and your family and friends. For example:

the time you usually get up in the morning; your favourite television programme; the type of coffee you prefer; etc.

Then, using the determiners in this unit, ask as many people as you can questions to find out how many people or their friends and relatives like the same things as you like or do the same things as you do. Some examples have been written for you.

What time do you get up in the morning?

What programme do you always try to watch?

Which brand of coffee do you buy?

UNIT 3.9
PREDETERMINERS:
all, both, half;
MULTIPLIERS: once, twice

An independent financial adviser will make sure that you are aware of all your options.
Both hypotheses were confirmed by the data.
It takes half an hour to get to the university from here.
The committee meets twice a month.

Predeterminers come before **central determiners** in a sentence. For example:
An independent financial adviser will make sure that you are aware of **all** your options.
Both hypotheses were confirmed by the data.
It takes **half** an hour to get to the university from here.

All can be used with **plural countable** nouns or with **uncountable** nouns. For example:
All students must register on Thursday.
In some countries **all** drinking water should be boiled.

Both is used only with **countable plural** nouns and can refer to only **two**, not more, people or things. For example:
Both applicants for the job were university graduates.

All, both and **half** can be followed by **articles, demonstratives**, or **possessives**. For example:
All the students arrived on time.
Both those shops sell soft drinks.
Half my time is spent looking for things I've misplaced.

All, both and **half** can also be used as **pronouns**.

Multipliers are used with nouns of **number** or **quantity**. For example:
twice the amount
three times the normal cost
double his weight
He ordered a **double** helping of chips with his fish.

Once, twice, three times, double, etc., can be followed by **a, every, each**, and occasionally **per**, to form expressions of **frequency**. For example:
The majority of British families go on holiday **once a** year.
The committee meets **twice each** month.

Task one

Tien and Rohaya, who are studying marketing, have conducted a survey of another group of students' opinions about six soft drinks. The results are set out in the chart below:

N = 20 students **Soft drink**	**(a)**	**(b)**	**(c)**	**(d)**	**(e)**	**(f)**
Popularity			10	10		
Cost						20
Packaging		14		6		
Availability	20					
Nutrition				5	5	
Colour		10	5			5

Soft drinks per week:

    one: 5 students
    two: 5 students
    three: 10 students

Read the following text and then, using the information in the chart, fill in the missing words with the correct predeterminers.

(a) In terms of popularity . . . . . . the students chose (c) and . . . . . . the students chose (d). . . . . . . the respondents thought (f) was the most expensive. More than . . . . . . the students thought (b) was the most attractively presented and less than . . . . . . the students chose (d). . . . . . . the students agreed (a) was the most widely available. There was less agreement on the next two characteristics; . . . . . . (d) and (e) were judged to have the same nutritional value but . . . . . . the students did not think soft drinks have any nutritional value at all. As for colour, ... the respondents chose (b) as the most attractive and (c) and (e) were chosen by the rest.

(b) The last question Tien and Rohaya asked was how often the students drank soft drinks. Five students reported that they drank a soft drink . . . . . . a week; another five said they drank a soft drink . . . . . . a week and . . . . . . the students said they drank soft drinks . . . . a week.

Task two

Make a similar survey among your friends or colleagues and write a report like the one that Tien and Rohaya produced. You can choose any topic to research: cars, films, television programmes, etc.

UNIT 3.10
POSTDETERMINERS 1:
cardinal numbers: one, two;
ordinal numbers: first, second;
general ordinals: next, last, etc.

In 1976 there was one doctor for every 870 citizens in Japan.
The first textbooks written to teach English as a foreign language were produced in the sixteenth century.
The next monthly prize will be awarded on 5 June.

The **cardinal** numbers (**one, two, three**, etc.) are **postdeterminers**. This means that they come after **predeterminers** and **central determiners**. For example:

A flight takes off or lands once every **thirty** seconds from Chicago's O'Hare Airport.
In 1976 there was **one** doctor for every **870** citizens in Japan.

They come before the **noun** and any **adjectives** in the sentence. For example:

We bought those **two** little red boxes in India last year.

The **ordinal** numbers (**first, second, third**, etc.) are also **postdeterminers** and occupy the same position in the sentence as the **cardinal** numbers: after **predeterminers** and **central determiners** but before the **noun** and any **adjectives** modifying the noun. For example:
The **first** textbooks written to teach English as a foreign language were produced in the **sixteenth** century.
In 1976 the **second** most visited country was Spain which had a total of 30 million tourists.
The **next** monthly prize will be awarded on 5 June.
Last year's profits reached £56.6 million.
We are expecting **further** supplies **next** week.

But **ordinals** precede **cardinals** if they are in the same phrase. For example:

The **first two** chapters of the book are an introduction to the whole theory of systems.

The **general ordinals** (**next, last, further, other**, etc.) generally precede any **cardinal** numbers that are in the same phrase. For example:
There is plenty of encouragement to be drawn from the **last** two years' performance of the team.
The **other** two books you might need to buy are very expensive.

Unit 3.10 Postdeterminers 1 – TASKS

Task one

Task one

How many of the following general knowledge questions can you answer?

(a) The first balloon to carry people was made by . . . . . .
(b) The next ascent in a balloon was made by another Frenchman, ...
(c) The first radio telephone service was opened in 1927 between . . . . . . and . . . . . .
(d) Which country won the World Cup three times and kept the Jules Rimet Cup?
(e) What is the second largest country in the world?
(f) Who was the last US President elected in the nineteenth century?
(g) In what year was the first commercial Concorde flight made?

Now working with a partner, ask and answer general knowledge questions using cardinal and ordinal predeterminers. Start with questions suggested by the cartoons below and then continue with other questions.

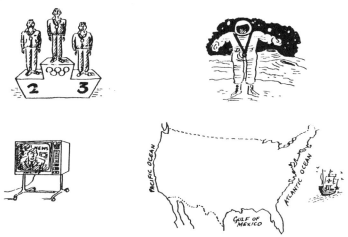

UNIT 3.11
POSTDETERMINERS 2:
quantifiers: more, many, much, less, few, little, several, etc.

Most new cars are built to go fast.
In 1975 Australians bought more toothbrushes than any other nationality.
The Japanese eat less meat than Australians, Americans or Canadians.
There is little risk of malaria in Kuala Lumpur or Penang.

The **quantifiers** (**more, many, much, less, few, little, several**, etc.) are **postdeterminers** because they are placed before **nouns** but after **central determiners**.

Many, few, several, can be used only with **plural countable** nouns. For example:
>There are **few** days in Bahia Felix, Chile, when it doesn't rain; it rains, on average, 325 days a year.
>In **many** parts of the world school examinations are set by an external agency.
>In a recent study of classroom behaviour in foreign language classes, **several** students were observed never to answer or ask questions.

Many and **few** have the following **comparative** and **superlative** forms:
>**many/more/most;**
>**few/fewer/fewest.**

Look at these examples:
>In 1975 Australians bought **more** toothbrushes than any other nationality.
>**Most** new cars are built to go fast.

Much and **little**, on the other hand, are used with **uncountable** nouns. For example:
>The Japanese eat **less** meat than Australians, Americans or Canadians.
>There is **little** risk of malaria in Kuala Lumpur or Penang.
>There isn't **much** time to finish this work.

Much and **little** have the following **comparative** and **superlative** forms:
>**much/more/most;**
>**little/less/least.**

With the **superlatives**, you must use **the** (see Unit 3.4). For example:
>All the students wrote a lot but Jim wrote **the most**.

There is a growing tendency to use **less** with both **countable** and **uncountable** nouns and it is becoming more acceptable. For example:
>There are **less** cars on this road since the motorway was extended.

However, **fewer** would be more correct in this example.

Many and much

In **spoken, informal** English we usually avoid using **many** and **much** in **affirmative** statements. They are more commonly used with **negative** statements or questions. For example:
>He hasn't **many** options.
>Have you got **much** work left to do tonight?

In **informal** English, we tend to use such expressions as **plenty of** or **a lot of** to express **many** in **positive** statements. For example:
>They've got **a lot of** ideas for raising money for charity.
>There's **plenty of** tea left if you'd like some.

Little/a little and few/a few

There is an important difference between **little** and **a little**, and between **few** and **a few**. There is a **negative/positive** contrast between the two. When **a** is used, then the quantity is meant to be a **positive** quantity but without **a** the quantity is **negative**. For example:

> **little** time (not much time)
> **a little** time (some time)
> **few** people (not many people)
> **a few** people (some people)

Few and **little** are often preceded by **very**.

Look at the examples in the chart:

Positive quantity	Negative quantity
I have **a little** time left before I have to go to the meeting. **A few** people went to the lecture. She has only been here for two months and she has already made **a few** good friends.	There's **little** time for this. **Very few** people like going to the theatre on their own. He is a very quiet man who has **few** friends.

Unit 3.11 Postdeterminers 2 – TASKS

Task one

Fill in the missing words in the following sentences with **few, a few, little** *or* **a little**, *according to the meaning of the sentences.*

(a) The difficulty of learning the Chinese script means that . . . . . . Westerners ever become literate in Chinese.

(b) Most British sports fans have . . . . . . interest in ice hockey; they are more interested in field hockey.

(c) There are still . . . . . . tickets left for the concert. Shall I get you one?

(d) I've managed to save . . . . . . money this month so I can buy the books I need for the course.

(e) Relatively . . . . . . English teenagers intend to continue in school after the age of 16.

(f) The article I am reading is interesting but it has . . . . . . new information on the subject of management systems.

Task two

Look at the following chart of Wimbledon tennis champions and, with a partner, ask and answer questions using the quantifiers in this unit. An example has been written for you.

Example:

John McEnroe has won fewer times than Bjorn Borg.

Wimbledon champions

Year	Women	Men
1977	Virginia Wade (GB)	Bjorn Borg (Sweden)
1978	Martina Navratilova (Czechoslovakia)	Bjorn Borg
1979	Martina Navratilova	Bjorn Borg
1980	Evonne Cawley (Australia)	Bjorn Borg
1981	Chris Evert-Lloyd (USA)	John McEnroe (USA)
1982	Martina Navratilova (USA)	Jimmy Connors (USA)
1983	Martina Navratilova	John McEnroe
1984	Martina Navratilova	John McEnroe
1985	Martina Navratilova	Boris Becker (W. Germany)
1986	Martina Navratilova	Boris Becker
1987	Martina Navratilova	Pat Cash (Australia)
1988	Steffi Graf (W. Germany)	Stefan Edberg (Sweden)
1989	Steffi Graf	Boris Becker

Task three

Look at all the written work you have done in your English class and find out what kind of errors you have made. Then write a report saying which are your most frequent errors and which your least frequent ones, comparing the different types of errors you have made and, if possible, giving reasons for the errors. An example has been written for you.

Example:

I have looked at six essays and six grammar tasks. I made more errors in the essays than in the grammar tasks because the latter are easier to do correctly.

SECTION 4: Modification

In Section 4 we look at words and phrases which tell us more about other words or groups of words – adjectives tell us more about nouns (the house/the red house); adverbs tell us more about verbs (he went/he went quickly). Adjectives and adverbs can themselves be modified. Modification helps us identify more clearly the elements contained in the information that is being conveyed.

UNIT 4.1
ADJECTIVES 1: position

A beautiful baby.
A big red balloon.
An Indian restaurant.
The wooden horse.
A rocking chair.

Adjectives describe **objects, people** and **animals** and they always come immediately **before** the **noun** they are describing. For example:

a **red** balloon;
a **beautiful** baby;
a **fast** horse;
a **big, white** house.

They can also be used as a **complement** (see Units 1.4, 1.5). In this case they come immediately **after** the **verb**. For example:

The house is **big**.

It is possible for several **adjectives** to describe the same thing. When this happens, if they come before the word, then they are separated by a **comma**. For example:

the **big, red** house;
the **beautiful, young, sleek** horse.

When the **adjectives** are used as **complements**, the final one is separated from the others by **and**. For example:

The house is **big and red**.
The horse is **beautiful, young and sleek.**

Types of adjectives

Adjectives can be divided into the following five main types:

(a) **Subjective** adjectives, which suggest the opinion of the speaker or writer – other people may disagree. For example:

That's a **beautiful** picture! – I don't think so.
That house is very **expensive**! – Not if you live in London.

(b) Adjectives which describe **characteristics**. For example:
        age (the **old** man);
        size (the **big** house);
        shape (the **round** pond);
        colour (the **yellow** Rolls-Royce).
(c) Adjectives formed from **proper names**. For example:
        the **Indian** restaurant;
        a **French** film;
        a **Chinese** laundry.
(d) Adjectives which tell us what **materials** things are **made of**. For example:
        the **wooden** horse.
    In this case a noun can used as an adjective. For example:
        He likes **cotton** socks.
(e) Adjectives which describe the **purpose** of the noun. For example:
        a **rocking** horse.

If we remember the **order** of these types of adjectives, then we have a possible order to put the adjectives into when more than one is used to describe a noun. There are no strict rules for the order, but the order above (summarised in the chart below) gives a general idea.

	Subjective	Characteristics	Proper names	Materials	Purpose	Noun
a	beautiful,	large, red,	Victorian			chair
a		large, old	Italian	oak		table
an	expensive	old,		iron,	frying	pan
a		dirty, old,	Russian,		army	coat

Adjectives in the **Characteristics** column have **no fixed order**.

The order of **subjective** and **characteristic** adjectives is often changed. For example:
    a **beautiful, large, red**, Victorian chair;
    a **large, red, beautiful** Victorian chair.
In both these examples the order is decided by the **feature** that the speaker or writer is **focusing on**. The adjectives describing this feature will come first.

Unit 4.1 Adjectives 1 – TASKS

Task one

(a) *Rewrite the following sentences, replacing the complements by putting the adjectives before the nouns.*

  (i) The bridge is beautiful and old.
  (ii) The river is dangerous, fast and deep.
  (iii) The day was dull, wet and cold.
  (iv) The prize will be valuable.
  (v) The football match was rough and exciting.

(b) *Rewrite the following sentences using the adjectives as complements.*

  (i) It was a large, grey van.
  (ii) He was a wealthy, young, Italian prince.
  (iii) It was a boring, long film.
  (iv) She was a clever, hard-working girl.
  (v) They were strong, Russian, wooden dolls.

Task two

Put the adjectives below before the nouns in the most suitable order.

(a) car – old, green, sports, British
(b) job – well-paid, important, responsible
(c) computer – beautiful, brown, American, small
(d) holiday – summer, long, hot
(e) train – fast, modern, long, beautiful
(f) boat – fast, sleek, racing
(g) painting – dark, old, sombre, classical
(h) house – haunted, lonely, big, empty
(j) restaurant – Italian, cheerful, cheap, crowded
(k) man – wise, Chinese, ancient, religious

UNIT 4.2
ADJECTIVES 2: comparison

Blackpool was hotter than London.
Lerwick was the sunniest place.

1. Comparatives

When we make **comparisons** between two things, we use the **comparative** form of the adjective. For example:

> On 8 June 1988, it was warm and sunny in Birmingham; but it was **warmer** in London. However, Birmingham was **sunnier** than London.

With adjectives of **one** or **two** syllables, the **comparative** is formed by adding **-er** to the adjective. For example:

> warm/**warmer**;
> cold/**colder**.

When the adjective ends in **-y**, we change the **y** to **i** and then add **-er**. For example:

> sunny/**sunnier**;
> lovely/**lovelier**.

When a **one-syllable** adjective ends with a **single consonant**, we **double** the consonant and then add **-er**. For example:

> sad/**sadder**;
> red/**redder**;
> big/**bigger**;
> hot/**hotter**.

When an adjective ends in **-ng**, we pronounce the **g**, and add **-er**.

> strong/**stronger**;
> long/**longer**.

We use **than** to link the two things we are comparing. For example:

> Blackpool was hotter **than** London.
> Cars are cheaper in Germany **than** they are in England.

Now look at this example:

> There are lots of cheap fares to the United States. It costs only £210 return to go from London to New York. It is **more expensive** if you want to go to Los Angeles.

With longer adjectives, we make the comparative form by putting **more** before the adjective. For example:

> **more** expensive;
> **more** beautiful;
> **more** dangerous.

We also use **more** when we are comparing statistics. For example:

There are **more** divorces among people in Wales than among those who live in the North of England.

When the number is lower, we use **fewer**. For example:

There are **fewer** divorces in the south-east of England than there are in Yorkshire.

WARNING BOX

> With **uncountable** nouns, the correct form to use is **less**. For example:
>
> People in Britain drink **less** tea than they used to.
>
> It has, however, become very common for people to use **less** instead of **fewer** when they are referring to **countable** nouns. For example:
>
> There are **less** divorces in the south-east of England than there are in Yorkshire.

2. Superlatives

To make the superlative form we add **-est** to the short adjectives. For example:

On 8 June 1988, Prestatyn was the **hottest** place in Britain; while Lerwick was the **sunniest** place.

With long adjectives, we put **most** before the adjective. For example:

From London, the **most expensive** places to fly to in America are Los Angeles and San Francisco.

WARNING BOX

> We always put **the** before a **superlative** form.

3. Summary

Positive	Comparative	Superlative
warm	warmer	warmest
cold	colder	coldest
sunny	sunnier	sunniest
pretty	prettier	prettiest
hot	hotter	hottest
big	bigger	biggest
expensive	more expensive	most expensive

Here are some irregular adjectives:

Positive	Comparative	Superlative
good	better	best
bad	worse	worst
little	less	least
many	more	most

Unit 4.2 Adjectives 2 – TASKS

Task one

Using the following chart, complete the sentences below. Then write more, similar comparisons.

WINTER WARMTH

**IF YOU WANT TO GET AWAY THIS WINTER
THEN BOOK NOW. OUR PRICES ARE
DIFFICULT TO BETTER AND INCLUDE
COACH FROM MORECAMBE AND
LANCASTER AREA AND INSURANCE. THE
HOLIDAYS WE HAVE ARRANGED ARE
DETAILED BELOW**

COSTA DEL SOL

6th	November Hotel Don Pablo 28 nights	£479
5th	February Hotel Angela 28 nights	£445
6th	January El Griego Hotel 35 nights	£399
18th	November El Griego Hotel 35 nights	£369
3rd	January El Griego Hotel 42 nights	£460
22nd	January El Griego Hotel 21 nights	£320
27th	November El Griego Hotel 21 nights	£269
2nd	February Hotel Palmasol 21 nights	£375
29th	January Las Palomas Sol 28 nights	£435
2nd	February Las Palomas Sol 28 nights	£410

BENIDORM

3rd	December Hotel Rosamar 28 nights	£440
7th	January Hotel Ruidor 28 nights	£305
10th	December Hotel Ruidor 28 nights	£445
14th	January Hotel Reymar/Riviera 28 nights	£305
31st	January Hotel Rosamar 28 nights	£385
21st	January Tropicana Gardens 21 nights	£355
4th	February Hotel Ruidor 28 nights	£335
7th	February Hotel Reymar/Riviera 28 nights	£340
7th	February Rio Park 21 nights	£260

ALGARVE

22nd	January De Lagos Hotel 28 nights	£375

MALTA

23rd	January Fortuna Hotel 28 nights	£360
9th	January Fortuna Hotel 28 nights	£295

MAJORCA

21st	January Hotel Palma Nova 21 nights	£285
11th	November Hotel Leo 84 nights	£799
6th	February Guadalupe Sol 28 nights	£405
30th	January Santa Lucia 28 nights	£365

*DON'T DELAY SPACE IS LIMITED AND
SELLING FAST*

HIGHGATE TRAVEL

ABTA 96412 23 Highgate, Kendal
TEL: 33603

(a) A holiday at the El Griego hotel costs . . . . . . than at the Hotel Don Pablo.
(b) A holiday at the Hotel Don Pablo is the . . . . . . holiday in the list.
(c) The . . . . . . date you can go is 6 November.
(d) The Hotel Leo is offering the . . . . . . stay.
(e) The Rio Park is . . . . . . than the Tropicana Gardens.

Task two

Complete the following chart from the information given in the text below.

The hottest place in Britain yesterday was Birmingham Airport, which recorded a temperature of 22°C. The lowest recorded temperature was 15°C in Colwyn Bay and Lerwick. Tenby had a higher tempertaure than Colwyn Bay, but it was colder there than it was at Anglesey. However, Anglesey had fewer hours of sunshine than Colwyn Bay, although throughout the day, it was hotter. The sunniest place in Britain was Newquay with 11.2 hours of sunshine. Wick had the most rain. It was warmer there than at Colwyn Bay, which had no rain at all; but it was colder than in Jersey, although it was sunnier than in Jersey.

AROUND BRITAIN

	Sun hrs	Rain in	Max C	F	
Scarboro	7.8	-	19	66	sunny
Bridlington	5.9	-	17	63	bright
Hunstanton	4.0	-	19	66	bright
Cromer	3.7	-	17	63	bright
Lowestoft	1.0	.02	18	64	bright
Clacton	1.8	-	19	66	cloudy
Southend	*	-	20	68	cloudy
Margate	1.6	-	20	68	dull
Folkestone	4.1	-	19	66	cloudy
Hastings	2.7	-	.9	66	cloudy
Eastbourne	3.5	-	19	66	dull
Brighton	2.4	-	18	64	cloudy
Littehmptn	3.7	-	20	68	cloudy
Bognor R	4.8	-	19	66	bright
Southsea	6.1	-	21	70	cloudy
Sandown	5.2	-	19	66	sunny
Bournemth	7.3	-	21	70	sunny
Swanage	6.7	-	20	68	sunny
Exmouth	6.8	-	20	68	bright
Torquay	9.1	-	22	72	sunny
Falmouth	6.2	-	20	68	sunny
Penzance	6.0	-	20	68	bright
Scilly Isles	3.6	-	18	64	sunny
Jersey	3.0	-	19	66	cloudy
Guernsey	5.5	-	19	66	sunny
Newquay	(a)	.02	19	66	sunny
Ilfracombe	*	.02	*	*	sunny
Minehead	7.8	.01	20	68	sunny
B'pool Airpt	5.7	-	17	63	bright
Morecambe	8.5	-	17	63	sunny
Douglas	*	-	17	63	sunny
(b)	4.5	-	22	72	sunny
Leeds	6.0	-	21	70	sunny
Nottingham	2.3	-	21	70	cloudy
(c)	3.3	-	19	66	bright
(d)	4.5	-	15	59	sunny
(e)	5.8	.02	17	63	bright
Aviemore	4.7	-	17	63	cloudy
Kinloss	7.3	-	19	66	sunny
(f)	8.1	.02	15	59	sunny
Stornoway	4.7	.01	16	61	shower
Tiree	7.5	.01	16	61	bright
(g)	5.7	.03	17	63	shower

* Denotes figures not available

Task three

Write a text similar to the one in Task two, using the chart below.

ABROAD

MIDDAY: t=thunder; d=drizzle; fg=fog; s=sun;
sl=sleet; sn=snow; f=fair; c=cloud; r=rain

	C	F			C	F	
Ajaccio	28	82	s	Luxor	38	100	s
Akrotiri	29	84	s	Madrid	27	81	s
Alex'dria	31	88	f	Majorca	30	86	f
Algiers	31	88	s	Malta	30	86	s
Amst'dm	17	63	c	Mexico C	15	59	d
Athens	33	91	s	Miami	29	84	f
Bahrain	35	95	s	Milan	29	84	s
Barcelna	24	75	f	Montreal	24	75	f
Belgrade	25	77	s	Moscow	29	84	f
Berlin	22	72	c	Munich	25	77	s
Bermuda	31	88	s	Naples	30	86	s
Biarritz	19	66	c	N Delhi	33	91	c
Borde'x	22	72	f	N York	26	79	c
Brussels	17	63	c	Nice	26	79	f
Budapst	23	73	c	Paris	26	79	f
B Aires	14	57	s	Peking	32	90	f
Cairo	34	94	s	Perth	14	57	s
Cape Tn	13	55	c	Reykjvik	14	57	f
C'blanca	25	77	s	Rhodes	28	82	s
Chicago	25	77	c	Rio de J	19	66	s
Ch'church	7	45	c	Riyadh	41	106	s
Cologne	22	72	f	Rome	27	81	s
C'phagn	19	66	f	Salzburg	25	77	s
Corfu	32	90	s	S F'risco	21	70	s
Dublin	17	63	f	Santiago	12	54	f
Dubrovnik	30	86	s	S Paulo	20	68	s
Faro	25	77	s	Seoul	24	75	r
Florence	32	90	s	Sing'por	31	88	s
Frankfurt	23	73	s	St'kholm	21	70	f
Funchal	22	72	f	Strasb'rg	27	81	s
Geneva	25	77	s	Tangier	24	75	f
Gibraltar	27	81	s	Tel aviv	30	86	s
Helsinki	24	75	f	Tenerife	26	79	s
Hong K	25	77	r	Tokyo	24	75	c
Innsbrck	26	79	s	Toronto	23	73	c
Istanbul	30	86	s	Tunis	34	93	s
Jeddah	38	100	s	Valencia	29	84	f
Jo'burg	19	66	s	Vanc'ver	23	73	s
L Palmas	24	75	s	Venice	28	82	s
Le Tquet	17	63	c	Vienna	23	73	s
Lisbon	23	73	s	Warsaw	21	70	f
Locarno	27	81	s	Wash'ton	31	88	f
L Angels	24	75	s	Wel'nton	10	50	c
Luxembg	22	72	f	Zurich	26	79	s

Hong Kong imports as many logs as Italy.

The following chart shows which countries import logs of broad-leaved trees. We can see that Japan imports the most.

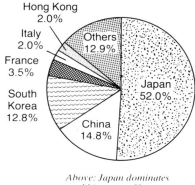

Above: Japan dominates world imports of logs from broadleaved trees

When we compare things that are **equal** we place **as . . . as** around the adjective. For example:
Hong Kong imports **as many** logs **as** Italy.

When we are saying they are **not the same**, we put **not as . . . as** or **not so . . . as** around the adjective. For example:
China imports a lot of logs, but **not so many as** Japan. It imports fewer than Japan.

Unit 4.3 Adjectives 3 – TASKS

Task one

Make **as . . . as** *or* **not so/as . . . as** *comparisons of the people and things in the pictures below to illustrate the following descriptions:*

(a) strong, (b) deep, (c) beautiful, (d) rich.

An example has been written for you.

Example:

The sea is not so deep where Jenny is as where her father is.

The Smiths   The Hamiltons

Task two

Read the following text, then complete the chart below.

In 1987, no writer was as successful as Jeffrey Archer, who sold more than a million copies of his novel *Matter of Honour*. Jeffrey Archer, however, is not considered to be so good a writer as John Le Carré, whose thriller *A Perfect Spy*, sold over 700,000 copies.

Probably none of the writers is as famous as Shirley MacLaine, whose autobiography sold only a little more than 170,000 but she is not so funny as Spike Milligan, the comedian, whose autobiography sold 158,124 copies in Britain. Although it was higher in the list than Noel Barber's book *The Other Side of Paradise*, Harold Robbins' *The Story Teller* did not make so much money. This is because it wasn't as expensive as Barber's book. In fact it was £1 cheaper. Generally, writers sell more books in their home country. This was not the case with Robert Goddard, whose sale of 81,806 copies of *Past Caring* in Britain was not as high as the number sold abroad.

From: TOP HUNDRED CHART OF 1987 PAPERBACK BESTSELLERS

Title	Genre	Author	Price	Home	Export	Total sales
Matter of Honour	(a)	(b) .... (Br)	£3.50	784,784	583,223	(c) ....
Hollywood Husbands	Novel	Jackie Collins (Br)	£3.50	597,654	402,500	1,000,154
(d)	Thriller	(e) .... (Br)	£3.95	511,853	234,472	(f) ....
Bolt	Thriller	Dick Francis (Br)	£2.95	377,894	175,763	553,657
(g)	Novel	Harold Robbins (US)	(h)	195,313	118,162	313,476
Other Side of Paradise	Novel	(j) .... (Br)	£3.95	159,955	122,337	282,292
His Way	Biography	Kitty Kelly (US)	£3.95	131,635	91,009	226,644
Goodbye Soldier	(k)	(l) .... (Br)	£2.95	158,124	17,751	175,875
Past Caring	Novel	(m) .... (Br)	£3.50	81,806	90,342	172,148
Dancing in the Light	(n)	(p) .... (US)	£3.50	49,960	120,228	170,188

Task three

Write a similar report to that in Task two on a topic of interest to you. You must provide the chart or list on which your report is based.

UNIT 4.4
ADJECTIVES 4: -ing, -ed endings

We are not amused.
The actor was not amusing.

Many people confuse adjectives that end in **-ing (interesting)** with their passive counterparts that end in **-ed (interested)**.

Look at these examples:

At the theatre, Queen Victoria said, 'We are not **amused**'.

She did not find the performance funny, because the actor was not **amusing**.

The **-ing** form of the adjective describes the actor or action or object. It describes the **active** effect.

The **-ed** form describes the feelings of the person affected by the action. It describes the **passive** effect.

Look at these examples:
The book is disappoint**ing**. Doris Lessing is usually a very good writer. (*Active.*)
He was disappoint**ed** by Doris Lessing's latest book. (*Passive.*)

Both **-ing** and **-ed** forms can be followed by the **infinitive**. For example:
It was disappoint**ing** for John and Elizabeth **to see** the scheme fail.
They were disappoint**ed to see** the scheme fail.

-ed forms can be followed by **by**. For example:
He was confus**ed by** the speaker.
He was bor**ed by** the lecturer. The lecturer was bor**ing**.
They can also be followed by other prepositions. For example:
He was disappoint**ed with** the book.
The government was surpris**ed at** the strength of the attack.
The following is a chart of some of the adjectives which end with **-ing** and **-ed**, and the prepositions which can follow the **-ed** form:

Adjective	Preposition				
	at	by	in	of	with
amazed	✓	✓			
amused		✓			
annoyed	✓				✓
astonished	✓				
bored		✓			✓
confused		✓			
depressed		✓			
disappointed		✓	✓		
disgusted	✓	✓			✓
embarrassed		✓			
excited		✓			
exhausted		✓			
fascinated		✓			
frightened	✓	✓		✓	
horrified		✓			
interested		✓	✓		
involved			✓		✓
satisfied		✓			✓
shocked	✓	✓			
surprised	✓	✓			
terrified		✓		✓	
tired				✓	
worried		✓			

Unit 4.4 Adjectives 4 – TASKS

Task one
Complete the following pairs of sentences with the appropriate form of the adjective and supply the preposition where necessary. An example has been written for you.

Example:
bore

"I find politics boring," said Margaret.

Margaret is bored with politics.

(a) **frighten**
Pamela thinks thunderstorms are . . . . . .
Pamela is . . . . . . thunderstorms.

(b) **involve**
Charles is very . . . . . . his work.
Charles finds his work very . . . . . .

(c) **fascinate**
'It's . . . . . . to watch the colours change,' said Tessa.
Tessa was . . . . . . the changing colours.

(d) **amuse**
Harold was very . . . . . . the play.
Harold found the play very . . . . . .

(e) **surprise**
Jeffrey was very . . . . . . the result of the trial.
'The result of the trial was very . . . . . .,' said Jeffrey.

(f) **exhaust**
Cathie found her last trip to India . . . . . .
Cathie was . . . . . . her last trip to India.

(g) **worry**
Roy finds Neil's behaviour very . . . . . .
Roy is . . . . . . Neil's behaviour.

(h) **satisfy**
Romy is very . . . . . . the results of the exam.
The results of the exam are very . . . . . .

(j) **excite**
It's . . . . . . for Susan to be going to China.
Susan is . . . . . . going to China.

(k) **depress**
The weather this month has been . . . . . .
Terry is very . . . . . . the weather this month.

Task two

Complete the following text by putting in the correct form of the adjective. Form the adjective from one of the verbs in the following list. You can use both forms of the same adjective.

amuse, bore, confuse, depress, disappoint, embarrass, excite, fascinate, interest, involve, shock, surprise.

Follow That Star is now showing at the Ritz cinema. Anyone who believes that science-fiction is what the cinema is good at and is (a) . . . . . . in space epics will be (b) . . . . . . by this film. It is very (c) . . . . Clearly the director thought it would be (d) . . . . . . for us to see what happens in space flight. When I saw the film, the audience was obviously not (e) . . . . . . in the story. Some people were (f) . . . . . . when the characters were eating standing on their heads; but nobody was (g) . . . . . . by the film. The film is very (h) . . . . I found myself (j) . . . . . . by some of the tricks which were meant to be either (k) . . . . . . or (l) . . . . My advice is to stay away from this (m) . . . . . . film.

Compare the following phrases:

in the corner   on/at the corner

(a) **in** the corner
   on/at the corner
(b) **in** the **beginning** *(time)* **(initially)**;
   in the **end** *(time)* **(finally)**.
(c) **at** the **beginning** of the book;
   at the **end** of the day.

The phrases beginning with **at** are more concerned with **place** – even when they refer to a **time**, where they indicate a **point** or **place** in **time**.

Note the following exception. We say:
   in the morning;
   in the afternoon;
   in the evening;
but **at** night.

in time   on time

(d) He arrived **in** time (before the last moment)
   He arrived **on** time (at the exact time)
(e) Sarah has already left and is **on** her way to London.
   Peter couldn't go on. A tree had fallen **in** his way.

On his/her way can be used metaphorically. For example:
   Peter's very ambitious and works hard. He's **on his way** to the top of his profession.
   Mary applied for the job, but David stood **in her way**. He had more experience.

By gives the idea of **near** or **by means of**. For example:

> *Place:* by the window; by the door (meaning near to).
>
> *Time:* by five o'clock; by next week; by New Year (meaning no later than and possibly before).
>
> *Manner:* by hand (meaning the person gave the letter or present, i.e. it wasn't posted).

WARNING BOX

> *Note the following exception. We say:*
> > **by** car;
> > **by** train;
> > **by** bicycle;
> > **by** plane, etc.,
> *but* **on** foot.

Other prepositions of **place** are as follows:
under, above, over, to, into, onto, towards.

Look at these examples:

> The cat's **under** the table;
> They slept **under** the stars.
> The cups are on the shelf **above** the plates.
> The bridge went **over** the river.
> He's going **to** Jakarta.
> The cat jumped **into** the box.
> The bird flew **onto** the table.
> He was last seen driving **towards** Berlin.

Other prepositions of **time** are as follows:
during, since, for.

Look at these examples:

> He was away in India **during** August.
> He hasn't been seen **since** the end of March.
> He hasn't been seen **for** three months.

There are many idiomatic uses of prepositions, which you will find in the dictionary.

In Appendix 3 you will find some verbs which are followed by prepositions, and in Appendix 5, some adjectives and the prepositions that follow them.

Unit 4.6 Prepositional phrases – TASKS

Task one

Complete the following sentences by putting in the appropriate preposition.

(a) The concert is taking place . . . . . . the park.
(b) Dinner will be served . . . . . . room 12.
(c) Mr Davidson goes to work . . . . . . bike.
(d) Rain is falling heavily . . . . . . the north-west.
(e) This train goes . . . . . . Lancaster and then Glasgow.
(f) It's dangerous to stand . . . . . . trees during a storm.
(g) The frightened horse jumped . . . . . . the fence and ran away.
(h) Her house stood . . . . . . the hill . . . . . . the race-course.
(j) Look up . . . . . . the sky. You can see Concorde.
(k) He's nearly . . . . . . the end of his essay now.

Task two

Complete the following text by putting in the appropriate preposition.

(a) . . . . . . 4 October 1936, 250,000 people fought the Blackshirts (b) . . . . . . Cable Street. The Blackshirts had wanted to march (c) . . . . . . the East End of London and cause trouble with the community there.

(d) . . . . . . the 1980s, many rock musicians have got together to protest against evils such as this. One group of bands is called the Cable Street Beat bands. They work (e) . . . . . . many parts of Britain, but especially (f) . . . . . . those areas where there are likely to be racist attacks. (g) . . . . . . 4 October, the anniversary of the original battle, the group hope to have several bands as members of the group and to stage a concert (h) . . . . . . London (j) . . . . . . the Electric Ballroom Centre. This will be followed by several concerts, and (k) . . . . . . the end of the series, they hope more than a million people will have heard their message. (l) . . . . . . stage, they will not only be providing good rock music, but will be firing a stern message (m) . . . . . . their audiences.

They fear many young people have never heard of the racist battles of the thirties and do not know about the Second World War. (n) . . . . . . 1945, people have tried to pretend these things aren't happening. (p) . . . . . . more than forty years, we've said that such events can't be repeated. These bands listen to such comments and look at our inner cities (q) . . . . . . despair. But they haven't given up all hope. (r) . . . . . . the end, they think most thinking young people will get their message of peace and love – even if it does seem sentimental to elderly cynics.

'You've only got to stand (s) . . . . . . a street corner for ten minutes to see what's really happening. And most people don't notice. It's like they're standing (t) . . . . . . the corner of a room, facing the wall with their eyes shut. It hasn't changed that much, except nowadays they arrive (v) . . . . . . car at the battle-fronts, whereas (w) . . . . . . the 1930s they came (x) . . . . . . foot or (y) . . . . . . bike.'

Task three

Write a report about something that happened in your home town. You can choose a recent event, or something that took place many years ago.

UNIT 4.7
INTENSIFIERS: very, too, enough

The dresses are very expensive.
People drive too fast on motorways.
Her work isn't good enough to pass the diploma exam.

The **intensifiers, very, too** and **enough**, qualify **adjectives** and **adverbs**. **Very** is used to add **emphasis**. For example:

> The shops used to stock nice, cheap dresses; but now there are only boutiques, and the dresses are **very** expensive.

This does not mean that the speaker can't afford the dresses in the boutiques; but that she thinks that they cost a lot of money.

Now look at this example:

> Above an altitude of 4,000 feet, he found it **very** difficult to breathe.

This doesn't mean that he couldn't breathe, only that he had difficulty in breathing.

Too is used to express the idea that something is **excessive**. For example:

> Clothes cost a lot in that shop. Many things are **too** expensive for me.

Another way of saying this might be:

> Clothes cost such a lot in that shop that I can't afford them.

Now look at this example:

> The police are looking out for people who drive **too** fast on motorways.

The police think that these people are dangerous. In Britain the speed limit is 70 mph on motorways. If you drive faster than that, you are driving too fast.

Another way you could say this is:

> The police are looking out for people who drive so fast on motorways that they are travelling over the speed limit and are dangerous.

WARNING BOX

> Some people confuse **very** and **too**.
>
> *Look at these examples:*
>
> The clothes in that shop are **very** expensive. They are **too** expensive for me; I can't afford them.
>
> Doug drives **very** fast; but he is always in control so it is not **too** fast for him.
>
> **Very** means **a great deal**; whereas **too** means that it is **excessive**.

Enough means sufficient or sufficiently. Unlike **very** and **too, enough** comes **after** the adjective or adverb. For example:

> Her work isn't good **enough** to pass the diploma exam.

Enough can also be used like an **adjective** with **nouns**. In this case, it comes **before** the noun. For example:

> The government hasn't allowed the authorities **enough** money to pay the new salaries.

214

Unit 4.7 Intensifiers – TASKS

Task one
Complete the following sentences by putting in the correct intensifier, **very, too** *or* **enough**.

(a) The film was . . . . . . long, but I enjoyed it.
(b) The stone-cutter was . . . . . . noisy, so the neighbours asked him to stop.
(c) There are not . . . . . . air-traffic controllers to handle all the flights over Europe in the summer.
(d) They weren't clever . . . . . . to understand the significance of what he said.
(e) Electronic companies are working . . . . . . hard to find ways of stopping people copying records.
(f) This is a . . . . . . important post and good communication skills are essential.
(g) Nowadays local education authorities can't recruit . . . . . . teachers for science subjects.
(h) The journal failed to attract a large . . . . . . readership, in spite of its being well written and attractively produced.
(j) It isn't true that there are . . . . . . many people in the world. It is just that we don't distribute the food and wealth properly.
(k) In spite of the changes made, the government's education bill is still . . . . . . confusing.

Task two
Rewrite the following sentences using **too, very** *or* **enough**.

(a) The mountain was high, but he climbed it in spite of the difficulties.
(b) The car went so fast that he didn't see the number.
(c) The house was so expensive that they couldn't afford to buy it.
(d) Of course cancer is a serious disease, but nowadays many cancers can be cured.
(e) He has got as much money as he needs to buy the car.
(f) He drove as fast as it was necessary to get there on time.
(g) Rank Xerox is an important company which has been responsible for significant developments in computing.
(h) The dinosaur wasn't as large as it needed to be to fight all its enemies.
(j) In the USA they didn't get as much rain as they needed in the summer of 1988.
(k) Britain imports so much toxic waste that many people consider it to be dangerous.

Task three
Make survey of your town and see how people feel about the facilities: where there are **very** *many things; where there are* **too** *many; where there is* **enough** *or there isn't* **enough**. *Then complete the chart below. Then consider what they are like. For example: are the buses* **too** *crowded? Is the airport* **very** *noisy? Are there* **enough** *restaurants?*

Facility	Very	Too	Enough

UNIT 4.8

RELATIVE CLAUSES 1: Form; defining, non-defining

Anne is one of those people who never seem to get tired.

His mother, who lives in London, is not a gypsy.

The Sierra is a car which was designed for the 1990s.

Relative clauses have two purposes: to **describe** something or to give us **additional information** about something.

1. The form of the relative clause

Look at these examples:

> Anne is one of those people. They never seem to get tired.
> The Sierra is a car. It was designed for the 1990s.

In both of the above examples, the second sentence is a **description** of something in the first sentence and completes the idea in the first sentence. Although they are grammatically complete, the first sentence in both of the examples is an incomplete **idea**.

Look at the first sentences again:

> Anne is one of those people.
> The Sierra is a car.

We need to know more to make sense of each statement. The second sentence in each case provides us with this information.

> Anne is one of those people. **They never seem to get tired.**
> The Sierra is a car. **It was designed for the 1990s.**

It is better to put the complete idea into one sentence, and we can do this by making the second sentence into a **relative clause**, as follows:

> Anne is one of those people **who never seem to get tired.**
> The Sierra is a car **which was designed for the 1990s.**

The **relative clause** is a **description** of the noun that immediately precedes **who** or **which**, and completes the idea.

In both of these examples the word replaced in the second sentence is the **subject** of the sentence:

> **They** never seem to get tired./**Who** never seem to get tired.
> **It** was designed for the 1990s./**Which** was designed for the 1990s.

The **relative pronoun** which replaces the subject of the sentence is **who** for people and **which** for things. **That** is also possible on occasions (see **2** below).

2. The role of the relative clause

The **relative clause** is a subordinate clause which describes a noun in the main clause. Sometimes it is important because by **defining** the object or person it helps to avoid any **confusion**. This is a **defining relative clause** (see **3** below). On other occasions, the **relative clause** is simply giving us **additional information** about the object or person. This is a **non-defining relative clause** (see **4** below).

In the examples in **1**, it is clear which should be the relative. But very often the speaker or writer has a choice.

216

Look at this example:
Marius couldn't afford to go abroad for a holiday. Marius was a teacher.
If we want to connect the information in these two sentences, we have a choice. For example:
Marius, **who was a teacher**, couldn't afford to go abroad for a holiday.
Marius, **who couldn't afford to go abroad for a holiday**, was a teacher.
We make our decision by deciding which is the most important piece of information, i.e. where we want to **focus** our information.. That is the **main clause**. The **relative clause** is the **subordinate** clause.

3. The relative clause as description (defining)

The **defining relative clause** is a description of the noun, which gives us information necessary to help us **identify** what we are talking about. It is important, and without the **relative clause**, we wouldn't have a full understanding of the topic. It answers the question WHICH ONE? or WHICH KIND OF? For example:
Anne is one of those people . . .
    Which kind of people?
    who never seem to get tired.
The Sierra is a car . . .
    Which kind of car?
    which was designed for the 1990s.

If you look at these examples again, you will see that **who** is used for **people** (and in some cases animals); **which** is used for **things**.

When the **relative clause** is a **description**, both **who** and **which** can be replaced by **that**. For example:
Anne is one of those people **that** never seem to get tired.
The Sierra is a car **that** was designed for the 1990s.

4. Relative clause as 'extra information' (non-defining)

On some occasions the **relative clause** is not describing the noun but is giving us some **extra** information about it. In this case it is not important to our understanding the topic generally. This is a **non-defining relative clause**.

Look at this example:
His mother is not a gypsy. She lives in London.
He has only **one** mother, so the information that she lives in London is not important in helping us to **identify** which mother we are talking about. So we can make one sentence by using a **non-defining relative clause**, as follows:
His mother, **who lives in London**, is not a gypsy.

Now look at this example:
Spycatcher was banned in Britain in 1988. It was on sale throughout the world.
In this case *Spycatcher* is a famous book, so the information that it was on sale throughout the world is not important in helping us to identify the book. Again, we use a **non-defining relative clause** to make one sentence, as follows:
Spycatcher, **which was on sale throughout the world in 1988**, was banned in Britain.
When the relative clause is giving **extra information** as in these cases, it must be **between commas**.

In this type of relative clause you **cannot use THAT**. You **cannot** say, for example:

*His mother, that lives in London, is not a gypsy.

In most cases the **non-defining clause** can be rewritten as two co-ordinating clauses (see Unit 5.4). For example:

His mother is not a gypsy, **and** she lives in London.

Spycatcher was banned in Britain in 1988, **yet** was on sale throughout the world.

5. Summary

Subject	Defining relative pronoun	Non-defining relative pronoun
people things	**who** or **that** **which** or **that**	**who** **which**

Unit 4.8 Relative clauses 1 – TASKS

Task one

(a) *Indicate by filling in the chart below, whether the relative clauses in the following sentences are defining or non-defining.*

(b) *Rewrite the sentences with non-defining clauses so that they contain two co-ordinating clauses.*

(a) Atlee was the Prime Minister who gave India independence.
(b) The film which made Albert Finney famous was *Tom Jones.*
(c) Danny Kaye, who was a Hollywood filmstar, did a lot of work for UNESCO.
(d) The table, which was made of walnut, was given him by his parents.
(e) The journey, which was over 500 miles, took her just six hours.
(f) She threw away the diary which contained the information about her father's illness.
(g) They can't understand the student who arrived yesterday.
(h) The judge, who was a kind man, gave the prisoner a light sentence.
(j) The newspaper attacked the judge who was too kind.
(k) The President of the USA was met by the Russian President, who was a year older.

Defining	Non-defining

Task two

*Although the text below is complete, it can be improved by adding relative clauses which will create a more complete picture of the situation. Go through the text and add the relative clauses at the appropriate places. Don't forget to enclose the non-defining clause with commas. You must decide which relative (**who, which, that**) to put at the beginning. The first one has been written for you.*

...... are full of vegetables
...... always come to live with the family in their final years
...... every member of the family will visit at least once a day
...... congregate around the square
...... have no room in their homes
...... all earn their living from fishing or market gardening like the rest of the islanders

The houses are low-lying detached residences. Many of the owners have built them themselves or inherited them from their parents. The houses have neat gardens. In a corner in each garden, there is a little shrine.

The houses are small, but the families are often large with ten or more children in addition to the grandparents.

In the middle of the square there is a large covered stand. At night the children from the families bring their mattresses to sleep on the stand.

Answer:

The houses which congregate around the square are low-lying detached residences.

Task three

Rudyard Kipling wrote a story called The cat that walked by itself.

Think up similar titles for the illustrations below.

UNIT 4.9
RELATIVE CLAUSES 2:
object of clause

He talked of Nehru, whom Churchill had imprisoned.
They are the people you would most like to see.
The picture he bought in Indonesia is much admired.

1. Defining relative clauses

(a) People
Look at this example:
They are the people. You would most like to see them.
In the example above, the **relative pronoun** will refer to **people** and will be the object of **see**. When the **relative pronoun** is the **object** of its clause, there are three ways of forming the **relative clause**, as follows:
  (i) They are the people **whom** you would most like to see.
  (ii) They are the people **who/that** you would most like to see.
  (iii) They are the people you would most like to see.

Many people think that **whom** must be used for the **object relative**, but now **whom** is used only in very formal situations. The most common construction is probably **(iii)** where **no relative pronoun** is used.

(b) Things
Look at this example:
The picture is much admired. He bought it in Indonesia.
In this example, the **relative pronoun** will replace **it** and will refer to **the picture**. The **relative clause** can be formed in two ways, as follows:
  (i) The picture **which/that** he bought in Indonesia is much admired.
  (ii) The picture he bought in Indonesia is much admired.
In the examples above, the more commonly used form is **(ii)**. That is the one where the **relative pronoun** is omitted.

WARNING BOX

> Whereas **who** may become **whom** for the **object pronoun, which** and **that** never change.

2. Non-defining relative clauses

In the **non-defining relative clause**, you must use **which** for **things** and **who** or **whom** for **people**, for the **object pronoun**. For example:
He talked of Nehru, **whom/who** Churchill had imprisoned.
The book, **which** she wrote for her mother, has now been filmed.

Continued

3. Summary

Object	Defining relative pronoun	Non-defining relative pronoun
people	**whom** (formal) **who/that** (informal) **(Ø)** *(usual)*	**whom** (formal) **who** (informal)
things	**which/what** **(Ø)** *(usual)*	**which**

Unit 4.9 Relative clauses 2 – TASKS

Task one

Below are some completed sentences followed by skeleton sentences. Join each pair together by making one of them a relative clause. An example has been written for you.

Example:
Nick made the desk from doors. **Jim/bought/doors/cheaply.**

Nick made the desk from doors Jim bought cheaply.

(a) They didn't like the new doctor. **hospital/appointed/him.**
(b) Lynette made the curtains from the material. **Edward/bought/in India.**
(c) The car was the envy of his neighbours. **he/bought/it.**
(d) Although not an architect, he lived in a house. **he/designed it/himself.**
(e) The football fans caused no trouble. **the police/watched/carefully.**

Task two

Although the text below is complete, it can be improved by adding relative clauses which will create a more complete picture of the situation. Go through the text and add the relative clauses listed at appropriate places. Don't forget to enclose any non-defining clauses in commas. You must decide which relative, if any **(who, whom, which, that)** *to put at the beginning of the clause. The first one has been written for you.*

...... I met in the café
...... the villagers trusted in times of danger
...... I had seen at the station when I arrived
...... the café-owner had taken on holiday in America
...... the men in the group jumped into immediately
...... one of the women laughingly handed to me
...... the villagers bought only one year before
...... the bell disturbed

It was almost midnight. After watching the films, I went with the people to the local fire-station. This was just a shed in the middle of the village. Inside the shed, there was a large, red fire-engine. They were all in a very merry mood and quickly put on the firemen's helmets. I soon realised that I also had to put one on. It was a very large one. I put it on and took my place on the fire-engine. Soon we were racing down the narrow lanes of the village. The fire-bell was clanging loudly and waking all the villagers. 'Fire! Fire!' shouted a man. He was running out of his house, half-asleep, wearing only his night-shirt.

Then to add to the confusion came the noises of the farm animals. They bellowed and jumped about in their stalls, frightened by the sound.

But the 'firemen' laughed and drove on into the night.

Answer:

It was almost midnight. After watching the films which the café-owner had taken on holiday in America....

Task three

(a) *Think of five people. Describe them by talking about something someone has done for them or to them.*

(b) *Think of five things you like. Describe them by saying something about what you have done with them.*

The picture she paid a lot of money for . . .
The girl, whose four brothers are also
missing, . . .

1. Preposition + relative pronoun

Look at this example:

Annette's favourite picture is that one. She paid at lot of money **for it**.

Here, the connecting word in the second sentence is **it**. **It** is governed by the preposition **for**. When we convert the second sentence into a **relative clause**, we can do it in several ways. For example:

Annette's favourite picture is that one **for which** she paid a lot of money.
Annette's favourite picture is that one **which/that** she paid a lot of money **for**.
Annette's favourite picture is that one she paid a lot of money **for**.

(It is often said that you shouldn't finish a sentence or clause with a preposition; but this happens very often.)

We can do the same when we are talking about a person. For example:

I met the old lady. You were very kind **to her**.

The second sentence above can be converted into a relative clause as follows:

I met the old lady **to whom** you were very kind.
I met the old lady **who/whom/that** you were very kind **to**.
I met the old lady you were very kind **to**.

When the **preposition** comes before the **relative pronoun**:
(a) it must be followed by **whom** (for people) or **which** (for things).
(b) **who** and **that** are not possible there.
(c) it is considered to be very **formal**.

2. Summary

| Type of use | Preposition and relative pronoun | |
	People	Things
formal informal	Preposition + **whom** **whom** (clause) preposition **who** (clause) preposition **that** (clause) preposition Ø *(clause) preposition*	Preposition + **which** **which** (clause) preposition **that** (clause) preposition Ø *(clause) preposition*

WARNING BOX

The examples above all have **defining clauses**. In **non-defining clauses, that** and the Ø option cannot be used.

When the **relative clause** is very long, it is better not to put the preposition at the end.

---

3. Whose

Look at this example:

The girl is six years old. **Her** brothers are also missing.

In this example, the connection between the two sentences is **the girl** and **her**. **Her** shows **possession**.

We can convert the second sentence into a **relative clause** by the use of the preposition **of + whom**, as follows:

The girl, the brothers **of whom** are also missing, is six years old.

Note that when we do this, we put the **noun** before the **relative pronoun**. However, it is considered to be very **formal** when we use **whom** to describe people. Usually, we use the relative pronoun **whose**, as follows:

The girl, **whose** brothers are also missing, is six years old.

Look at these examples:

Hughes is a dull leader. His party has failed

Hughes is a dull leader **whose** party has failed.

You are the generation. Your fathers fought the Great War.

You are the generation **whose** fathers fought the Great War.

Unit 4.10 Relative clauses 3 – TASKS

Task one

(a) *Rewrite the following pairs of sentences as one sentence, using a relative clause. The focus in each case is the first sentence.*

(b) *Write as many variations as possible.*

(c) *State which is formal and which is informal.*

(d) *State whether the relative clause is defining or non-defining.*

Example:

That's the book. I've heard so much about it.

That's the book about which I've heard so much.

(Formal, defining)

That's the book which I've heard so much about.

(Informal, defining)

That's the book I've heard so much about. (Informal, defining)

 (i) Sir Winston Churchill was a great leader. His biography has just been completed.

 (ii) That club is very expensive. Many entertainers belong to it.

(iii) That school was founded in the fifteenth century. Only children of rich families go to it.

 (iv) The manager didn't want to tell the staff. His company had gone bankrupt.

 (v) The Swiss company has increased its bid. Its previous offer was £9.95 a share.

Task two

Think of ten people you know and say something about them, using a relative clause beginning with **whose**. *An example has been written for you.*

Example:

She's the woman whose car was stolen.

UNIT 4.11
RELATIVE CLAUSES 4:
adverbs as relative pronouns; special use of that

**No. 170 is the house where he was born.
1979 was the year when Thatcher became
Prime Minister.**

When the relative clause refers to **place** or **time** and would normally begin with **in which** or **on which**, we can replace both of these with **where** or **when**.

1. Place

Where is used when the relative pronoun refers to **place**. For example:

No. 170 is the house. He was born there.
No. 170 is the house **where/in which** he was born.

Rome is the city. She lived in Rome for fifteen years.
Rome is the city **where/in which** she lived for fifteen years.

The idea of place can be extended to many other things, such as books, films, plays, documents, etc. For example:

That's the book **where** the young boy meets the convict in the graveyard.
That's the film **where** Robert Redford and Paul Newman jump into the ravine.

It is often possible to transfer the preposition to the end of the relative clause, in which case there are other alternatives. For example:

Rome is the city **which/that** she lived **in** for fifteen years.
Rome is the **city** she lived **in** for fifteen years.

However, it is **unlikely** that the preposition would be transferred to the end of a **long** relative clause. It is **unlikely** that we would say the following:

That's the film *which* Robert Redford and Paul Newman jump into the ravine *in*.

2. Time

When can be used when the relative pronoun refers to **time**. For example:

1979 was the year. Thatcher became Prime Minister that year.
1979 was the year **when/in which** Thatcher became Prime Minister.

That was the day. My father died that day.
That was the day **when/on which** my father died.

With **time** relatives, it is **unusual** to transfer the preposition to the end of the clause. It is **unlikely** that we would say the following.

That was the day *which* my father died *on*.

It is more common, however, to use **that** or **Ø** in the **time** relative clause without the preposition. For example:

1979 was the year **(that)** Thatcher became Prime Minister.

3. Summary

Reference to	More usual	Less usual
place	**where** **which** . . . preposition **that** . . . preposition **Ø**. . . preposition	*in/on which*
time	**that** **Ø**	*when* *on/in which*

Unit 4.11 Relative clauses 4 – TASKS

Task one

Find alternatives for the relative pronouns in the following passage.

There are some times in which important events occur, so that you never forget what you were doing at the exact time at which the event happened, nor the place in which you were when it happened.

The day on which the war broke out, Dad was visiting the town in which he had been born. He went there to visit his old mother, my grandmother. She had been having problems with her neighbours since the day on which grandfather had died. When Dad heard the news, however, he hurried back quickly, because he wanted to find the papers in which it said he was no longer required to join the army.

It was also the day on which Mum saw a tulip tree for the first time. She was in the garden in which the mayor of the town had greeted the Prime Minister on his visit.

Task two

(a) *Think of five important times in your life and say why they are important to you.*

Example:

That's the day when I got my first job.

(b) *Think of five important places and describe why they are important.*

Example:

Rome—that was the place where I first met Liz.

The bear wearing a funny hat . . .
The bike tethered by a rope . . .
The city walls, built in AD 700 . . .

When the relative pronoun is the **subject** of its clause, we often reduce the relative clause by using the **participle** form of the verb (see Unit 1.3) and leaving out the relative pronoun.

Look at this picture and the description:

In the cartoon, the bear, wearing a funny hat, is sitting on a bike tethered by a rope.

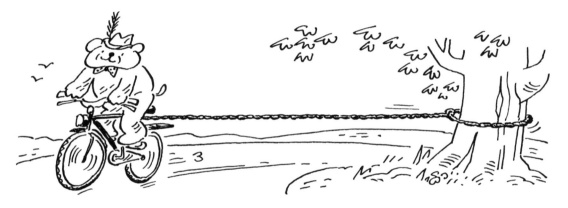

The description could be rewritten as follows:
> In the cartoon, the bear, **who is** wearing a funny hat, is sitting on a bike **which is** tethered by a rope.

In both cases, the writer has reduced the relative clause as follows:
> the bear, **who is wearing** a funny hat *becomes*
> the bear, **wearing** a funny hat

> a bike **which is tethered** by a rope *becomes*
> a bike **tethered** by a rope.

In the same way as when these non-finite forms were used to replace adverbial clauses (see Unit 1.3), **no time** is indicated by the form of the verb used.

The two clauses, **the bear, wearing a funny hat** and **the bike tethered by a rope**, could each be rewritten in several ways, as shown in the following chart.

the bear	who is who was who will be	**wearing**	a funny hat
	who has who who will etc.	**worn** **wore** **wear**	
the bike	which is which was which will be which is being etc.	**tethered**	by a rope

As was stated in Unit 1.3, the **time** and **form** used is dictated by its context of the rest of the sentence.

If you look again at the charts above, you will notice the following points:

The **present participle** represents the **active** voice of the verb.

The **past participle** represents the **passive** voice.

(See also Unit 1.3.)

Unit 4.12 Relative clauses 5 – TASKS

Task one

(a) *Read the following text and state whether the participles in bold type are active or passive.*

In the room, there was a very small man, **dressed** in Bedouin clothes, **offering** me a glass of tea. I accepted and sat down on some cushions **placed** against the wall. The room, **decorated** in a very ornate and traditional style, seemed to me to be very long and there were couches and cushions the length of each wall. The cushions, **taking up** about a third of the space, were very brightly coloured. In the centre of the room was a tray, **filled** with glasses and a pot of tea. Very quietly and suddenly, another man, **looking** like the brother of the man already in the room, but **wearing** Western clothes, entered, bowed and sat down beside me. The room suddenly seemed crowded.

(b) *Rewrite the text, making the participles in bold type full finite verbs.*

Task two

The following verses from some poems have been altered by expanding the reduced relative clauses. Restore them to their original form. An example has been written for you.

Example:
Archbishop Boethius
Who is known affectionately to his flock as Yellowface

Archbishop Boethius
....
known affectionately to his flock as Yellowface.
....

(a) I saw a naked man who was smoking a cigarette.
I cannot tell you how shocked I was.
He was by no means the only passenger who was smoking a cigarette,
But he was the only naked passenger who was smoking a cigarette.

(b) When the pistol muzzle that was oozing blue vapour
Was lifted away
Like a cigarette that has been lifted from an ashtray.

(c) At home I used to sit in a winged chair by the window
That overlooked the river and the factory chimneys.

(d) At a clandestine press conference in the Kerry Mountains,
Which was organised by the dissident playwright Dr Joe Pat Sheehy

(e) But then one day she solved the problem
For all us nosey-parkers
Who lurked about the drawing rooms of Paris.

Task three

Find a picture in which a lot of things are happening which remind you of your home town or of your country. Describe some of the things you can see in it, using active and passive participle forms. Some examples have been written for you.

Example:

Look at the old woman walking over the bridge.

You can see a boat tied to a tree.

SECTION 5: Discourse

In discussing grammar, we are usually concerned with language at clause or sentence level. Discourse looks at more extended chunks of language.

In looking at discourse, we can see how different parts are linked together. For example:

how reference is carried across sentences and clauses;
how ideas are connected;
how sentences are connected;
how clauses within sentences are connected;
how various parts of the discourse are focused;
how the topic is established;
how the topic changes.

UNIT 5.1
PRONOUNS

I seem to have a good memory for names no matter how long ago I heard them but faces are a different matter.
What sort of community do you live in? Is it large or small, in town or country, affluent or hard-up?

Pronouns are used in place of **nouns**.

Look at these examples:

I seem to have a good memory for **names** no matter how long ago I heard **them** but faces are a different matter.

Here **them** replaces **names** to avoid repetition of the noun **names**.

What sort of **community** do you live in? Is **it** large or small, in town or country, affluent or hard-up?

Here **it** replaces **community**.

Pronouns can also replace **noun phrases**. For example:

Considering the problems **the regional Water Authorities** have to cope with, **they** do a remarkable job of providing us with a liquid which is generally safe and palatable.

Here **they** replaces **the regional Water Authorities.**

But **pronouns** can also refer directly to the **outside world** or **situation**.

Look at these examples:

We all recognise the benefits of a healthier diet.

We are becoming more conscious of the principle that '**we** are what **we** eat'.

I seem to have a good memory for names no matter how long ago I heard them but faces are a different matter.

What sort of community do **you** live in? Is it large or small, in town or country, affluent or hard-up?

These **pronouns, I, you, we**, are not substituting for a noun or noun phrase in the text. They refer directly to **people outside** the text itself.

Finally, **pronouns** can refer to a **whole clause, sentence** or **idea**.

Look at these examples:

Many people think that if a cat wags its tail it is angry but **this** is only partly true.

Here, **this** refers to the **whole sentence** about what people think tail-wagging means.

When atoms bind together to form molecules, they usually share their electrons equally. **This** is called a covalent bond.

Here, **this** refers to the **process** of binding together to form molecules.

1. Personal pronouns

Personal pronouns have a different form when they are **subject, object** or **possessive** forms.

Look at the following chart:

Subject	Object	Possessive
I	me	mine
you	you	yours
he	him	his
she	her	hers
it	it	its
we	us	ours
they	them	theirs

Look at these examples:

That newspaper's combined circulation is 2,565,000. **Ours** is 3,832,000.

Here, **ours** stands for **our combined circulation**.

In this car you'll sail around corners, not sway around **them**.

Here, **them** refers to **corners**.

We/us/our is often used by academic writers, advertisers and others who want to give the reader a sense of involvement in the text or who are inviting the reader to share the writer's commitment to the text and what it has to say. For example:

We have already seen how the events of the past few years have changed **our** perceptions. Now let us look to the future.

> The **possessive pronouns** – **my, your, his, her, its, our, their** –which come **before a noun** are **central determiners** (see Unit 3.6).

2. Reflexive pronouns

Reflexive pronouns refer back to the subject. The singular form **-self** is used with **singular object pronouns** – **myself, yourself, himself, herself, itself**. The plural form **-selves** is used with **plural object pronouns** – **ourselves, yourselves, themselves**. For example:

She hurt **herself**.

Millipedes protect **themselves** by rolling up into little balls.

The dog hurled **itself** at the intruder.

3. Indefinite pronouns

The **indefinite pronouns** – **some, any** and **every** – can be combined with **-one, -body** or **-thing**, as follows:

anyone, anybody, anything
someone, somebody, something
everyone, everybody, everything

No can be combined with **-body** or used with **one** as two words, as follows:

no one, nobody

In both British and American English, **everyone, anyone** and **someone** are used more often than the compounds with **-body**.

The **indefinite pronouns** – **anyone, anybody, everyone, everybody, someone, somebody, no one, nobody** – are grammatically **singular** but there is an increasing tendency, even in formal English, to follow these pronouns with a **plural** pronoun. For example:

I certainly wouldn't advise **anyone** to leave **their** house empty for long periods. It is much safer to rent the house.

This avoids the awkwardness of using **his or her** or **his/her**:

I certainly wouldn't advise **anyone** to leave **his or her** house empty for long periods.

One way of avoiding the problem is to put the subject into the plural, as follows:

I certainly wouldn't advise **people** to leave **their** houses empty for long periods.

4. Determiners and pronouns

Many words, such as the following, can function either as **determiners** (see Units 3.5, 3.7-3.9) or **pronouns**.

all	what	more	either
least	each	no	fewer
less	this	these	enough
many	one	most	little
much	whose	few	neither
some	both	any	several
which	that	those	

We distinguish between the two forms by checking whether the word is followed by a **noun** or not. **Determiners** are always followed by a noun; **pronouns** stand alone as they refer to the whole noun phrase in these cases.

Look at these examples:

Determiners	**Pronouns**
Many people in Britain have become vegetarian.	But **most** continue to eat meat.
Which sports do you watch on television?	**Which** do you actually go to watch in person?

In the first example, **most** is a pronoun which stands for **most people**; in the second example, **which** stands for **which sports**.

5. Demonstrative pronouns

The **demonstrative pronouns** – this, these, that, those – can be preceded by **pre-determiners** such as **all, both, half**. For example:

All these are to be moved over there.

I'll take **both those**.

But the construction with **of** is much more frequently used. For example:

All of these are to be moved over there.

I'll take **both of those**.

WARNING BOX

When **all, both, half** are followed by **of** and a noun, you must use the article **the**. For example:

All of the books

Both of the boys

Half of the pages

When the quantifiers, **some, any, many, few**, etc. are used with **of** and a noun, you must also use the article **the**. For example:

Some of the people

Many of the students

Most of the books

Unit 5.1 Pronouns – TASKS

Task one

Read the following texts and make a list of all the pronouns. Then fill in the chart below with the pronouns and the nouns, noun phrases or clauses, or the concept that the pronouns replace. The first one has been written for you.

(a) Elephants make up for the damage they do to woodlands by scattering seeds and fertilising them. In the Luangwa Valley in Zambia, the *Sclerocarpya caffra* tree is a favourite food of elephants. They eat the fruits, completely strip the bark from the tree and apparently kill it. But zoologists found that the bark grows back rapidly and they also found dozens of seeds intact in the elephants' droppings. The elephants had eaten the fruit and dropped the seeds in well-drained soil, away from predators that might eat them.

(b) Dr Samuel Johnson, who compiled *A Dictionary of the English Language* in the eighteenth century, wrote: 'Knowledge is of two kinds. We know a subject ourselves, or we know where we can find information upon it'. But a new problem faces the modern educated person. We now have an excess of information and even an excess of sources of it. This is often called the 'information explosion' but some have said that it should be called the 'publication explosion'.

Pronoun	Noun/noun phrase/clause/concept
they	elephants

Task two

Read the following texts and fill in the missing words with suitable pronouns.

(a) Herons are under threat in Greece and to raise public awareness of ...... the Hellenic Ornithological Society has been carrying out a scientific study to monitor the birds and guard their nexts.

(b) The populations of ...... of the most poorly nourished nations are growing at nearly four per cent a year. At that rate, ... will double within 20 years. ...... is happening despite the best efforts of family planning agencies.

In both adults and children chronic malnutrition is made worse by a 'hungry period' during the annual rains. ...... happens when the previous year's crops start to run out before the next year's harvest.

(c) Talking in one's sleep is ...... of the most common phenomena and ...... that is of more concern to the observer than to the sleeper. Laboratory observation suggests that ...... is widespread and most people are likely to do ...... Sometimes ...... wake up aware that ...... have been talking. Often ...... do not.

(d) Anyone can set ...... up in business as an estate agent – ...... don't need any qualifications. So how do ...... go about finding .... can trust? Last year a report showed that half of ...... don't think ......'re getting good value for our money from ......

Task three

The following passages have been written without any pronouns or determiners. Read them, then decide which nouns should be replaced by pronouns and determiners and rewrite the passages.

(a) Just when people were learning to live with the idea of 'safe sun' as far as people's skin is concerned, along came the scientists and doctors to tell people that people's hair is sun-sensitive too. Sand, salt and chlorine can strip hair of the hair's oils, leaving the hair rough and the ends split. Most in danger is a person's parting. A person's parting is subject to the same carcinogenic ultra-violet rays that a person's skin is.

(b) Adam White is a photographer. Yesterday Adam White flew to the United States to photograph the President. Adam White's assignments take Adam White all over the world.

Adam White owns a large house in Sussex where Adam White lives with Adam White's wife Jane and Adam and Jane White's two children, Margaret and Peter. Adam, Jane, Margaret and Peter White have three cats, two dogs, a horse and fifteen ducks. Adam, Jane, Margaret and Peter White have lived in the house for five years, ever since Adam and Jane White sold Adam and Jane White's house in London and moved south.

UNIT 5.2
IT AS INTRODUCTION WORD

It was discovered that sunlight helped to prevent tooth decay.
It's fun riding a motorbike.
It's impossible to judge when the golf-boom will peak.
It's raining.
It's a lovely day.

It is a pronoun. Because it is a pronoun, we expect that it will refer back to some other noun or noun phrase and replace it, as in the following example:

Exposure to sunlight decreases the risk of a heart attack. **It** also seems to prevent other infections.

Here, **it** has replaced **exposure to sunlight**. There are, however, occasions when **it** is used in the **subject position** without any reference.

1. Talking about the weather

Look at these examples:

It's raining.
It's a lovely day.

Here, **it** has no meaning and cannot be replaced. We **cannot** say:

*Raining is.
*A lovely day is.

We also have such expressions as **It's ten o'clock already!** In such expressions, **it** plays a similar role to the one it has in talking about the weather. But some people say that, here, **it** has replaced **the time**.

2. Anticipating a noun clause

Look at these examples:

It's a pity (that) **he came so late**.
It's a shame (that) **he lost his job**.

When **it** anticipates a noun clause after such phrases as **it's a pity, it's a shame,** etc., it is possible, but **very unlikely**, that the noun clause would replace **it**. For example:

That he came so late is a pity.
That he lost his job is a shame.

3. Impersonal passive

Look at these examples:

It was discovered in the 1930s that sunlight helped to prevent tooth decay.
It is known that ultra violet light kills bacteria.

When an **impersonal passive** is used, the impersonal **it** and the passive form lend **authority** to a statement, without the speaker having to name the authority. In this case, it

UNIT 5.3
SO, NEITHER/NOR

The committee disagrees, and has said so in a report.
Americans are too fat. So says one who admits to being overweight.
The members complained of the inefficiency; so did the official report.

So can be used with a verb to replace a clause.

Look at this example:
    The committee disagrees. **It** has said **so** in a report.
In the second sentence, **it** and **so** are replacing information from the first sentence. **It** is a **pronoun** and is replacing the noun **committee** (see Unit 5.1); **so** is replacing a whole clause. Without **so**, the sentence would be rewritten as follows:
    The committee disagrees. It has said **that it disagrees** in a report.

Now look at this example:
    Americans are too fat. **So** says one who admits to being overweight.
Here, **so** has replaced the clause **Americans are too fat**.

In the last example, **so** has been placed at the beginning of the clause. This has the effect of keeping the focus on the original clause.

In the last example there is also inversion, so that the subject comes after the verb. It is not necessary. It is possible to say **So he says**, but **So one who is overweight says** is **unlikely** for reasons of style. The inversion form is unlikely to occur with other verbs, though it is possible with **think**. Here it is also stylistically better. It would be possible to say the following:
    Americans are too fat. One who admits being overweight says so.
There is, however, an imbalance, where the longer part of the sentence comes at the beginning (see Units 5.2, 5.9).

In addition to **say**, there are many other verbs that can be followed by **so**. For example:
    He hopes so
        thinks so
        supposes so
        does so.
The negative is usually **not**. For example:
    He hopes not
        does not
        says not.

WARNING BOX

But: he **doesn't think** so.

When **so** is placed at the beginning of the clause, the **negative** is formed by putting **not so**, at the beginning of the clause. For example:

Not so, says one who is overweight.

So is also used to replace **part** of a clause or a phrase.

Look at this example:

The members complained of the inefficiency. **So** did the official report.

Here, **so** does not replace the whole clause but only the predicate, and has the meaning of **also**, as follows:

The members complained of the inefficiency. The official report **also** complained of the inefficiency.

In this case, **so** always comes at the **beginning** of the sentence and is then followed by the **auxiliary verb + subject**. For example:

The Foreign Ministers have arrived in Geneva. **So has the Secretary-General**.

The **negative** is formed with **neither** or **nor**. For example:

The two ministers didn't announce any decision. **Nor/neither** did their spokesmen.

Unit 5.3 So, neither/nor – TASKS

Task one

*In the following dialogue two people are discussing a new plan concerning members of the staff of their institute who spend working time on overseas visits. Complete the dialogue, filling in the missing words with the correct form of the words in brackets to make a clause with **so** or **not**. The first two have been written for you.*

Example:

(a) **I think so.**

(b) **I don't think so.**

Tim: Will you reach an agreement on the plan to curtail overseas visits?

Art: I (a) **(think)**. We've almost finished discussions now.

Tim: What about an agreement on research projects?

Art: No, I (b) **(think)**. In fact, I (c) **(hope)** because I don't think the agreement as it stands gives us a very good bargain.

Tim: We could renegotiate it later.

Art: I (d) **(suppose)**.

Tim: The head of the unit (e) **(say)** last week. He said he would reopen discussions immediately any agreement was signed.

Art: If he (f) **(do)**, that would make any agreement rather silly, don't you think?

Tim: I (g) **(suppose)**. But it would get us over the position we are in now where we need somewhere to start further discussions. In a way it would take us a step forward.

Art: I (h) **(hope)**. But we mustn't make ourselves look silly. It will seem to everyone that either we don't know our own minds, or that we're trying to trick them.

Tim: I (j) **(think)**. People will realise that it's only a stage in the negotiations. I don't think they'll see us as two criminals.

Art: I (k) **(hope)**. But your credibility is weak at the moment.

Tim: Do you really (l) **(think)**?

Art: Don't you see anything you don't want to?

Tim: I (m) **(suppose)**. That's how I survive.

Task two

*Read the following information about the people and then complete the sentences about them below, using **so, neither/nor**. Some examples have been written for you.*

Examples:

Sara was born in March.

So was Marc.

Miles is going to the USA next year.

So are Helen and David.

Rowan didn't go to university.

Nor did Marc and Sara.

246

David

Born:	12-5-49
Married:	15-10-78
Children:	3 – 2 boys, 1 girl
Educated:	University – read physics
Work:	pilot
Sport:	most sport, esp. swimming; but not football
Arts:	not much; doesn't go to the theatre
Plans:	will go to USA next year
Wants:	to start his own business

Marc

Born:	29-3-63
Married:	not yet
Children:	None
Educated:	school until 16
Work:	clothes shop manager
Sport:	only likes tennis
Arts:	theatre and cinema
Plans:	will get married next year in USA
Wants:	to own his own shop

Miles

Born:	16-6-54
Married:	16-7-78
Children:	2 girls
Educated:	university – read history
Work:	teacher
Sport:	nothing
Arts:	cinema, music, dance
Plans:	work in USA next year
Wants:	to be a writer

Sara

Born:	9-3-54
Married:	31-8-76
Children:	2 girls
Educated:	school until 18
Work:	secretary
Sport:	most sport, esp. tennis; but not football
Arts:	likes the theatre
Plans:	will go to France next year
Wants:	to be a teacher

Rowan

Born:	4-5-38
Married:	10-7-60
Children:	5 – 4 boys, 1 girl
Educated:	school until 15
Work:	housewife
Sport:	only likes climbing
Arts:	doesn't like theatre but goes to cinema
Plans:	to buy a house in France next year.
Wants:	to be a writer

Helen

Born:	29-6-49
Married:	15-10-78
Children:	3 – 2 boys, 1 girl
Educated:	university – read physics
Work:	journalist
Sport:	all sport, esp. swimming and climbing
Arts:	not much
Plans:	to spend next year in USA
Wants:	to sail round the world

(a) David read physics at university.
(b) Marc didn't stay at school after 16.
(c) Sara doesn't like football.
(d) Helen has only one daughter.
(e) Rowan didn't get married in the 1970s.
(f) Rowan wants to be a writer.
(g) David got married in October.
(h) Marc plays tennis.
(j) Sara won't go to the USA next year.
(k) David wants to have his own business.

Task three

Think of six cities, either in your own country or around the world, and make comparisons of the kind in Task two.

UNIT 5.4
CO-ORDINATING CONJUNCTIONS

In the USA, the number of psychiatrists has increased ninefold since 1948 and the ranks of clinical psychologists have expanded fifteen times.
The official language is Arabic, but there are also other officially recognised languages.

Co-ordinating conjunctions link two clauses of equal importance. The most commonly used co-ordinating conjunctions are and and but. There are others, such as yet, either . . . or/ neither . . . nor, not only . . . but also.

1. And

And is a neutral link between two clauses. It can link **facts**, such as statistics; and it can link **events** in a narrative.

Look at these examples:

> In the USA, the number of psychiatrists has increased ninefold since 1948 **and** the ranks of clinical psychologists have expanded fifteen times.

When **and** is used to link clauses that state **facts**, the order of the clauses will depend on how the speaker wishes to **focus** the message (see Unit 5.9). We could say:

> In the USA, the ranks of clinical psychologists have expanded fifteen times since 1948 **and** the number of psychiatrists has increased ninefold.

This would not change the **meaning**; it would give a different **focus** to the message.

Look at this example:

> He went into the theatre **and** bought a ticket.

Here, the order of the clauses indicates the order in which the **events** occurred. If we change them around, the **events** occur in a different order. For example:

> He bought a ticket **and** went into the theatre.

2. But

The use of **but** signals that the second clause says something **unexpected** or something which is in **opposition** or in **contrast** to the first clause. For example:

> In Iraq, the official language is Arabic, **but** there are also other officially recognised languages.

Here, the second clause seems to contradict the first one.

As with **and**, when we are dealing with **facts** like the above, the order of the clauses will depend on the **focus** the speaker wishes to put on the statement (see Unit 5.9). Thus, we could say:

> There are other officially recognised languages in Iraq, **but** the official language is Arabic.

This would not alter the **meaning** of the statement; there would only be a shift in **focus**.

And and but

Compare these examples:

> In the USA, the number of psychiatrists has increased ninefold since 1948 **and** the ranks of clinical psychologists have expanded fifteen times.

In the USA, the number of psychiatrists has increased ninefold since 1948 **but** the ranks of clinical psychologists have expanded fifteen times.

The use of **and** indicates a **neutral** statement of the facts. When we use **but**, we draw attention to the **difference** in the increase – fifteen times for clinical psychologists as opposed to only nine times for psychiatrists.

3. Yet, even though

Yet signals a similar intention to **but**, in that it is introducing an idea in **opposition** or in **contrast** to the first one presented. The effect, however, is more one of **concession** than direct opposition. For example:

Disasters often make dramatic headlines, **yet** there is some good news here.

It would be possible to rephrase the example by using the **subordinate conjunction even though** (see Unit 5.8):

Even though disasters often make dramatic headlines, there is some good news here.

4. Either . . . or

Either . . . or indicates a **choice** or an **alternative**. For example:

Either all nations stop hunting the blue whale **or** it will become extinct.

Each member (of the Scottish YHA) must use **either** (a) a sheet sleeping bag of the approved type **or** (b) a down sleeping bag along with a sheet sleeping bag . . .

WARNING BOX

As with other double conjunctions, when we use **either . . . or**, the **same part** of the sentence must follow each conjunction. The following sentences are **incorrect**:

*All nations stop *either hunting* the blue whale *or it* will become extinct.

Either each member must use (a) a sheet sleeping bag of the approved type *or (b) a down sleeping bag* along with a sheet sleeping bag . . .

The **negative** form is **neither . . . nor**.

And, but, or also co-ordinate **lexical** items. For example:

Boris had marched **and** shared quarters with Berg.

He wanted not just one **but** three copies of the report.

Would you like tea **or** coffee?

5. Not only . . . but also

Not only . . . but also is similar to an emphatic use of **and**. For example:

Not only had Boris marched with Berg, **but** he had **also** shared quarters with him.

WARNING BOX

The position of **also** can be immediately after **but** or immediately before the **main verb**.

As with **either . . . or**, there must be the **same parts** of the sentence after each part of the conjunction (see **4** above).

When we begin with **not only**, the order of the clause after **not only** is like that in the **question** form. For example:

Not only were the police late, but (also) they did not bring a search warrant.

This also applies to clauses beginning with **neither** and **nor**. For example:

The police were late; **nor did they bring a search warrant**.

There are several other words after which the same pattern is followed. Usually these words have a **negative** aspect. These are some of them:

hardly, rarely, seldom, only, never, not.

Hardly had he arrived when the announcement was made.
Seldom have I seen a better performance.
Only now **has she** agreed to take part.
Never have I been so humiliated.
Not even for a million dollars **would I** take part in a marathon.

Unit 5.4 Co-ordinating conjunctions – TASKS

Task one

Using co-ordinating conjunctions combine as many sentences as you can in each of the groups of sentences below. Make any changes necessary such as replacing nouns with pronouns or leaving out words in order not to repeat them unnecessarily. Don't forget which conjunctions are followed by the question form.

Group one
there are eleven service centres for small businesses in England
they handle 27,000 new counselling cases
there are 180 counselling offices
they need government support

Group two
he soon faced cash-flow problems
he needed help from a local investment fund
he had little money of his own
Robin Aspden set up his own frozen food firm
he would have had to work for a poor company all his life

Group three
the best rate for pedalling is 100 rpm
cyclists should pedal faster
cyclists should pedal longer
cyclists should not go too fast
cyclists should not go faster than 115 rpm

UNIT 5.5
CONNECTERS 1: contrast, result, difference

The behaviour of apes and monkeys is very illuminating. . . However some recent books have over-emphasised the similarities between man and monkeys.

Connecters link together two sentences of **equal** importance. As with co-ordinating conjunctions and clauses (see Unit 5.4), the **order** of the two sentences cannot be changed without altering the **meaning**.

A co-ordinating conjunction must always come at the beginning of its clause, but the position of **connecters** is variable. If you put the connecter at the **beginning** or **end** of the clause, it is the connecter itself which is highlighted. For example:

It was only a short article. **However**, Janet felt entitled to call herself a writer from the day it was accepted by a magazine.

It was only a short article. Janet felt entitled to call herself a writer from the day it was accepted by a magazine, **however**.

When the **connecter** comes at other points in the sentence, it is the word that precedes it that is stressed. For example:

It was only a short article. Janet, **however**, felt entitled to call herself a writer from the day it was accepted by a magazine.

It was only a short article. Janet felt entitled, **however**, to call herself a writer from the day it was accepted by the magazine.

This is made made clearer in spoken language, where there would usually be a pause surrounding the connecter.

As in the case of conjunctions and clauses, the different relationships between sentences are made clear by the selection of a connecter, regardless of position in the sentence. In this unit, we look at three relationships: **contrast, result** and **difference.**

1. Suggesting a contrast

Look at this example:

The behaviour of apes and monkeys is very illuminating. . . . **However**, some recent books have over-emphasised the similarities between man and monkeys.

However is the **connecter** which shows the link between the two sentences. You can see this clearly in the following chart:

The behaviour of apes and monkeys is very illuminating.	However	some recent books have over-emphasised the similarities between man and monkeys.

The first sentence is very **positive**. The second sentence expresses a **negative** view. There is always this kind of **opposition** with this type of **connecter**. Another **connecter** which expresses a similar relationship is **nevertheless**.

Look at this example:

> I didn't like *The Singing Detective* the first time it was shown on television. Nevertheless, I shall watch it again because so many people liked it.

The connecters **however** and **nevertheless** express a similar relationship between clauses to the **co-ordinating conjunctions but** and **yet**.

2. Result

Look at this example:

> In the eighteenth century when these three opened up the study of sociology, to be considered a scientist was important in any field of study. **Therefore**, all three wanted to be considered scientists.

Therefore shows that the idea expressed in the second sentence is a **result** of what is stated in the first sentence. Alternatively, the idea of the first sentence is the **cause** of the idea in the second sentence.

The following are other **connecters** which express the same relationship:

consequently, so, thus.

3. Emphasising difference

We have seen in **1** above how we can express a contrasting or opposing idea. We can emphasise the **difference** by using **on the other hand**.

Look at this example:

> Durkheim and Pareto take a different approach. This is possibly because Durkheim is a French philosopher. Pareto, on the other hand, is Italian.

Here the writer is drawing attention to an important **difference** between these two famous sociologists.

On the other hand usually comes at or near the **beginning** of its sentence or clause.

The **subordinating conjunction** which expresses a similar relationship is **whereas** (see Unit 5.8).

Unit 5.5 Connecters 1 – TASKS

Task one

Read the following text and place the connecters in bold type in the appropriate column in the table below.

On the one hand, Suleiman the Magnificent (1495(?)–1566) was a statesman, warrior, administrator and law giver. **On the other hand**, he was also a poet and patron of the arts.

His fleets dominated the Eastern Mediterranean and North Africa and ravaged the coasts of Italy and Spain. **Consequently**, his armies were the terror and admiration of the West. Vast wealth flowed from his victories, and this was increased by trade in spices, coffee and raw silk, as well as precious gems, rock-crystal and porcelain. The arts, **however**, flourished and Suleiman's architects transformed the face of the great cities of his empire. **Thus** Istanbul, as seat of his court, exercised a powerful attraction to craftsmen from Europe, Iran and the Ottoman Empire. They produced works of art – textiles, carpets, illuminated manuscripts, goldsmith's work, arms and armour – which were the envy of Europe.

His family life was not free from trouble, **however**. His younger son Mehmed, whom he made his heir, died early. **Consequently**, a struggle grew up among his younger sons. Mustafa, the eldest, considered himself to be the heir. Suleiman's wife Hurren opposed Mustafa and supported the other sons. A civil war threatened. It would be wrong to blame Hurren for all the troubles. **On the other hand**, she did present Mustafa as a traitor. He was, **therefore**, summoned to his father's presence. Suleiman did not discuss the troubles with him, **however**. While Mustafa was with his father, he was seized and executed.

Making concessions/ contrasting ideas	Showing results/ consequences	Emphasising difference

Task two

Read the following passage and use connecters to fill in the missing words.

This is a time when the Earth's woodlands are disappearing at an alarming rate. One of the world's poorest, most densely populated countries has, (a) . . . . . ., pioneered the first successful replanting of a tropical forest. There was, (b) . . . . . ., often the possibility of failure. Large areas were laid waste during the war years. (c) . . . . . ., there were large areas of grassland, which easily caught fire in the intense heat in the dry season. (d) . . . . . ., many young saplings were burnt in these fires. So, the scientists made a forest cover of strong, exotic trees. When these trees were tall enough, they planted the weaker young saplings. It has taken the Vietnamese more than a decade to bring back only a small number of species of trees. (e) . . . . . ., the recovering patch of the Ma Da woods stands out as a fragment of green.

Task three

(a) *Think of (or imagine) a famous person in history and then make notes about his/her life.*
(b) *Write a short passage connecting the notes together, after the style of Task one.*

First, we may use the syllabus to provide a
resumé. . . . Second, it can be the basis of
an agreed action. . . . Third, it will be
useful. . . .
Clearly the man is unaware of his true
motivation, and furthermore is likely to
make up other reasons for his action.

Connecters can be used to list ideas and events in a particular **order** in a sentence, to signal a **summary**, to introduce a **repetition** that **clarifies** a previous statement or idea, and to introduce **extra information**.

1. Order

The following example lists **ideas** – the reasons for having syllabuses:

> **First**, we may use the syllabus to provide a resumé. . . . **Second**, it can be the basis of an agreed action. . . . **Third**, it will be useful. . . .

The writer here is looking at the different ways in which something can be **viewed** and not in order of their importance. Often, however, the suggestion is that the first view is more important than the second or third. The order is in terms of **importance** if we use **Firstly . . ., Secondly . . .**, etc.

When we come to the end of the list, we use **connecters** such as **finally** or **lastly**. For example:

> Finally, the traditional four skills . . . provide another basis for syllabus design.

Making a list is one way of putting things in **order**, another is to show the **order in which things happened**. In this case, we use **First. . . . Then. . . . Finally. . . .** For example:

> **First**, the books were in a room at the front of the house; **then** they spread into the one next to it; and **finally** into what used to be the backyard.

Here, the writer is setting out the **order** in which the **changes were made** in his house as he bought more books. Such an ordering can also be expressed by using **To start with. . . . Then. . . . After that. . . .**

When we come to the end of the list, we use **connecters** such as **finally** or **lastly**. In both cases, these connecters usually come at the **beginning** of the sentence or clause.

2. Summary

When we come to the end of what we want to say or write about, we signal that we are about to make a **summary** of what we have said or come to a **conclusion** with phrases such as **to sum up** or **in conclusion**. For example:

> **To sum up**, there's no better car in its price range on the market.

These connecters come at the **beginning** of the sentence or paragraph.

3. Clarity

Sometimes, to make sure we have been understood, we repeat what we have said, but in another form. We can signal this by using a **connecter**. For example:

> **To put it another way**, is popularity a function of personality?

The writer is here making sure the reader has **understood** what he was talking about and has rephrased his question. Another way of signalling that you are doing this is to use the phrase **in other words**.

We also use **to put it another way** and **in other words** to rephrase what another person has said, especially when that person has been very hesitant about expressing an idea which is **unpleasant**. For example:

A: I'm sorry, but, you see, . . . it's not me, but it's difficult with you here. . . .

B: **In other words**, you want me to leave!

4. Extra information

Look at this example:

Clearly the man is unaware of his true motivation, and **furthermore** he is likely to make up reasons for his action.

With this type of connecter, the second clause **adds to the information** we have in the first. Other connecters expressing the same relationship are **also, in addition, besides, moreover**.

The **co-ordinating conjunctions** which express similar relationships are **and** and **not only . . . but also**.

Unit 5.6 Connecters 2 – TASKS

Task one

Read the following text, then fill in the missing words, using connecters from the following list:

Ordering (ideas): first, second, third, finally.
(narrative): first, then, next, finally.
Summing up: to sum up, in conclusion.
Making something clear: to put it another way, in other words.
Adding more: furthermore, moreover, also, in addition, besides.

The village we arrived at was on the edge of the estuary. (a) . . . . . . I got out of the car, (b) . . . . . . Soeprapto drove it into the shade under a tree, (c) . . . . . . he and the man got out. They looked a bit embarrassed as they came over to see me.

Soeprapto suggested that it would be interesting for me to look round the village. (d) . . . . . ., they didn't want me to go with them to meet the man's brother.

I nodded agreement. They seemed relieved and walked off.

Although the villagers seemed very busy, a large number of them found time to gather round the car and try to touch it. The little red car was creating a lot of lively amusement. The way the people approached the car was very orderly. (e) . . . . . . the person would give a casual, uninterested glance; (f) . . . . . . he would say something to a friend. (g) . . . . . . they would join hands and walk to the car. All the time they looked cautiously at me to see if I was becoming angry. (h) . . . . . ., when they were sure I was quite happy, the two of them would touch the car rather shyly and in a slightly frightened manner. They seemed to think that by touching the car, they might be arousing demons. Black magic was never far away in this part of Java.

Task two

(a) *Here are some instructions for repairing uneven legs on chairs. Using connecters for ordering, summing up or adding more, write a continuous description of what you have to do. (It doesn't matter if you do not know all the technical terms.)*

  (i) Trim a piece of wood to suit the shape of the leg.
 (ii) Drill pilot screw holes into both the chair leg and the wood block.
(iii) Screw the wood block into place.
 (iv) Fill the joint between the wood block and the leg with wood filler.
  (v) After the filler has set, rub it smooth.

(b) *Rewrite the following text, which tells you how to get rid of scorch marks on furniture, as a list of instructions like those in* (a) *above.*

First take a sharp knife to scrape away the mark completely. Then rub with fine glass paper. You will then need to apply transparent French polish. Furthermore, several applications will be necessary. Also you will need some more fine glass paper. Wait for the French polish to dry. Then smooth the area carefully. Finally apply metal polish to bring back the shine.

Task three

Set out some instructions for some work to be done as in (a) *above. Then rewrite the instructions as in* (b).

UNIT 5.7
SUBORDINATE CONJUNCTIONS 1: place, time, manner

When these trees gained sufficient height, the foresters planted several other species. More forests have been lost in Vietnam since the war ended than during it. Wherever you go in the north-west, you find signs of new growth.

There are many kinds of **subordinate clause**, and we have looked in detail at two: **conditional clauses** (see Units 2.35–2.39) and **relative clauses** (see Units 4.8–4.12). In this unit and Unit 5.8 we look at several other types.

Like **co-ordinating conjunctions** (see Unit 5.4) and **connecters** (see Units 5.5, 5.6), **subordinate conjunctions** signal the **relationship** between the two clauses they connect. The two clauses are **not equal**, however. The **subordinate clause** is always dependent on the main clause. It can come either before or after the main clause (see Unit 5.9).

Some **conjunctions** can introduce **subordinate clauses** of different types. **Since**, for example, introduces **time** clauses (see 1 below) and **reason** clauses (see Unit 5.8).

1. Place

Subordinate clauses expressing **place** are introduced by **where** or **wherever**. For example:
> **Wherever you go in the north-west**, you can see the signs of growth.

Where very often introduces a **relative clause** (see Unit 4.11).

2. Time

There are many aspects of **time** which **subordinate conjunctions** express. The examples below show their use to describe an event that occurred at a **particular point** in time, two events that occurred at the **same time**, and looking back to a **particular time** in the **past**.

Look at this example:
> **When the strong trees gained sufficient height**, the foresters planted several other species.

Here, the writer is telling us the **particular point in time** when something happened. Other conjunctions which express this relationship are **as, after, until, before, as soon as**.

Look at these examples:
> The Prime Minister will step forward **as the Queen leaves the stand**.
> **After the war ended in 1975**, Vietnamese scientists attempted to replant several species of trees.

Don't wait **until it's too late.**
With Xerox, she'll have the reports ready, **before the first person has arrived.**
Come **as soon as you can.**

WARNING BOX

The **future** tense is **never** used after these conjunctions. We say:
> The work will be finished, **when you get back.**

We **do not say:**
> *when you will get back.

In the next example, the two events are happening **at the same time:**
> **While Curie worked on her research,** others were trying to seek a more simple solution.

As can also be used to express this relationship between the clauses.

When we are looking back to a **particular time** in the **past** we can use **since**. For example:
> More forests have been lost in Vietnam **since the war ended** than during it.

Here the reference is to a **specific point in time** that is **past**.

3. Manner

Subordinate clauses can describe **how** something happened or was done. They are introduced by **as** or **as if**. **As** compares something which is **real**, and is used in the same way that **like** is used to compare two **lexical** items. For example:
> He worked hard, **as his father had done all his life.**

We can assume it is a **fact** that his father worked hard all his life.

As if makes the comparison with something **unreal**. For example:
> He ran the race, **as if it was the last he would ever run.**
> He was very tired and looked **as if he hadn't slept well.**

There is no suggestion that this will be the last race he will run, or, in the second example, that he hadn't slept well. In fact, the suggestion is the opposite, i.e. he did sleep well, but he looks tired, as if he hadn't.

4. Summary

Use	Subordinate conjunction
Time Place Manner	when, as, after, since, until, before, as soon as, while. where, wherever. as, as if.

Unit 5.7 Subordinate conjunctions 1 – TASKS

Task one

Below are several parts of sentences. Connect as many as you can by using one of the subordinate conjunctions from the following list. Some examples have been written for you.

Examples:

As air-traffic increases in South-East England, a major catastrophe seems possible in Britain.

When you see this sign, you are sure of a friendly welcome.

Time: **when, as, after, since, until, before, as soon as, while.**
Place: **where, wherever.**
Manner: **as, as if.**

air-traffic increases in South-East England
she looked at her opponent directly
buy now
you'll find the meal has been prepared
businessmen throughout Europe are re-examining their positions
there is a higher growth in industry
you do anything else
she knew she would win
you like it
you see this sign
open this letter
prices are still at last year's level
there are higher taxes
1992 approaches
you are sure of a friendly welcome
a major catastrophe seems possible in Britain

Task two

Read the following text and fill in the missing words, using the appropriate conjunctions from the list in Task one.

David Lewis has just been sacked as the Managing Director of Poseur. It seemed to have happened very suddenly, (a) ...... the rest of the board had been holding conspiracy meetings at midnight. (b) ...... he took over the company in 1980, Lewis has made Poseur one of the big names in High Street. (c) ...... you go throughout Britain, you will find a Poseur store or one of its subsidiaries such as Curtains. It seemed at one time that (d) ...... one shop had been opened, negotiations were being finalised to take over another. (e) ...... there was a town without a Poseur, Lewis would bring his team to look over the place.

(f) . . . . . . he came on the scene, the fashion business had gone into decline. After the swinging entrepreneurs of the 1960s had retired to the country, clothes seemed to lose their attraction, except for chic punk. Lewis changed all that. (g) . . . . . . he came along, Poseur was an uninteresting, down-market tailors. Lewis transformed it, (h) . . . . . . he did with so many others later on. We shall miss him; but we are sure it will only a temporary set-back for him. (j) . . . . . . there's an empty shop for sale, David Lewis will soon be on his way there.

Task three

Think of a person who has been in the news recently and write a report about them, similar to the one in Task two.

UNIT 5.8
SUBORDINATE CONJUNCTIONS 2:
concession, contrast, cause and effect, result, purpose

He may respond to questions, even though he is still asleep.
. . . in Britain 'syllabus' refers to the content . . . whereas 'curriculum' refers to the totality of what is to be taught.
He wants things to be neutral, because he does not want people to impose their ideas.

1. Concession

Even though forms a relationship between clauses similar to that formed by **however** and **nevertheless** (see Unit 5.5). We use **even though** when the main action is something which appears **unlikely**, given the situation in the subordinate clause.

Look at this example:
He may respond to questions, **even though he is still asleep**.
Here, the writer is talking about what **might** happen when someone is walking in their sleep. Other conjunctions which can be used to express this idea are **though** and **although**.

WARNING BOX

> **Even though cannot** be shortened to **even**. It is **wrong** to say:
> *He may respond to questions, *even he is* still asleep.

2. Contrast

Contrast clauses are similar to **concession** clauses. They usually point out the **differences** between two situations. We can use **whereas, while** or **although** to introduce them. For example:
. . . in Britain, 'syllabus' refers to the content . . . **whereas 'curriculum' refers to the totality of what is to be taught**.
Hirst refers to the 'programme of activities', **while Kerr refers to the activities**.

3. Cause and effect/reason

Cause and effect and **reason** clauses answer the question WHY? We can use the conjunctions **because, since, as** and **for** to introduce them. For example:
He wants things to be neutral, **because he doesn't want people to impose their ideas**.
The writers did not speak **since they scarcely knew each other**.

4. Result

Result clauses tell us the **result** of something.

Look at this example:
The director was **so** moved **that he promised his support**.
Here, **so** and **that** are separated and surround the word that affects the result. This is often an **adjective** or **adverb**. When it is a **noun**, we use **such a . . . that**. For example:
In 1960, President de Gaulle of France met Prime Minister Shastri of India. Mr Shastri was **such a small man that** President de Gaulle had to bend down to talk to him.

5. Purpose

Purpose clauses tell us the **purpose** for doing something. To introduce them we use **so that** or **in order that**. For example:

We took Katy home, **so that she could arrange her meeting.**

In clauses signalling **purpose, so that** are never separated.

6. Summary

Concession	Contrast	Cause & effect	Result	Purpose
even though though although	whereas while	because since as for	so . . . that such a . . . that	so that in order that

Unit 5.8 Subordinate conjunctions 2 – TASKS

Task one

Using subordinate conjunctions from the following list, make as many sentences as you can by linking the clauses below. Some examples have been written for you.

Examples:

Although it can be very harmful, people judge the success of a holiday by the sun-tan.

Whereas it once was considered the sign of people who did dirty, physical jobs, nowadays you must have a tan.

Concession: **even though, though, although.**
Contrast: **whereas, while.**
Cause and effect: **because, since, as, for.**
Result: **so . . . that, such a . . . that.**
Purpose: **so that, in order that.**

people judge the success of a holiday by the suntan
suntan is now considered beautiful
the British insist on going out in the hot sun
it can be very harmful
people try many methods to protect themselves from the sun
nowadays you must have a tan
it can be very painful
it was once considered the sign of people who did dirty, physical jobs
British people lie out in the mid-day sun
the only real protection is to avoid the sun altogether
people get wrinkles in their skin at a young age
some cosmetics are packed in exotic bottles
there are now many tanning cosmetics
they may not be good for you
with the sun, the skin dries
in the nineteenth century, 'pale and interesting' was fashionable
it won't show for twenty years
with fast planes, it is more dangerous than before
the skin can react to the sun slowly

Task two

Read the following text and fill in the missing words with subordinate conjunctions chosen from the list in Task one.

(a) . . . . . . only a few years ago the two major powers in the world wouldn't talk to each other, their leaders now seem unable to keep apart. (b) . . . . . . there is still a lot which divides them ideologically, they both feel that there is more that unites them (c) ...... the safety of the world is at stake. Before their meetings, the threat to world peace was (d) ...... strong (d) ...... nobody felt there was any chance of a real and lasting peace. Their meetings began (e) ...... such fears could be dispelled. Even so, few people thought these meetings would get very far, (f) ...... there was too much distrust on both sides. All that has changed (g) ...... two people have started to talk to each other. (h) ...... there can be few who expect that soon there will be no more wars, there are many who now feel that peace has a chance. (j) ...... the momentum is maintained, all governments should review their policies and look for similarities in their beliefs rather than stress the differences, (k) ...... this will be hard for many for them. (l) ...... there is still much to do, let us start as soon as possible.

Task three

Comment on a recent piece of news in the same way as the text in Task two.

UNIT 5.9
TOPICALISATION

For me, a glass of Veuve Cliquot says
summer. It conjures up visions of . . .
cloudless skies and long warm evenings.
The Cliquot label even looks summery.

Topicalisation is about how we organise our messages to **focus** the attention of the listener or reader. In written discourse, this can mean that we change the neutral order of a sentence – subject–verb–object (see Units 1.3 and 1.4). This is also frequently the case with spoken discourse. With spoken discourse, however, we are also able to make use of such features as pitch, movement and stress.

Look at these examples from two advertisements:
> (a) **For me**, a glass of Veuve Cliquot says summer.
> *(Advertisement for Veuve Cliquot wine.)*
> (b) **I**'m a great believer in instant technology
> *(Advertisement for Polaroid cameras.)*

In both of these advertisements, the advertisers have used a famous personality to advertise the products. In (a), the actor Paul Eddington, who at the time was the most popular actor in Britain, talks about Veuve Cliquot. In (b) Eddy Shah, who at the time was associated with introducing modern technology into newspaper production, is talking about Polaroid cameras. In both cases, the advertiser wants the reader to identify with the personality, and so in both cases, the **focus** is on the person speaking. In (b) this is done through the conventional sentence structure – subject–verb–object. **I** is at the beginning and is the **topic** of the sentence.

In (a), however, the speaker has had to reconstruct the sentence, so that reference to himself comes at the beginning. The neutral sentence order would have the adverbial phrase at the end of the sentence (see Unit 1.4):

A glass of Veuve Cliquot says summer **for me**.

By transferring **for me** to the beginning of the sentence, the speaker becomes the **topic** of the sentence and thus its **focus**.

Sentences are divided into two parts: **theme** and **rheme**. The **theme** is at the beginning and tells the listener/reader what the sentence is about; the **rheme** tells us **more** about the theme. You can see this in the following chart:

Theme	Rheme
For me	a glass of Veuve Cliquot says summer.
I	'm a great believer in instant technology.

In many cases, the **theme/topic** is also the grammatical **subject** of the sentence.

Now look at this advertisement:
> **In twelve weeks**, you could be speaking a new language with Linguaphone's help.

Here, the reader's attention is drawn to the short **time** it will take to speak a new language.

Compare this with the following possible alternative versions:

With Linguaphone's help, you could be speaking a new language in twelve weeks.

You could be speaking a new language in twelve weeks with Linguaphone's help.

Shifting the **prepositional phrase** is only one way of high-lighting special information in the sentence.

Look again at the two newspaper reports in Unit 2.24. They are both discussing the same incident but, by the use of the **passive**, the **focus** has been shifted from the police action to the criminal in the second extract. In this case the sentence **object** in the first extract has been raised to the **subject** in the second.

Sentences do not operate in isolation. They are part of a continuing discourse – spoken or written – and although the **focus** may be different in each sentence, the speaker's or writer's choice will be affected by what has gone before.

Look at the whole paragraph for the wine advertisement:

For me a glass of Veuve Cliquot says summer. It conjures up visions of . . . cloudless skies and long warm evenings. The Cliquot label even looks summery . . .

After the first sentence, the writer has chosen to **focus** on the **name of the wine**. It is this that links the sentences in the paragraph together.

There is a choice available to the writer. The rest of the paragraph could have focused on the personality, or it could have focused on **summer**. For example:

For me a glass of Veuve Cliquot says summer. **Visions of** . . . cloudless skies and long warm evenings **are conjured up**.

In this case, however, although it would have been acceptable, the **focus** on the **wine** would have been lost.

Topic is another way of linking the parts of a discourse together. In the original paragraph, while the two themes **(Veuve Cliquot** and **summer)** are maintained, the **topic** has shifted from the **personality** to the glass of wine, to the bottle.

This is not the complete answer. We have to bear in mind the **context** of the event. Sometimes people talking together share a knowledge about the topic they are talking about which is not available to the casual listener, so that the conversation seems absurd. For example:

A: Were there any copies left?
B: It's at four o'clock after lunch.
A: Oh! Leave a note on my desk then.

Although to the outsider this conversation seems bizarre, the two people involved knew what it was about and so left out certain pieces of information and changed topics with abandon. In fact, they were two university lecturers talking about some handouts that one had given to the other for a comprehension exercise.

Unit 5.9 Topicalisation – TASKS

Task one

Find five advertisements and discuss how the advertiser has focused the information. What reasons can you give for the sentence topic that has been chosen?

Task two

(a) *Think of an event that has been in the news recently. The event can be international, national (your home country) or local (the place where you live). Make notes on what you think are the important features of the event.*

(b) *Make notes on your own attitude to the event.*

(c) *Write your own report on the event.*

(d) *Underline the focus in each sentence and discuss how you shifted the topic.*

(e) *Consider how far your report reflects the points you made in (a) and (b).*

Appendices

APPENDIX 1:
THE ZERO ARTICLE

In the following charts, the left column lists common expressions that **do not have any article** or, as it is sometimes said, use **zero article**. The right column lists examples of the same words in other contexts when they **do have an article**.

With zero article (idiomatic use)	With an article (normal use)
Institutions of life and society	
be in / go to { bed	Don't sit on the bed.
class	The class starts at 2.00
hospital *(British English, not American)*	The hospital is near the prison/jail.
prison, jail	
town	The town is very old.
be at school	We visited the school.
go to sea	He sat by the sea and dreamed.
be in/be at church	They are building a new church in the town.
go to { college	The college was opened last year.
university *(British English, not American)*	The university is outside the city.
live on/off campus	It has quite a large campus.
get out of bed	
in/out of court (of law)	The court is sitting this month.

With zero article (idiomatic use)	With an article (normal use)
Means of transport and communication	

travel leave come go	} by {	bicycle bus car boat ship train plane	She bought a bicycle. Take the blue bus. You could win a car. We built a boat. The ship sails at noon. The train left at 1.00. The plane is delayed.
communicate/ communication	} by {	radio telephone telex/fax post (*British*) mail (*American*) satellite	Turn on the radio. May I use the telephone? He sent a telex. The post has arrived. Has the mail come? You can't see the satellite.

With zero article (idiomatic use)		With an article (normal use)
Times of day and night		
at	{ dawn/daybreak sunrise/sunup sunset/sundown noon/midnight dusk/twilight	Let's watch the dawn. The sunrise was lovely. He's watching the sunset. I'm going in the afternoon. It's hard to see in the twilight.
at/by before after all	night morning/noon/evening dark/nightfall/midnight day/night/week/year	I woke up in the night. In the evening we watched a film. Cats can't see in the dark. It will take him a week to do the work.

With zero article (idiomatic use)	With an article (normal use)
Seasons	

The article is usually omitted when we speak of seasons generally but not when we refer to a particular year.

in	(the) spring/summer/winter/autumn. (**fall** *in American has* **the**)	The summer of 1985 was very cold.

With zero article (idiomatic use)		With an article (normal use)
Meals		
come for ⎫	⎧ breakfast	They serve a good breakfast.
have ⎪	⎪ lunch/dinner	The lunch was terrible.
before ⎬	⎨ tea	They ordered a large tea.
after ⎪	⎪ supper	There was a cold supper.
at/for ⎭	⎩ brunch/drinks/cocktails	The drinks weren't very cold.

The article is usually omitted when we refer to **meals** as a **routine** or social institution but not when we refer to **one particular** meal. For example:

We always have dinner at 7.30
   but
I had a huge dinner yesterday.

Illnesses

We do not use articles with most **illnesses** such as diabetes, pneumonia, influenza. Some people, however, still use **the** with such common infectious diseases as (the) flu, (the) measles, (the) mumps, (the) chicken pox and with the condition (the) hiccups.

Some **conditions** require the indefinite article, **a**. For example:

a cold, a temperature, a fever, a headache.

Many **names** do not have an article. These names include **personal names, geographical names** and names connected with certain **times of the year**. (See Appendix 2 for examples of names that take **the**).

Personal names

Personal names – a first or Christian name, a surname or both first and surname, with or without a title such as Dr, Mr, Mrs, Miss or Ms – have no article before the names. For example:

Anne Smith;
Ms Anne Smith;
Dr Anne Smith;
Mr Paul Smith;
Professor Simon Evans;
Miss Anita Peabody;
President Kennedy;
Captain Lewis;
Chief Inspector Johnson.

If we use a surname in the **plural** to refer to a married **couple** or to a whole **family**, then we use **the**. For example:

The Smiths (Dr Anne Smith and her husband, Mr Paul Smith, and their children.)

Geographical names

No article is used before **continents** or **countries.** For example:

North/South America, Europe, Southeast Asia, Africa.
Canada, England, Scotland, Australia, Zimbabwe.

The is used with names ending with a **compass point.** For example:

The Middle East, the Southeast, the Northwest, etc.

The is sometimes used for a few countries such as **The** Sudan and **The** Lebanon, but this use is less common now. (See Appendix 2 for uses of **the** with plural geographical names.)

No article is used before **cities, lakes** and **mountains** (see Appendix 2 for the use of **the** with mountain ranges). For example:

London, Penang, Ipoh, Asunción, Naples.

Lake Michigan, Lake Titicaca, Lake Windermere.

Everest, Ararat, Mont Blanc.

The article is normally omitted with names of **streets, buildings, airports, cathedrals, stations, parks**. For example:

Oxford Street, Buckingham Palace, Changi Airport, Canterbury Cathedral, Euston Station, Kew Gardens, Park Avenue, Reading Gaol, Schipol Airport, St Mary's Church, Waterloo Station, Windsor Safari Park.

May/June 1988

ACADEMIC staff threatened with compulsory redundancies at Lancaster University say they are prepared to fight their battle through the courts.

SPRING/SUMMER

PUNCH
WEEKLY

Temporal names

We do not use an article when we refer to names of **holidays** or **festivals** or **days** of the week and **months** of the year or **years** when we want to refer to the period as a time in the **calendar**. For example:

Ramadan, Christmas, New Year's Day, Dominion Day, Passover, Easter, Chinese New Year, ANZAC Day.

Monday to Friday, January to December.

1702 (seventeen-oh-two), 1814 (eighteen fourteen), 1954 (nineteen fifty-four), 1975 (nineteen seventy-five), 1989 (nineteen eighty-nine).

However, when we refer to a ten-year period or a decade, **the** is used with the **plural**. For example:

the 1900s (the nineteen hundreds), the '30s (the thirties), the '50s (the fifties).

A can be used with days of the week when no particular day is referred to. For example:

I left Santos on a Tuesday.

You arrive on a Wednesday.

Days of the week can have a plural, but **months** of the year do not have a plural. For example:

Lots of people hate Mondays.

The shops are closed on Wednesdays.

APPENDIX 2:
THE WITH PLURAL NOUN PHRASES

The is used with plural nouns or noun phrases to refer to a whole class of people in two special cases that refer to groups of people.

1. National/ethnic groups

The is used with nouns of nationality that refer generally to a whole group of people of a **nationality** or **ethnic group**. For example:
> the Americans, the Arabs, the Australians, the Asians, the Belgians, the Brazilians, the Canadians, the Chinese, the Danes/Danish, the French, the Finns/Finnish, the Germans, the Indians, the Peruvians, the Saudi Arabians, the Swedes/Swedish, the Swiss.

When the nationality nouns end in **-sh** or **-ch** you must use **the**. For example:
> **the Spanish**;
> **the Dutch**.

Nationality nouns with **-sh** and **-ch** endings can also be used as **adjectives**. For example:
> **Welsh** rugby;
> **Swedish** furniture.

With nationality nouns ending in **-s, the** is optional: you can omit it if you prefer. For example:
> **(The) Argentinians** are very keen on football.

When **-s** nouns are used as adjectives, then they drop the final **-s**. For example:
> Traditional Indonesian puppet performances are very popular with both tourist and **(the) Indonesians**.

2. General groups

The second special case is the use of **the** with an adjective to refer to a **whole group of people**. For example:
> **the** unemployed;
> **the** poor/rich;
> **the** blind/deaf.

Certain **names** are always preceded by **the**, as follows:

Plural names in general:
> **the** Netherlands;
> **the** United States;
> **the** USSR;
> **the** Smiths.

Geographical names:

Mountain ranges (plural and singular)
    the Alps;
    the Himalayas;
    the Andes.
    the Sierra Nevada;
    the Caucasus.
(*Mountain peaks,* on the other hand, are not preceded by **the**):
    Pike's Peak, Everest, Annapurna.

Groups of islands:
    the Bahamas;
    the Canaries.

Rivers:
    the Thames;
    the Danube.

Oceans and seas:
    the Pacific (Ocean);
    the Baltic (Sea).

Canals:
    the Suez Canal;
    the Panama Canal.

Other geographical features followed by an **of** *phrase:*
    the Straits of Malacca;
    the Gulf of Mexico;
    the Isle of Man.

Public institutions and facilities:

Government:
    the Kremlin;
    the Senate;
    the Department of Education.

Universities (only when they include an **of** phrase):
> **the** University **of** Lancaster (*but* Lancaster University);
> **the** University **of** Malaya (*but* Oxford University, McGill University, Harvard University).

Museums, libraries, etc.:
> **the** British Museum;
> **the** National Library;
> **the** BBC.

Hotels:
> **The** Ritz;
> **The** Merlin Hotel.

Theatres, cinemas, clubs, etc.:
> **the** Royal Exchange;
> **the** Odeon;
> **the** Yacht Club.

All newspapers and some journals:
> *The Independent;*
> *The Guardian;*
> *The ESPecialist;*
> *The Economist.*

The is part of the name of these newspapers and periodicals and is usually spelt with a capital letter. If, however, there is another determiner before the name, then **the** is omitted. For example:
> Have you seen **my** *Economist?*
> Where is **today's** *Guardian?*
> I'd like **a** *Times* and **a** *Telegraph* please.

Most magazines and many journals, however, have no **the**. For example:
> *Time, Nature, TESOL Quarterly, Newsweek, Good Housekeeping, Reader's Digest.*

APPENDIX 3:
MULTI-WORD VERBS

Multi-word or **phrasal verbs** can be very difficult to learn. This is because you cannot always understand what they mean, even if you understand what each of the words means. For example, **to look up** might mean **to look up at the sky** but it more often means to consult a reference book and find out the meaning of something or to contact someone. For example:

She **looked up** the word 'phrasal' in the dictionary.

He **looked up** his friends when he went to Chicago.

To look up can, therefore, have both a **literal** meaning and a **non-literal** meaning.

There are a great many **multi-word verbs** that have a **non-literal** meaning and more are being coined all the time. They are extremely common in spoken or colloquial English and it is only by listening to people speaking English, listening to the radio or watching television programmes that you will be able to increase the number of **multi-word verbs** that you can understand and use.

The following list defines some of the most common **multi-word verbs** with **non-literal** meanings and also gives some rules for **word order** with these verbs.

1. Verb + adverb (without an object)
This is a type of **intransitive** verb and has **no object.**

The new students are **getting on** very well. *(Settling down and succeeding in their work.)*

The Boeing 747 **took off**. *(Left the ground and flew into the air.)*

2. Verb + adverb + object
This is a type of **transitive** verb and has an **object.**

It's impossible to **make out** what he wants. *(Understand.)*

Have you **handed in** your application yet? *(Submitted.)*

The object can be either a noun or noun phrase or a pronoun. If the object is a **noun** or **noun phrase**, it can come either at the **end** of the **multi-word verb** or **between** the verb and the adverb:

Have you handed in your application yet?

Have you handed your application in yet?

If the object is a **pronoun**, then it must come **between** the verb and the adverb:

Have you **handed** it **in** yet?

3. Verb + preposition + object
With this type of phrase, the **object**, whether it is a **noun** or a **pronoun**, must come **after the preposition**:

Some people can't **cope with** very loud music. *(Accept or endure it.)*

Some common **prepositions** in these **multi-word verbs** are:

across, after, for, into, over, past.

4. Verb + adverb + preposition

These verbs always have a **non-literal** meaning. Like type **3**, the **object** always comes **after the preposition**:

> I'm not going to **put up with** his bad temper any longer. *(Accept or tolerate.)*

Examples

Type 1

She's very **run down**.	*(Tired or ill.)*
The prices of houses are still **going up**.	*(Rising.)*
Don't **stay up** too late.	*(Remain out of bed.)*
The pain will soon **wear off**.	*(Gradually disappear.)*

Type 2

We can **put up** your cousin for the week end. ⎫
We can **put** your cousin **up** for the week end. ⎬ *(Provide a bed and food.)*
We can **put** her **up** for the week end. ⎭

They **called off** the meeting. ⎫
They **called** the meeting **off**. ⎬ *(Cancelled.)*
They **called** it **off**. ⎭

He **brought up** the children on his own. ⎫
He **brought** the children **up** on his own. ⎬ *(Took care of them until they were adults.)*
He **brought** them **up** on his own. ⎭

I can't **work out** why he said that. ⎫
I can't **work** it **out**. ⎬ *(Understand.)*

Type 3

Anne **looked after** my cat when I was in India. ⎫
Anne **looked after** her/it when I was in India. ⎬ *(Fed and took care of.)*

The police **are looking into** the matter. ⎫
The police **are looking into** it. ⎬ *(Investigating.)*

John **will see about** booking the tickets. ⎫
John **will see about** it. ⎬ *(Will make arrangements.)*

I **came across** a photograph of my father in
an old magazine. ⎫
I **came across** it in an old magazine. ⎬ *(Found by chance.)*

Type 4

Trish **is looking forward** to getting a good job. ⎫
Trish **is looking forward to** it. ⎬ *(Anticipating with pleasure.)*

You'll have to **get down to** some serious study this term. ⎫
You'll have to **get down to** it this term. ⎬ *(Start to work seriously on.)*

John **will get round/around to** the work as soon as he can. ⎫
John **will get round/around to** it as soon as he can. ⎬ *(Find time to do it.)*

Women should **stand up for** their rights. ⎫
Women should **stand up for** them. ⎬ *(Defend and advocate.)*

APPENDIX 4:
IRREGULAR VERBS

There are over 150 verbs in English which do not form the **Past** and the **past participle** by adding **-ed** to the stem or infinitive form. However, many of these verbs are rarely used and occur only in literary or older texts. The following chart, therefore, contains only the words that are in **common use**.

There is a group of verbs that have two forms for the **Past** and the **past participle**. Generally, in **British** English, the **irregular** form is used but in **American** English the **regular** form is more usual.

Present Simple/infinitive	Past Simple	Past participle
Verbs with both regular ~~and irregular forms~~		
	British/U.S.	British/U.S.
burn	burnt/burned	burnt/burned
dream	dreamt/dreamed	dreamt/dreamed
lean	leant/leaned	leant/leaned
learn	learnt/learned	learnt/learned
smell	smelt/smelled	smelt/smelled
spell	spelt/spelled	spelt/spelled
spill	spilt/spilled	spilt/spilled
spoil	spoilt/spoiled	spoilt/spoiled
Verbs with irregular forms		
be	was/were	been
beat	beat	beaten
become	became	become
begin	began	begun
bend	bent	bent
bet	bet	bet
bite	bit	bitten
blow	blew	blown
break	broke	broken
breed	bred	bred
bring	brought	brought
broadcast	broadcast	broadcast
build	built	built
burst	burst	burst

Present Simple/infinitive	Past Simple	Past participle
Verbs with irregular forms *(continued)*		
buy	bought	bought
catch	caught	caught
choose	chose	chosen
come	came	come
cost	cost	cost
cut	cut	cut
deal	dealt	dealt
dig	dug	dug
do	did	done
draw	drew	drawn
drink	drank	drunk
drive	drove	driven
eat	ate	eaten
fall	fell	fallen
feed	fed	fed
feel	felt	felt
fight	fought	fought
find	found	found
fly	flew	flown
forbid	forbade	forbidden
forget	forgot	forgotten
forgive	forgave	forgiven
freeze	froze	frozen
get	got	got *(British)*
get	got	gotten *(American)*
give	gave	given
go	went	gone/been
grind	ground	ground
grow	grew	grown
hang	hung	hung *(for objects)*
hang	hanged	hanged *(for people)*
have	had	had
hear	heard	heard
hide	hid	hidden
hit	hit	hit
hold	held	held
hurt	hurt	hurt
keep	kept	kept
know	knew	known
lay	laid	laid
lead	led	led
leave	left	left

Present Simple/infinitive	Past Simple	Past participle

Verbs with irregular forms *(continued)*

lend	lent	lent
let	let	let
lie	lay	lain
light	lit/lighted	lit/lighted
lose	lost	lost
make	made	made
mean	meant	meant
meet	met	met
pay	paid	paid
put	put	put
read	read	read
ride	rode	ridden
ring	rang	rung
rise	rose	risen
run	ran	run
say	said	said
see	saw	seen
seek	sought	sought
sell	sold	sold
send	sent	sent
set	set	set
sew	sewed	sewn/sewed
shake	shook	shaken
shine	shone	shone
shoot	shot	shot
show	showed	shown
shrink	shrank	shrunk
shut	shut	shut
sing	sang	sung
sink	sank	sunk
sit	sat	sat
sleep	slept	slept
slide	slid	slid
speak	spoke	spoken
speed	sped/speeded	sped/speeded
spend	spent	spent
split	split	split
spread	spread	spread
spring	sprang	sprung
stand	stood	stood
steal	stole	stolen
stick	stuck	stuck

Present Simple/infinitive	Past Simple	Past participle
Verbs with irregular forms *(continued)*		
sting	stung	stung
strike	struck	struck
swear	swore	sworn
sweep	swept	swept
swim	swam	swum
swing	swung	swung
take	took	taken
teach	taught	taught
tear	tore	torn
tell	told	told
think	thought	thought
throw	threw	thrown
understand	understood	understood
wake	woke	woken
wear	worn	worn
weave	wove	woven
win	won	won
wind	wound	wound
write	wrote	written

Compound *verbs ending in* **irregular** *verbs form the* **Past** *and the* **past participle** *in the same way as the* **simple irregular** *verb:*

overcome	overcame	overcome
undertake	undertaken	undertook
upset	upset	upset

APPENDIX 5:
ADJECTIVES FOLLOWED BY PREPOSITIONS

There are no rules to govern the use of **prepositions**, especially when they follow **verbs** or **adjectives**. From the chart below you will see that some **adjectives** can be followed by different **prepositions** and that this affects their meaning and use.

Appendix 5 should be considered as a quick reference for the more commonly used **adjectives**; but there are very many more than are listed here, and you should refer to a good learners' dictionary. **Adjectives** which are derived from the **past participle** form of a verb, such as **surprised, interested, disappointed,** etc., are not included here and are listed in Unit 4.4.

Adjective + preposition	Example
Acceptable to	The contract was **acceptable to** all of those involved. *compromise*
Afraid of	Children are often **afraid of** the dark.
Ambitious for	Dick was very **ambitious for** his children. *eager or excited*
Angry about	Charles was **angry about** the way in which the new policy matter was handled.
Angry with	Jon is very **angry with** Gerry at the moment.
Capable of	Tony is very **capable of** forgetting the date of his children's birthdays.
Careful of	You should be very **careful of** promising to help. You may find there's a lot to do alone.
Close to	The castle is very **close to** the railway station. It's about a two-minute walk.
Conscious of	Robert is very **conscious of** the fact that Roger doesn't like him and his work.
Dependent on	Sandra is **dependent on** Michael for her job.
Different from/to	Pinter's latest play is very **different from/to** his earlier ones.
Envious of	Liz is very **envious of** Charles' success.
Expert at	The cat was **expert at** getting through its new door.
Familiar to	I couldn't remember her name, but her face was very **familiar to** me.

Adjective + preposition	Example
Famous for	Scotland is **famous for** its whisky.
Fond of	But she's also very **fond of** him.
Glad of	Edward was **glad of** extra money from the trip.
Good at	Mary was **good at** persuading people to do things for her.
Good for	Eating an apple a day is supposed to be **good for** you.
Grateful to	Bobby was very **grateful to** Sheila for lending him the money.
Happy with	They were very **happy with** the arrangements that had been made.
Impatient at	Joan was **impatient at** the thought of having to wait two hours for the plane.
Impatient for	Pamela was **impatient for** the film to come on television.
Impatient with	Now he is old, Paul gets **impatient with** the children.
Important for	It was very **important for** him to be at the meeting.
Important to	Although he said nothing during the meeting, it was **important to** the director that he was present.
Independent of	Although he worked at the university, he felt quite **independent of** the department.
Innocent of	The captain said he was **innocent of** any negligence.
Intent on	Marc is **intent on** becoming a soldier when he grows up.
Jealous of	Roy was **jealous of** the way Barry managed to organise his holiday in Senegal.
Kind of	It was **kind of** Jim to meet her.
Kind to	Elizabeth is very **kind to** animals.
Quick at	Lee is **quick at** understanding the main point of the argument.
Similar to	That decision is **similar to** the one we made at our meeting last week.
Sorry for	His mother was **sorry for** him, after he had tried so hard and still failed.
Successful in	Keith is very **successful in** his work.

ANSWER KEY

1.1 Task one

Transitive: receive; saves; invited; clean; own; takes.
Intransitive: went; wait; swam.
Intensive: was.

1.1 Task two

(a) is shivering; (b) have turned; (c) are walking; (d) is wearing; (e) seems; (f) is; (g) see; (h) traverses; (j) covered; (k) are tramping.

1.2 Task one

Modal auxiliary: must(n't).
Primary verb: was; don't; 've; don't; has been; were; had.
Lexical verb: born; brought; lived; was; left; worked; became; wrote; know; know; seen; want; married; died; married; became; wasn't; grown (up); said; marry; ignored.

1.2 Task two

(a) should consider *(modal auxiliary, lexical)*; (b) is *(lexical)*; (c) should rush *(modal auxiliary, lexical)*; (d) take *(lexical)*; (e) is *(lexical)*; (f) have *(lexical)*; (g) seems *(lexical)*; (h) take *(lexical)*; (j) is *(primary)*; (k) engineered *(lexical)*; (l) have *(lexical)*.

1.3 Task one

Finite: are not; are; have; cost; have.
Non-finite: offering; compared; built; displayed; interested; looking.

1.3 Task two

(a) Holding the reins, the jockey controls the horse.
(b) Hurt by the fall, she couldn't . . .
(c) Wanting a holiday in France, Mehdi has . . .
(d) Living in Madras, Balan often . . .
(e) Having been found out, Philby escaped . . .
(f) Given a computer as a present, she . . .
(g) Awarded the top prize, Malcolm decided . . .
(h) Seeing the house, Anne . . .
(j) Having been seen by a top Hollywood producer, she thought . . .
(k) Leaving the university, Esme had . . .

1.4 Task one

(a) They sold the house last week.
Last week they sold the house.
(b) The wedding was in June.
(c) Seamen have gathered at Dover from all over the country.
From all over the country, seamen have gathered at Dover.
Seamen have gathered from all over the country at Dover.
(d) Elizabeth Taylor has houses in many parts of the world.
(e) Alice doesn't live here any more.
(f) Spencer remained at Cookham for a few days.
Spencer remained for a few days at Cookham.
(g) He didn't like being on his own.
(h) He fell in love with Patricia two years later.
Two years later he fell in love with Patricia.
(j) Scottie played the bugle beautifully in the army.
In the army, Scottie played the bugle beautifully.
(k) Put the casserole into a warm oven.

1.4 Task two

(b) by the door; (g) at the gate for hours; (h) in the Great Hall.

1.5 Task one

(a) wrong; (b) right; (c) wrong; (d) wrong; (e) right; (f) wrong; (g) wrong; (h) right; (j) right;
(k) wrong.

2.2 Task one

(a) spells; is; stand out.
(b) One reason why the advertisers have used the Present Simple tense is to suggest that they are stating general truths or making statements of fact which everyone would agree with.

2.2 Task two

(a) (i) has; (ii) is; (iii) is; (iv) includes; (v) are.
(b) (i) eat; (ii) own; (iii) prefer; (iv) go; (v) buys/reads, buys/reads.

2.2 Task three

(a) do . . . eat/buy; (b) do . . . own; do . . . rent . . . live; (c) do . . . do; (d) are; (e) do . . . buy/read.

2.3 Task one

(a) are . . . operating; are planning; will determine; fly; are looking.
(b) Three Present Continuous forms.
(c) British Airways want to give an impression of urgency and to stress that they are definitely planning to employ new people. The use of this form also stresses that there is a definite time limit and that anyone who is qualified and interested should apply immediately.
(d) If they had used the Present Simple form, they would have been saying that employing people with the special skills they need is something they do all the time and there might not actually be any jobs available at the time of the advertisement. The use of the Present Perfect Form would mean that they have already employed people for the available jobs.

2.3 Task two

(a) (i) am standing; (ii) is shining; (iii) look; (iv) see; (v) is; (vi) is coming; (vii) is bringing; (viii) expect.
(b) Four -ing forms.
(c) look, see, is, expect should not have the Present Continuous form.

2.3 Task three

(a) talking; (b) planning; (c) having individual tutorials.

2.4 Task one

(a) 'having lunch' refers to an event.
(b) 'have' means to suffer from.
(c) statement of fact or opinion.
(d) expresses an action/activity.
(e) refers to an event.
(f) statement of fact.
(g) statement of fact.
(h) refers to an event/activity.

2.4 Task two

(a) does . . . look; is; is getting/gets; is sitting/sits; is having/has; looks;
(b) deal; says;
(c) need; looks; have;
(d) lives;
(e) come; says; do; see; am.

2.5 Task one

been	fell, fallen	left, left	sell, sold
became	feed, fed	lend, lent	sent, sent
begin, begun	feel, felt	let, let	show, showed
bet, bet	found, found	lit/lighted	shut, shut
bite, bit	forget, forgotten	lit/lighted	sat, sat
broke, broken	got, got (gotten in US)	make, made	speak, spoken
bring, brought	give, gave	meant, meant	spent, spent
buy, bought	go, gone	meet, met	stand, stood
choose, chosen	had, had	pay, paid	take, taken
came, come	hear, heard	put, put	taught, taught
cost, cost	hide, hidden	read, read	tell, told
cut, cut	hit, hit	ring, rung	thought, thought
did, done	hold, held	ran, run	understand,
drew, drawn	kept, kept	say, said	understood
drive, driven	know, known	saw, seen	write, written
eat, ate	lead, led		

2.5 Task two

(a) *Group 1:* fly, be, begin, bite, break, choose, do, draw, drive, fall, forget, get (in USA), give, go, know, ring, see, take, write.
    Group 2: buy, bring, feed, find, get (in UK), have, hear, hold, keep, lead, leave, lend, light, lose, make, mean, meet, pay, read (same form but different pronunciation), say, sell, send, stand, teach, tell, think, understand.

Group 3: bet, cost, cut, hit, let, put.
(b) become, run, come.
(c) Group 2.

2.6 Task one
(a) loves, preferred, is, made, took, got, notice, dates, dates, are.
(b) shows, is, can, is.
(c) had, were, were, did, bumped, knocked, sued, were.
(d) lost, ruled.

2.6 Task two
  (i) He may no longer be depressed; he is probably still depressed.
 (ii) She means that it rained some time in the past; it is raining now.
(iii) The office is on Main Street; the office may still be on Main Street or it may have moved.

2.6 Task three
15 June

Dear Edward

I **was** really excited **when I wrote this letter** because I **had** just booked my tickets for my trip to Australia. I **left on 15 January** and **was** in Sydney for two weeks. I **stayed** with two old friends, Jim and Cathy, who have a flat on Sydney Harbour and they **took** me to all the places of interest in and around Sydney like the Opera House, Bondi Beach and even on a trip into some of the parks and the country outside Sydney. It **was** summer **then** in Australia so I **got** lots of sun.

It **was** a long way to go from London and I only **had** two weeks' holiday but if I **didn't go** this year I **might never go** at all. So I just **had** to be content with two weeks and do as much as possible while I **was** there.

You said in your letter that your final exams **were** at the beginning of February. I hope you **did** well in them and that you **got** a chance to take a holiday before you **started** your new job at the end of February.

You must write and tell me all about the job, your new flat and everything as soon as you are settled in.

Write and give me all your news.

Lots of love

2.7 Task one
(a) She was talking to her sister on the phone.
(b) Jim was putting the children to bed.
(c) They were watching the match on television.
(d) We were sitting in the garden.
(e) The neighbours were making such a lot of noise.
(f) I was writing a letter to you.

2.7 Task two
(a) working in the garden/gardening;
(b) having a bath/shower/swim;

(c) getting dressed/undressed;
(d) swimming/sunbathing.
(e) cooking/baking/painting;
(f) studying/doing research/preparing to teach a class;
(g) sleeping/just going to bed/just getting up/relaxing at home;
(h) sunbathing/getting dressed or undressed/training;
(j) doing some electrical work/doing some carpentry;
(k) painting;
(l) taking the dog for a walk/washing the dog/playing with the dog;
(m) listening to music/listening to a lecture/practising English;
(n) painting her nails/toenails/getting ready to go out;
(p) making a cup of tea;
(q) talking on the phone.

2.9 Task one

(a) Zurbriggen . . . (past); World cities . . . (future); Troops . . . (future); BAe . . . (past); Gadafy . . . (future); Whitbread . . . (future); Bell . . . (past).
(b) Zurbriggen has kept World Cup.
World's cities will tackle urban health problems at pioneering Liverpool conference.
Troops will guard civilian gaols.
BAe has called for shake-up of airbus.
Gadafy will withdraw troops.
Whitbread will axe 300 London jobs.
Bell has sold television stations.

2.9 Task two

(a) (i) will begin; will become. (ii) will begin; will spread. (iii) will become. (iv) will begin; will be.

2.9 Task three

(a) 3; (b) 2; (c) 1.

2.9 Task four

The Chancellor, HRH Princess Alexandra is to/will preside at a ceremony for the conferment of higher and honorary degrees on Thursday, 3 December. Sir Ronald Halstead is to/will receive the honorary degree of Doctor of Science, M. Maurice Lévy is to/will receive the honorary degree of Doctor of Science and Dr Derek Whiteside is to/will receive the honorary degree of Doctor of Letters.

2.10 Task one

I: are you going to do.
A: I'm going to do.
I: going to be.
A: is going to miss you; are going to feel.
I: going to see; is going to watch.

2.10 Task two

(a) Geoff
I'm going to buy a personal organiser . . .; I'm going to delegate . . .; I'm going to set aside regular times . . .; I'm going to hold fewer meetings.

The other members of the family precede their original statements with **I'm going to** in the same way as Geoff.

(b) Geoff is going to delegate more to his staff;
he's going to set aside regular times for meetings with his staff;
he's going to hold fewer meetings.

I'm going to start a time log;
I'm going to keep an up-to-date shopping list;
I'm going to make a schedule of household chores and assign something to everyone;
I'm going to get to the office half-an-hour earlier.

Anne is going to buy a filing cabinet to keep her notes in;
she's going to put her books in alphabetical order on the shelves;
she's going to practise typing for thirty minutes a day;

Charles is going to make a weekly study schedule;
he's going to do his homework every evening;
he's going to limit his phone calls to twenty minutes each;
he's going to get Anne to take the dog for a walk every other day.

2.10 Task three

(a) He's going to fall off;
(b) the tins are going to crash down;
(c) it's going to rain;
(d) I'm going to feed her;
(e) he's going to be arrested;
(f) he's going to write out a ticket;
(g) the cat's going to catch the mouse;
(h) she's going to answer the telephone.

2.11 Task one

(a) (She/He or I)'ll be meeting my friends for coffee; I'll be staying up all night writing essays; I'll be falling asleep in the Physics lecture; I'll be eating junk food; I'll be going to discos; I'll be photocopying articles; I'll be queuing for the launderette.
(b) If you wrote the answers using **be going to + infinitive**, this would suggest that they were making definite plans to do these things. In fact, they are simply saying that these things will happen as a matter of course, without planning.

2.11 Task two

300 million people will be watching the Grand National at Aintree where thirty-six horses will be running.

One million spectators will be watching the London Marathon. Over 25,000 runners will be taking part.

60,000 spectators will be watching the British versus Brazilian Schoolboys football game at Wembley Stadium.

20,000 viewers will be watching Severiano Ballesteros, Sandy Lyle and Greg Norman in the US Masters Golf Championship at Augusta, Georgia.

2.12 Task one

(a) (i) 17.27; (ii) 7.03; (iii) 2.24; (iv) 23.01; (v) 4.43.

2.12 Task two

S: 's/is; *J:* 's/is; 's/is; *S:* does (it) finish; *J:* starts; *S:* 's/is not finished (USA)/doesn't finish (GB); *J:* doesn't start; *S:* sounds; 's/is.

2.12 Task three

We cannot give you all the possible sentences but if you check with your partner or with another group you can probably find any mistakes that might have been made. If you're working on your own and do not have anyone to help you check your sentences, then check:

You used the **Present Simple** form in the clause that starts with the conditional or time conjunction.

You did not use any **will/shall** or **'ll** in the clauses that start with conditional or time conjunctions.

All of your sentences make sense.

2.13 Task one

(a) 'm having; 'm putting; 'm putting; 'm having; 'm having; 'm getting.
(b) **There'll be** is not in the Present Continuous form because it is a conclusion or result and is not one of the things she is planning to do. **Can** is a modal verb (see 2.25).
(c) Will/shall + infinitive.
(d) I think I'll have a party tomorrow night. I'll put all the living room furniture upstairs so there'll be lots of room for everyone to stand and move around. I'll put all the food on the dining-room table and everybody can just mill around and help themselves. I'll have a huge turkey, fried chicken, plenty of bread, salads and little things like pickled onions and olives and cheese. I'll have all the drinks on the sideboard. And I'll get an entertainer to play the guitar.

2.13 Task two

Dear Bill

Lisa and I are planning to completely re-do the kitchen next week. Perhaps you'd like to come and help with some of the work?

We're painting the kitchen ceiling and tiling the wall above the sink. We're painting the other walls and putting two new shelves on the wall over the counter. We're replacing the floor tiles, putting up new curtains and installing a new cooker.

It'll be hard work but it'll be great when we're finished.

All the best,

2.14 Task one

(a) Sorry, I'm about to start the dinner.
(b) Sorry, I'm about to wash the car.
(c) Sorry, I'm about to go to the cinema.
(d) Sorry, I'm about to hang up the clothes.
(e) Sorry, I'm about to take a shower.

2.15 Task one
(a) are to join forces.
(b) is to address.
(c) are to begin.
(d) is to transfer.
(e) is to become.

2.16 Task one
was going to buy; was going to delegate; was going to do.

2.17 Task one
(a) has worked; has given; has visited; has hosted; has made; started; led/have led.
(b) has been; has stolen.

2.17 Task two (suggested answers)
(a) have never owned one./haven't owned one for . . . years.
(b) has had very few complaints.
(c) he has never been there before./he hasn't been there for . . . years.
(d) have raised . . . of dollars.
(e) he has never made a film/directed a film with Elizabeth Taylor.

2.18 Task one
(a) renewed;
(b) has come, have been dumping, are;
(c) said, have been pressing, said;
(d) disagreed, has/has had, banned/has banned, have passed.

2.19 Task one
(a) When he had gathered the data on crime, he wrote a report.
(b) When she had taken an exam, she went on holiday.
(c) When they had saved enough money, they bought a video recorder.
(d) When she had arranged a loan, she went into business.
(e) When the team had won a gold medal, they were interviewed by the BBC.
(f) When he had learned to type, he went to university.
(g) When I had filled in the forms, I got a visa for Senegal.
(h) When he had consulted a mechanic, he bought a new car.
(j) When they had bought the house, they discovered serious faults.

2.19 Task two
has discovered; has been called; found; brought; had been shot; confirmed; was; had examined.

2.20 Task one
(a) The air traffic controllers had been striking for two weeks.
(b) I had been driving for ten hours.
(c) They had been experimenting for six years.
(d) They had been working for eighteen months.
(e) She had been saving for six months.

(f) He had been planning to go for three months.
(g) They had been writing it for eighteen months.
(h) He had been taking lessons for six months.
(j) He had been doing research for three years.
(k) He had been working for twenty-five years.

2.21 Task one

(a) By the year 2000 the world population will have doubled/will have reached 10 billion.
(b) By 1997 they will have been married for forty years.
(c) In/By 1998 he will have owned the house for ten years.
(d) In twelve months' time she will have saved £360.
(e) By the end of July she will have driven 620 miles.

2.22 Task one

(a) (i) She always works hard and is accustomed to the hard work.
     (ii) She worked hard in the past but now she doesn't work as hard as before.
(b) (i) They often eat fish for dinner and so they are accustomed to eating fish.
     (ii) There are two possible interpretations: In the past they ate fish for dinner but now they eat less fish OR the people [they] referred to are no longer together as a group – they eat separately possibly because they don't live together any longer.
(c) (i) In the past he lived on his own but now he lives with someone else.
     (ii) He has lived alone for some time and is accustomed to it.
(d) (i) In the past I drove a car but now I don't.
     (ii) I drive quite a lot and I am accustomed to driving.

2.23 Task one

(a) Stephen Spender's novel *The Temple* was unearthed by John Fuller at Texas University.
(b) Peaches can be bought there for 10p each.
(c) Jim was laughed at as he fell into the water.
(d) –.
(e) –.
(f) The cuckoo was heard very early this year.
(g) Cars can be parked in the street behind the hotel.
(h) Bookings cannot be accepted after 30 September.
(j) –.
(k) Princess Anne has been given the title of Princess Royal by (her mother) the Queen.

2.23 Task two

(a) The weathermen in general and the BBC's Mr Michael Fish in particular were cleared (by a report yesterday) of irresponsible forecasting before last October's storms in which ten people were killed and 15 million trees were destroyed across the south of England.
(b) A candidate in next week's election has been shot dead. Bombs were thrown and shots were fired at the candidate at close range. Next Wednesday's elections are being/will be boycotted by the main opposition parties.
(c) No extra staff were hired. Instead, a hundred workers were transferred from other duties and some of the workload was transferred to Liverpool.
(d) Two women politicians have been given new posts by Mrs Thatcher after the resignation of Lord Stoddart, following a heart attack. His job as Energy Spokesman has been taken by Baroness Nicol while Baroness Ewart-Biggs has been made a Whip.

2.24 Task one

(a) Hilary climbed it in 1953.
(b) It was designed by Adam.
(c) His secretary always bought every newspaper.
(d) Prayers were said by the headteacher.
(e) The other car was driven by somebody who was drunk.

2.24 Task two

Nick had been followed by the police all day. He was seen leaving his flat at 7.30 in the morning, taking a bus to Regent Street and entering the airline office by a side door. He came out again at 1.00 and was tailed to the language school where he usually worked. He stayed in the school until 8.00 that evening and then went with Maria in her car for a drink. He was driven home by Maria at about 11.30. He was still being followed by the police but he had exhausted them.

2.25 Task one

	Type	Characteristic
(a)	central	modal + bare infinitive
(b)	central	modal + bare infinitive
(c)	central	modal + bare infinitive
(d)	marginal	modal + to + infinitive
(e)	semi-auxiliary	preceded by another modal
(f)	central	modal + bare infinitive
(g)	semi-auxiliary	negative formed with **do**
(h)	semi-auxiliary	interrogative as with verb **to be**.
(j)	marginal modal	modal + bare infinitive
(k)	central	modal + bare infinitive

2.25 Task two

The following are all acceptable answers:
(a) can/ought to/should/might/may/could.
(b) be able to.
(c) could/will/should/might/may.
(d) could/will/ought to/should/can/might/may.
(e) can/could/will/should/might/may.
(f) can/could/will be able to/ought to/should/might.
(g) can/could/will/will be able to/ought to/should/might/may.
(h) can/could/will/ought to/should.
(j) could/should/might/may.
(k) could/should/might/may.

2.26 Task one

(a) **Ability:** can, cannot (can't); could; be able to.
(b) **Advisability:** should; ought to.
(c) **Certainty (primary use):** will, will not (won't).
(d) **Exemption:** need not (needn't); not have to.
(e) **Necessity:** need.
(f) **Obligation:** must; have to; should.
(g) **Permission:** may; can.

(h) **Prohibition:** may not; must; cannot.
(j) **Request:** can; could; would.
(k) **Certainty (secondary use):** will, will not (won't); would.
(l) **Near certainty:** should; could; might.
(m) **Possibility:** can; may; might; could.
(n) **Impossibility:** cannot (can't); could not (couldn't); would not (wouldn't).
(o) **Probability:** must; could; should.

2.27 Task one

Ability: (e), (f), (h).
Permission: (c), (j).
Request: (k).
Prohibition/refusal: –.
Possibility: (b), (g).
Impossibility: (a), (d).

2.27 Task two

(a) You couldn't see the film because you were not 18. *(Prohibition.)*
(b) Medical expenses could have been very expensive. *(Possibility.)*
(c) The baby could say/was able to say a few words. *(Ability.)*
(d) You could have become very famous. *(Possibility.)*
(e) Could you have told me the way to the town hall? *(Ability.)*
(f) Surely that can't have been/couldn't have been Jack. *(Impossibility.)*

2.28 Task one

(a) **Obligation:** (iii), (x).
   Necessity: (iv), (vi).
   Exemption: (i), (viii), (ix).
   Prohibition: (v).
   Probability: (ii), (vii).
(b)   (i) You didn't have to pay the whole amount in advance.
     (ii) That must have been/had to have been Charlie. He had said he would be here about then.
    (iii) A separate cheque had to accompany each application.
     (iv) You needed to add some more sugar to that.
      (v) You were not to/not allowed to walk on the grass.
     (vi) You had to be there by 9.00, if you wanted to be sure of a seat.
    (vii) As a senior official, you must have had great influence over the committee's decisions on appointments.
   (viii) You needn't have waited for me.
     (ix) You didn't need smallpox vaccinations any longer for anywhere.
      (x) Books had to be returned on or before the date stamped below.

2.28 Task two

(a) Children under 18 mustn't be admitted.
(b) Dogs must be kept on a lead.
(c) Cheques can be accepted only with a bank card./Cheques must be/need to be accompanied by a bank card.
(d) With Visa you need not wait. With Visa you don't have to wait.
(e) You need/must have/have to have seventy-five tokens to get the coffee pot!

2.29 Task one

(a) **Permission:** (i), (ix).
   Prohibition: (vi).
   Possibility: (ii), (iii), (iv), (v), (vii), (viii), (x).
(b) (i) Might I have had/Could I have had longer to complete the assignment?
   (ii) It might have been/could have been Rosalie, but I doubt it.
   (iii) The house repairs might have/could have cost more than the house was worth.
   (iv) The sea might have been cool for bathing, but the beaches were warm with the sun.
   (v) You might not have been aware of the advantages of this scheme.
   (vi) Nobody could leave the hall before the exam had finished.
   (vii) They could/might have had what you want/wanted, but I doubted it. They only stocked torches in small numbers.
   (viii) That tree looked dangerous. It might have/could have fallen down.
   (ix) You could withdraw up to £250 at any time.
   (x) There might have been/could have been a heavy frost during the night.

2.29 Task two

Suggested captions:
(a) May I have another piece of cake?
(b) Dogs may not come in.
(c) He might be from Mars.
(d) Careful! It may break.
(e) I might stay at the Connemara.

2.30 Task one

Obligation: (e).
Advisory: (a), (c), (d), (f), (g), (j), (k).
Near certainty: (b), (h).

2.30 Task two

(a) You should get a new starter motor/You should park your car in a garage/You should buy a new car, etc.
(b) You should see a doctor/You should try yoga/You should give up coffee, etc.
(c) You should book the tickets early.
(d) You should reserve a seat/You should get there early, etc.
(e) You shouldn't have criticised them.
(f) You should have kept them in a safe/the bank/You should report it to the police.
(g) You shouldn't go to see that film.
(h) You should read the book.
(j) You should get up earlier.
(k) You should study harder/You shouldn't go out so often.

2.31 Task one

(a) Photocopies will not be accepted. *(No past expression.)*
(b) At that price it would be a BMW they're offering. *(Guess.)*
(c) Would you post this for me, please? *(Polite form.)*
(d) Tourist offices would give you all the information you need. *(Advice.)*
(e) It's a big dog. It would be an Alsatian. *(Guess.)*

2.31 Task two
(a) At that price they'll be very poor quality.
(b) At that price the service will be poor.
(c) He will have had an accident.
(d) Tom will be at the cinema.
(e) That will be a supermarket.

2.32 Task one
(a) Would you mind if I stayed for another month? Could I stay for another month?
(b) Would you mind if I borrowed your car? Could I borrow your car?
(c) Would you mind lending me your tools?
Would you mind if I borrowed your tools?
(d) Would you mind if I watched television? Could I watch television?
(e) Would you mind if I had/took a day's holiday?
Replies: No, not at all. No, that's fine; go ahead. No, that's no trouble.

2.32 Task two
(a) Would/could you help me move the furniture?
(b) Would/could you play in the team?
(c) Would/could you take these documents to . . ., please?
(d) Would/could you help me start the car?
(e) Would/could you help that person?
Replies: Yes, of course. Sure. All right. OK.

2.32 Task three
Polite:	**Impolite:**
(a) Yes, of course.	No, I couldn't.
(b) Yes, certainly.	No, I won't.
(c) Not at all.	Yes, I would.
(d) Yes, of course. Sorry.	No, I couldn't.
(e) Not at all. Yes, of course I will.	Yes, I would.

2.33 Task one
(a) Hadn't you better . . .
(b) would rather
(c) 'd better
(d) would rather
(e) would rather
(f) had better
(g) Wouldn't . . . rather
(h) would rather
(j) 'd better
(k) Hadn't you better . . .

2.34 Task one

can (possibility)	will (certainty)	will (certainty)
need (necessity)	might (possibility)	should (advisability)
can (possibility)	might (possibility)	can (possibility)
will (certainty)	might (possibility)	might (possibility)
will (certainty)	might (possibility)	might (possibility)
will (certainty)	might (possibility)	can (possibility)
can (possibility)	will (certainty)	may (possibility)
will (certainty)	might (possibility)	

2.34 Task two

Here is a copy of the original text. Many alternatives are possible, so discuss your own version with your teacher.

P L A N   W E L L   A H E A D

Check the requirements for your destination

Find out about the health risks in the country you are visiting, and the precautions you can take, by reading the chart on page 5. And check on the vaccinations you need, using the advice on pages 9–14. You can get more information from your travel agent and the Embassy or High Commission in London of the country concerned.

Consult your doctor at least 2 months before departure

He will advise you and arrange vaccinations. Some of these car take time to become effective and cannot be given at the same time as other vaccinations. Tell your doctor where you are going and if you are taking your children with you. This is particularly important if they have not had their full course of childhood vaccinations. Rather earlier arrangements may be needed if you require vaccination against tuberculosis (see page 9).

Paying for medical treatment abroad

How much you need to pay depends on the country you are visiting and the existence of any special arrangements for free or reduced cost medical treatment:

■ If you are visiting a European Community country you will need form E111. Read pages 15–22. You may need medical insurance as well.

■ If you are visiting a country which has a reciprocal health care agreement with the UK, read pages 23–26. Consider the need for supplementary medical insurance.

■ If you are visiting any other country medical insurance is **essential.** Check with your travel agent on the amount of insurance you will need and include enough cover to allow for the extra cost of travelling home in an emergency.

2.34 Task three

(a) You can only turn left here.

(b) Non-residents can have lunch in this hotel.

(c) You should place your purchases on this platform.

(d) Your Kodak film can be developed and printed here.

(e) You must have a permit to go riding here.

(f) You can't camp beyond this point.

(g) You don't have to pay to go in.

(h) Newcastle United will play Derby County on Wed. 28 Feb.

(j) This road could/might/may subside.

(k) You shouldn't give this cold and influenza mixture to children under 5.

2.35 Task one
(a) had been . . . would have got rid of . . .
(b) had gone . . . would have lost . . .
(c) had learned/learnt . . . would be/would have been . . .
(d) are . . . will mean . . .
(e) cut . . . will buy . . .
(f) receive . . should ask . . .
(g) had woken . . . would have been . . .
(h) hear . . . means . . .
(j) do not hear . . . will drown.
(k) will have . . . make . . .

2.35 Task two
(a) If you do not sell the house, you will not have to pay any commission. *(Possible.)*
(b) If you had invested £1,000 in 1974, it would be worth £20,000 today. *(Impossible.)*
(c) If we start early, we will see the wonderful sunrise. *(Possible.)*
(d) If Jane had stayed on, she would be Director of Studies now. *(Impossible.)*
(e) If you believe that, you'll believe anything. *(Possible.)*
(f) If you do not enclose postage, only the cassettes will be returned. *(Possible.)*
(g) Awards will be withheld, if sufficiently high standards are not attained. *(Possible.)*
(h) If you are successful in the second stage, you can/will join the semi-final. *(Possible.)*
(j) If we receive the form before 26 March, we will send you a special free gift. *(Possible.)*
(k) If you do not contact us tomorrow, we shall contact you the day after. *(Possible.)*

2.36 Task one
Past habit: (b);
Present habit: (a);
Deduction: (e);
Future possibilities: (c), (d), (f), (g), (h).

2.36 Task two
(a) If you keep the lights on all night, burglars will know you are not at home.
(b) Should the price of that house get any higher, I won't be able to afford it.
(c) If you go I won't ask you again.
(d) If he arrives after dark, he may not find the house easily.
(e) If we don't leave now, we will be late.
(f) Bother him now and he'll forget the time he started cooking the meat.
(g) If you see Sally give her my love.
(h) If you don't read that paper tonight, you'll fail the exam.
(j) Elect me and I'll bring about changes in the social welfare system.
(k) If you return this form within seven days, you'll get a free gift.

2.37 Task one
Impossible now or improbable future: (d), (e), (h), (j).
Non-existent past (present reference): (b), (f).
Non-existent past (past reference): (c), (g), (k).

2.37 Task two

(a) If he didn't have to see his mother in London, he could drive to Edinburgh.
     Had he not got to see his mother in London, he could drive to Edinburgh.
(b) If he had some money, he could buy some new shirts.
     Had he some money, he could buy some new shirts.
(c) If the dance class weren't full, he could attend it.
     Were the class not so full, he could attend it.
(d) If the ice hadn't melted, he could go skating.
     Had the ice not melted, he could go skating.
(e) If he hadn't failed his exams, he could study at the university.
     Had he not failed his exams, he could study at the university.

2.37 Task three

(a) If she had been good with words, she could have been a writer.
     Had she been better with words, she could have been a writer.
(b) If she had saved hard enough, she could have bought a large house in London.
     Had she saved hard enough, she could have bought a large house in London.
(c) If she had been seriously interested in politics, she could have been Prime Minister.
     Had she been seriously interested in politics, she could have been Prime Minister.
(d) If they hadn't wanted only men in those days, she could have been a pilot.
     Had they not only wanted men in those days, she could have been a pilot.
(e) If she hadn't disliked heights, she could have been a trapeze artiste.
     Had she not disliked heights she could have been a trapeze artiste.

2.38 Task one

Suggested answers:
(a) Unless you wait until next week to change your money, you'll lose on the exchange rate.
(b) Unless you take that book back to the library, you'll have to pay a heavy fine.
(c) The candidate must get 75%, otherwise she won't/doesn't stand a chance of being admitted to the course.
(d) They'll have to hurry or we'll miss the train.
(e) Unless you drive more slowly, you'll have an accident.
(f) You have to order that magazine, or you'll never get it. It's so popular.
(g) You must have a lot of money, otherwise you can't think of living in London.
(h) Unless you start early, you'll get held up in the traffic.
(j) Unless he attends the next meeting, they'll ask him to resign.
(k) You must do what the doctor tells you or you won't get better.

2.38 Task two

Suggested answers:
(a) He won't see the Prime Minister unless his Private Secretary agrees.
(b) Unless his wife books the tickets, he won't go to the theatre.
(c) Unless he wins a lot of money, he won't fly in Concorde.
(d) He won't become very rich unless he becomes a successful songwriter.
(e) He'll have to borrow some money or he won't be able to buy a house.
(f) Unless he does a lot of hard training, he will not be able to go to the moon.
(g) Unless he finds a sponsor, he will not be able to race at Le Mans.
(h) He will never be chairman of his company unless he gets support from the committee.
(j) He must build a strong boat, otherwise he won't be able to sail round the world.
(k) Unless he learns to swim, he can't be a sailor.

2.39 Task one

Impossible now: (c), (h).
Improbable future: (b), (e), (j).
Non-existent past: (a), (d), (f), (g), (k).

2.39 Task two

(a) I wish I hadn't driven around that bend so fast.
(b) If only you had got here earlier!
(c) They wish they were soldiers.
(d) If only I had been a scientist!

2.40 Task one

to get; debating; having; to finish talking; to see; to become; being; winning; suffering; appearing.

2.41 Task one

(a) (i), (b) (i), (c) (i), (d) (i), (e) (ii), (f) (i), (g) (i), (h) (ii).

2.41 Task two

to say; to go; to send; smoking; to buy; putting; calling; to make; attacking; helping.

2.42 Task one

(a) He can try teaching English, opening a restaurant or selling luxury homes.
(b) Jane forbids her children to play loud music at night.
(c) He would like to travel by plane.
(d) He likes travelling.
(e) She would like to be Senior Editor/She would like to have been Senior Editor.
(f) He allowed her to go to the party.
(g) He will want to try to climb Mont Blanc.

2.42 Task two

consulting/to consult; to give; to claim; investing/to invest; to gamble; giving; to make; to invest; to deduct.

2.43 Task one

(a) He said that whatever the politicians try/tried to do, capitalism and socialism will/would always have to exist side by side.
(b) He complained that human beings always behave/behaved contrarily.
(c) He said that he would be in Rome on Saturday.
(d) He declared that the British monarch cannot/could not be a Catholic.
(e) She said that Ray was/had been ill for three years before he died.
(f) She said that Wordsworth wrote about nature and the countryside.
(g) He said he'll lose the game next week.
(h) They said they didn't see/hadn't seen any sharks while they were there.
(j) They said they had to move so often that they can/could never make any friends.
(k) He said we would never believe it but that Los Angeles was once/had once been a small country town.

2.43 Task two

Agnes: I never go out after dark
Fred: It's very dangerous nowadays
A: It can make things difficult. I never go to the cinema any more.
F: I haven't been for ages.
A: Well, I don't miss going.
F: No. I don't either. They don't make films like they used to any more.
A: And anyway, now everyone has a video.
F: Yes; so you can watch films at home.
A: But I used to like going to the cinema.
F: Yes. It did make a nice night out.
A: But there are no films worth seeing.
F: You're right. They only make violent films now and not the good adventure stories they made when I was young.

2.44 Task one

Lee heard a noise and wondered what it was. Juliet didn't know, so Lee asked her what it could have been. Juliet said it was probably Concorde. Lee wondered if it always went that fast and Juliet told him that it did. Lee asked her if she had ever flown in it but she said that she hadn't because it was too expensive. So Lee asked her if she would like to. Juliet replied that she wouldn't because she wasn't terribly interested. Then she asked Lee if he would like to fly in Concorde and he said he would. He reckoned it would be an exciting experience. So Juliet urged him to take her with him if he went.

2.44 Task two

Dr R: Why are you interested? Has your research on the size of worms' eggs uncovered anything of interest and value to mankind?
Colleague: I feel it has.
Dr R: How is it valuable?
C: I think it could stop some illnesses
Dr R: Oh you do, do you? Whatever makes you think that?
C: I can't really answer that. What do you think about research generally?
Dr R: My decision to abandon my research is my answer!

3.2 Task one

Countable: bank, brain, canal, engineer, gasket, group, joke, jump, knot, nodule, option, peer, quarrel, ultimatum, utensil, van, yawn, year.
Uncountable: advice, cash, electricity, independence, kinetics, logic, methane, realism, scenery, silk, tedium, zeal, zest.
Both countable and uncountable: air, balance, ceramic, decision, duty, flight, fruit, history, hope, industry, language, money, night, office, paper, quality, right, thought, variety, water, work.

3.2 Task two

an honest man	an efficient machine	a hydroplane	a newspaper
an unusual event	a horror film	an example	a hovercraft
a history book	a useful tool	a hitchhiker	an appointment
a/an hysterical child	a wastepaper basket	a year	

3.3 Task one

Non specific reference: an atomic nucleus, a proton, an electron, an antineutrino, an insulated lining, a device, a box
In complement position: a fundamental tenet
One: a dozen
Per: a year, a year.

3.4 Task one

(a) The, the, Ø; (b) the, the/a; (c) a, the; (d) the, Ø; (e) an, the; (f) Ø, a; (g) Ø/the, The/Ø, Ø/the; (h) the, the; (j) A, the; (k) Ø/a, the, the; (l) –; (m) the, the; (n) the; (p) Ø, the, Ø, A; (q) Ø, Ø/the; (r) –.

3.4 Task two

Mentioned before: the thing; the big one; the destruction.
Specified in the noun group: the trail; the . . . bridge; the river; the town; the turn; the irony.
By context, local: The Smiths.
By context, global: the Eiffel Tower; the years; the police; the first burglar-engineers; The world; the century; the world's; the poorest land; the world.

3.4 Task three

Jones out of Rome marathon

Steve Jones, **the** world's second-fastest marathon runner, withdrew from **the** British team yesterday because of torn ligaments suffered when he ran in **the** UK 10,000 metres championship seeking selection for a second event at **the** world championships.

Jones had been selected for **the** marathon in Rome after finishing second in **the** Boston marathon but chose to run **the** track race in **the** hope that he might win a second place.

3.5 Task one

(a) (i) This action kit; (ii) This series; (iii) These changes; (iv) these countries; (v) that case; (vi) those principles.

Sentence	Time reference	Space reference
(ii)		This series
(iii)	These changes	
(iv)		these countries
(v)	that case	
(vi)	those principles	

3.6 Task one

(a) their, their; (b) your, your, their; (c) its; (d) our/your/their; (e) your, your, your, your, your; (f) our/their/your.

3.6 Task two

(a) Modern professional traffic **engineers** will need to continue to develop **their** skills to provide the sound, unprejudiced advice that decision-makers should have. The pattern of work can vary considerably and **they** will have to attend meetings with clients and make site visits and surveys. **They** will need to be computer-literate and be able to write clear and concise reports.

(b) An important skill for **teachers** is classroom management. **They** must be able to motivate **learners** to achieve **their** potential and to fulfil **their** aims. **They** must exercise patience and adopt a positive attitude towards **their** learners. This means encouraging slow **learners** when **they have** trouble grasping certain points as well as providing interesting and motivating activities for fast **learners**. If **learners** who **are** quick to absorb new materials **are** not given challenging work, **they** will rapidly lose interest in the whole process of learning and **they** will stop paying attention in class. **They** may even drop out of the course altogether.

3.7 Task one
(a) no, no, some; (b) some/a few, no; (c) either, neither.

3.8 Task one
(a) whose; (b) what; (c) which; (d) which; (e) which/what; (f) what; (g) which; (h) whose.

3.9 Task one
(a) half, half, All, half, half, All, both, half, half; (b) once, twice, half, three times.

3.10 Task one
(a) Montgolfier brothers; (b) J.A.C. Charles; (c) Great Britain and the USA; (d) Brazil; (e) China; (f) McKinley; (g) 1976.

3.11 Task one
(a) few; (b) little; (c) a few; (d) a little; (e) few; (f) little.

4.1 Task one
(a) (i) It is a beautiful, old bridge.
    (ii) It is a fast, deep, dangerous river.
   (iii) It was a dull, wet, cold day.
   (iv) It will be a valuable prize.
    (v) It was a rough, exciting football match.
(b) (i) The van was large and grey.
    (ii) The prince was young, wealthy and Italian.
   (iii) The film was long and boring.
   (iv) The girl was hard-working and clever.
    (v) The dolls were strong, Russian and wooden.

4.1 Task two
(a) old, green, British sports car;
(b) important, responsible, well-paid job;
(c) beautiful, small, brown, American computer;
(d) long, hot, summer holiday;
(e) beautiful, long, fast, modern train;
(f) sleek, fast racing boat;
(g) dark, old, sombre, classical painting;
(h) big, lonely, empty, haunted house;
(j) cheap, cheerful, crowded, Italian restaurant;
(k) wise, ancient, religious, Chinese man.

4.2 Task one

(a) less; (b) most expensive; (c) earliest; (d) longest; (e) cheaper;

4.2 Task two

(a) 11.2; (b) Birmingham Airport; (c) Anglesey; (d) Colwyn Bay; (e) Tenby; (f) Lerwick; (g) Wick.

4.3 Task one

(a) A is not so strong as B; (b) Pool B is not so deep as pool A; (c) A is not so beautiful as B; (d) B is not so rich as A.

4.3 Task two

(a) novel; (b) Jeffrey Archer; (c) £1m +; (d) *A Perfect Spy*; (e) John Le Carré; (f) 700,000+; (g) *The Story Teller*; (h) £2.95; (j) Noel Barber; (k) autobiography; (l) Spike Milligan; (m) Robert Goddard; (n) autobiography; (p) Shirley MacLaine.

4.4 Task one

(a) frightening, frightened by; (b) involved in, involving; (c) fascinating, fascinated by; (d) amused at/by, amusing; (e) surprised at/by, surprising; (f) exhausting, exhausted by; (g) worrying, worried by; (h) satisfied with, satisfying; (j) exciting, excited at/by; (k) depressing, depressed by.

4.4 Task two

(a) interested; (b) disappointed; (c) boring; (d) interesting; (e) involved; (f) surprised; (g) amused; (h) depressing; (j) bored; (k) shocking; (l) surprising; (m) disappointing.

4.5 Task one

(a) He works hard.
(b) She dances in a lively manner.
(c) Rachel sings badly.
(d) The film was shown recently.
(e) George fights aggressively.
(f) Rocky learns quickly.
(g) The book analyses the situation in China well.
(h) The spy behaved in a very friendly way.
(j) He examined the scene of the accident quietly and seriously.
(k) Becker received the trophy proudly.

4.6 Task one

(a) in; (b) in; (c) by; (d) in; (e) to; (f) under; (g) over; (h) on . . . by/near; (j) at; (k) at.

4.6 Task two

(a) On; (b) in; (c) to; (d) In; (e) in; (f) in; (g) On; (h) in; (j) at; (k) at; (l) On; (m) at; (n) Since; (p) For; (q) in; (r) in; (s) at; (t) in; (v) by; (w) in; (x) on; (y) by.

4.7 Task one

(a) very; (b) too; (c) enough; (d) enough; (e) very; (f) very; (g) enough; (h) enough; (j) too; (k) very.

4.7 Task two

(a) The mountain was very high, but . . .
(b) The car went too fast for him to see the number.
(c) The house was too expensive for them to buy.
(d) Of course cancer is a very serious disease, . . .
(e) He has got enough money to buy the car.
(f) He drove fast enough to get there on time.
(g) Rank Xerox is a very important company . . .
(h) The dinosaur wasn't large enough to fight . . .
(j) In the USA they didn't get enough rain in the summer of 1988.
(k) Britain imports too much toxic waste.

4.8 Task one

Defining: (a), (b), (f), (g), (j).
Non-defining: (c), (d), (e), (h), (k).

4.8 Task two

The houses **which congregate around the square** are low-lying detached residences. Many of the owners, **who all earn their living from fishing or market gardening like the rest of the islanders,** have built them themselves or inherited them from their parents. The houses have neat gardens, **which are full of vegetables**. In a corner in each garden, there is a little shrine, **which every member of the family will visit at least once a day.**

The houses are small, but the families are often large with ten or more children in addition to the grandparents, **who always come to live with the family in their final years**.

In the middle of the square there is a large covered stand. At night the children from the families **who have no room in their homes** bring their mattresses to sleep on the stand.

4.8 Task three

The man who climbed tall trees.
The bird that couldn't fly.
The train that sailed on the sea.
The house that had no door.
The flowers that danced in the sun.
The clock that had no hands.

4.9 Task one

(a) They didn't like the doctor **the hospital appointed**.
(b) Lynette made the curtains from the material **Edward bought in India**.
(c) The car **he bought** was the envy of his neighbours.
(d) Although he wasn't an architect, he lived in a house **he had designed himself**.
(e) The football fans **the police were watching carefully** caused no trouble.

4.9 Task two

It was almost midnight. After watching the films **which the café-owner had taken on holiday in America,** I went with the people **I met in the café** to the local fire-station. This was just a shed in the middle of the village. Inside the shed, there was a large, red fire-engine, **which the men in the group climbed onto immediately**. They were all in a very merry mood and quickly put on the firemen's helmets. I soon realised that I also had to put one on. It was a very large one, **which one of the women laughingly handed to me**. I put it on and took my place on the fire-engine. Soon we were racing down the narrow lanes of the village. The fire-engine bell, **which the villagers had bought only one year before,** was clanging loudly and waking all the villagers. 'Fire! Fire!' shouted a man **I had seen at the station when I arrived**. He was running out of his house, half-asleep, wearing only his night-shirt.

Then to add to the confusion came the noises of the farm animals **that the bell had disturbed**. They bellowed and jumped about in their stalls, frightened by the sound.

But the 'firemen', **whom the villagers trusted in times of danger**, laughed and drove on into the night.

4.10 Task one

 (i) Sir Winston Churchill, whose biography has just been completed, was a great leader. (Informal, non-defining)
 (ii) That club, to which many entertainers belong, is very expensive. (Formal, non-defining)
   That club, which many entertainers belong to, is very expensive. (Informal, non-defining)
   That club many entertainers belong to is very expensive. (Informal, defining)
(iii) That school, to which only children of rich families go, was founded in the fifteenth century. (Formal, non-defining)
   That school, which only children of rich families go to, was founded in the fifteenth century. (Informal, non-defining)
   That school only children of rich families go to was founded in the fifteenth century. (Informal, defining)
 (iv) The manager, whose company had gone bankrupt, didn't want to tell the staff. (Informal, non-defining)
   The manager whose company had gone bankrupt didn't want to tell the staff. (Informal, defining)
 (v) The Swiss company whose previous offer was £9.95 a share has increased its bid. (Informal, defining)
   The Swiss company, whose previous offer was £9.95 a share, has increased its bid. (Informal, non-defining)

4.11 Task one

There are some times **when** important events occur, so that you never forget what you were doing at the exact time **when** the event happened, nor the place **where** you were when it happened.

The day **that** the war broke out, Dad was visiting the town **where** he had been born. He went there to visit his old mother, my grandmother. She had been having problems with her neighbours since the day grandfather had died. When Dad heard the news, however, he hurried back quickly because he wanted to find the papers **where** it said he was no longer required to join the army.

It was also the day **when** Mum saw a tulip tree for the first time. She was in the garden **where** the mayor of the town had greeted the Prime Minister on his visit.

4.12 Task one

(a) dressed – passive; offering – active; placed – passive; decorated – passive; taking up – active; filled – passive; looking – active; wearing – active.

(b) In the room, there was a very small man, **who was dressed in Bedouin clothes**, and **who offered me a glass of tea.** I accepted and sat down on some cushions **which were placed against the wall.** The room, **which was decorated in a very ornate and traditional style,** seemed to me to be very long and there were couches and cushions the length of each wall. The cushions, **which took up about a third of the space,** were very brightly coloured. In the centre of the room was a tray, **which was filled with glasses and a pot of tea.** Very quietly and suddenly, another man, **who looked like the brother of the man already in the room,** but **who was wearing Western clothes,** entered, bowed and sat down beside me. The room suddenly seemed crowded.

4.12 Task two

(a) I saw a naked man smoking a cigarette.
I cannot tell you how shocked I was.
He was by no means the only passenger smoking a cigarette,
But he was the only naked passenger smoking a cigarette.

(b) When the pistol muzzle oozing blue vapour
Was lifted away
Like a cigarette lifed from an ashtray.

(c) At home I used to sit in a winged chair by the window
Overlooking the river and the factory chimneys.

(d) At a clandestine press conference in the Kerry Mountains,
Organised by the dissident playwright Dr Joe Pat Sheehy . . .

(e) But then one day she solved the problem
For all us nosey-parkers
Lurking about the drawing rooms of Paris.

5.1 Task one

Pronoun	Noun/noun phrase/clause/concept
they	elephants
them	seeds
they	elephants
it	caffra tree
they	zoologists
them	seeds
we	the readers/people
ourselves	the readers/people
we	the readers/people
we	the readers/people
it	a subject
we	modern educated people
it	information
this	excess of information
some	people
it	excess of information

5.1 Task two

(a) this. (b) some; they; This; This. (c) one; one; it; it; we; we; we. (d) himself/herself/themselves; you; you; one; you; us; we; them.

5.1 Task three

(a) Just when **we** were learning to live with the idea of 'safe sun' as far as **our** skin is concerned, along come the scientists and doctors to tell **us** that **our** hair is sun-sensitive too. Sand, salt and chlorine can strip hair of **its** oils, leaving **it** rough and the ends split. Most in danger is **our** parting. **It** is subject to the same carcinogenic ultra-violet rays that **our** skin is.

It would also be possible to write:

Just when **you** were . . . **your** skin . . . **you** that **your** hair . . . is **your** parting . . . **your** skin is.

Or:

Just when **people** . . . **their** skin . . . **them** that **their** hair . . . is **their** parting . . . **their** skin is.

(b) Adam White is a photographer. Yesterday **he** flew to the United States to photograph the President. **His** assignments take **him** all over the world.

He owns a large house in Sussex where **he** lives with **his** wife Jane and **their** two children, Margaret and Peter. **They** have three cats, two dogs, a horse and fifteen ducks. **They** have lived in the house for five years, ever since **they** sold **their** house in London and moved south.

5.2 Task one

(a) –.
(b) Remembering the expiry date is important.
(c) Arriving early pays.
(d) –.
(e) Travelling first class makes a lot of difference.
(f) Queen Elizabeth is said to always take her own water when she travels.
(g) It's a shame/It's a pity;
(h) That the film contained damaging information was known in government circles.
(j) –.
(k) Being here is lovely.

5.2 Task two

(a) It's a pity/It was known/It's a shame;
(b) It's claimed;
(c) It was learned/It was known;
(d) It's going;
(e) It's difficult;
(f) It's dangerous;
(g) It's a shame/It's a pity/It's claimed;
(h) It's;
(j) It was a capital offence;
(k) It was known/It was learned.

5.3 Task one

(c) I hope not; (d) I suppose so; (e) said so; (f) If he did so; (g) I suppose so; (h) I hope so; (j) I don't think so; (k) I hope not; (l) Do you really think so? (m) I suppose not.

5.3 Task two

(a) So did Helen; (b) Nor did Rowan; (c) Nor does David; (d) So do David and Rowan; (e) Nor did Marc; (f) So does Miles; (g) So did Helen; (h) So does Sara; (j) Nor will Rowan; (k) So does Marc.

5.5 Task one

Concessions/contrasts: however, however, however.
Results/consequences: consequently, thus, consequently, therefore.
Differences: on the one hand; on the other hand; on the other hand.

5.5 Task two

(a) however; (b) however; (c) Thus; (d) Consequently; (e) However.

5.6 Task one

(a) First; (b) then; (c) then; (d) in other words; (e) First; (f) then; (g) Next; (h) Finally.

5.6 Task two

(a) First trim a piece of wood to suit the shape of the leg; then drill pilot screw holes into both the chair leg and the wood block. Next screw the wood block into place. Then fill the joint between the wood block and the leg with the wood filler. Finally, after the filler has set, rub it smooth.

(b)   (i) Take a sharp knife to scrape away the scorch mark completely.
    (ii) Rub with fine glass paper.
   (iii) Apply transparent French polish.
   (iv) Do this several times and use some more fine glass paper.
    (v) Wait for the French polish to dry.
   (vi) Smooth the area carefully.
  (vii) Apply metal polish to bring back the shine.

5.7 Task two

(a) as if; (b) since; (c) Wherever; (d) as soon as; (e) Wherever; (f) Before; (g) When; (h) as; (j) Wherever.

5.8 Task two

(a) Although; (b) Even though; (c) since; (d) so; that; (e) so that; (f) as/since; (g) because; (h) Although; (j) in order that/So that; (k) although; (l) Since.

Index